Contents

Contents

Foreword

The Pensions Commission was appointed in December 2002 with the remit of keeping under review the adequacy of private pension saving in the UK, and advising on appropriate policy changes, including on whether there is a need to "move beyond the voluntary approach."

In June 2003 we published our work plan, setting out the analysis we would conduct in the period before our First Report. We made it clear that the First Report would focus on a detailed description of the present position, but would not make policy recommendations.

We have now published that First Report and this document contains its appendices.

The style of the main report and the appendices is deliberately detailed and fact-based. We want to make clear the facts on which our analysis is based, enabling experts and interested parties to point out where we are wrong, or where we have missed key issues. We also make explicit the deficiencies of the data sources available, and the extent to which we have had to make judgments. And where, particularly in our modelling, we have had to make assumptions on variables such as rates of return or costs, we have made these explicit, enabling people to judge how far different assumptions would lead to different conclusions.

We are now launching the consultation phase of our work, details of which are set out in Chapter 9 of the main report. We would like to receive written submissions by the end of January 2005. In about a year we will produce a Second Report, which will include specific policy recommendations.

List of figures

List of figures

List of tables

Data adequacy to support evidence-based policy

The Pensions Commission's terms of reference asked us to comment on the adequacy of available data to support evidence-based pension policy: *'To keep under review the regime for UK private pensions and long-term savings, taking into account the proposals in the Green Paper, assessing the information needed to monitor progress.'*

This Appendix responds to that request. Its overall conclusion is that present data sources are significantly deficient as a basis for some aspects of evidence-based policy making. This is in part because they have not been designed to answer the questions we now need to consider and in part (in the case of aggregate national data) because of significant errors in past data gathering and analytical approaches. Some improvements will come on stream over the next year, but these will not transform data availability in the key areas where information is currently deficient. Recommendations on policy in the Pensions Commission's 2005 Report will therefore necessarily be based on the judgements from imperfect data which we present in this year's report.

The sections below expand on this summary conclusion, commenting in turn on:

1. Data on individual wealth and savings behaviour, and on individual pension scheme participation. The problems here are severe.

2. Data from employers, schemes and administrative sources on trends in pension provision, membership and contribution rates. The problems here are moderate.

3. Department for Work and Pensions (DWP) modelling capabilities: the validation of the first version of the dynamic microsimulation model, Pensim2, needs to be completed by the end of February 2005.

4. Aggregate national data (e.g. in the Office for National Statistics (ONS) "UK National Accounts") on total levels of pension contributions and benefits. The problems here have been exceptionally severe, but are now being addressed by the ONS.

5. Some other areas of analysis where data is deficient:
   – The healthy/unhealthy ageing debate
   – Consumption patterns in old age
   – People's attitudes and expectations

Under each of these headings we assess the adequacy of existing data, identify steps already in hand which will deliver improvements, and where appropriate make specific recommendations for further actions. These recommendations are pulled together in the final section of this Appendix.

1. Information on wealth, savings and pensions

In Chapter 4 of the Report we consider the adequacy of current levels of pension saving by age, gender and income level. In Chapter 5 we analyse whether people have significant other sources of wealth (non-pension financial assets and housing assets) which could fill gaps in retirement provision. But to do those analyses we had to draw on multiple imperfect data sources, and to make reasonable judgements amid considerable uncertainty.

The ideal dataset: To assess the information sources which are available it is useful to define the ideal dataset for policy development in this area. Ideally we would like to know, for representative samples of individuals by age, gender, income, and other key characteristics, the following data:

■ Pensions stocks and flows: What level of rights people have already accrued in Defined Benefit schemes (DB), or what Defined Contribution (DC) funds they already own. What type of pension scheme they are members of, and either (for a DB scheme) the rate of accrual of rights or (for a DC scheme) the level of employer and employee contributions being made. Information on both current and deferred pensions is important. And information on what state pension rights have been accrued is required to complete the picture.

■ Membership of different types of scheme by age, gender, and income band, but also by employment status (whether employed or self-employed), company size, and business sector.

■ Non-pension financial assets and liabilities: Stocks and (to a lesser) extent flows. What stocks of financial wealth, net of liabilities, people now own, broken down by type of asset and liability. And some indication of annual savings flows into financial assets and repayments of debt.

■ Housing net assets and flows: Gross housing wealth and mortgage debt outstanding. And an indication of the pace at which housing debt is being paid off (whether via repayment mortgages or via the accumulation of endowment savings or other linked policies).

Ideally, moreover, this data would include:

■ Longitudinal data to allow analysis of changes over time, and of how individuals accumulate assets throughout their lifetime.

- The clear separate identification within couples of individual wealth and of shared wealth.

- Good data on the cross-correlation between different categories of wealth holdings. The ability to match data across different sources would also be beneficial.

- Individual measures of asset holding which when multiplied up to the total population level produce a good match to aggregate national statistics, thus giving us confidence in conclusions.

Presently available data sources leave us very far short of this ideal.
The key problems are:

- Pensions: There is an almost total lack of quantitative data at the individual level on stocks of existing pension rights/fund assets or on flows of new pension savings. Most data on pensions is of a "yes/no" type, telling us whether people are members of different schemes, and in some cases which type of schemes, but with no data on the accumulated value of existing pension rights, and little on the level of contributions being made.

- Non-pension financial wealth: Imperfect aggregation, and imperfectly defined categories. Multiple surveys of wealth exist, but when aggregated up these often produce totals up to 50% short of believed national aggregates. And the data split between categories of wealth is often frustratingly imprecise (e.g. with unclear use of distinctions such as "savings" versus "investments").

- Housing wealth: On the whole the problems here are less severe, with better aggregation to national totals. But there is imperfect capture of information on endowment mortgages intended (provided capital values are sufficient) to pay off mortgages.

These problems partly reflect the generic problems of data gathering. But the problems are exacerbated in the pension and wealth area because:

- Pensions are very complex: The vast majority of people could not express the value of their accrued DB rights or state system rights in a single figure, even if they were able to give a good (but complex) description of the nature of their arrangements. Many people have several different current and deferred pension arrangements. In particular knowledge of what employers are contributing is poor. Getting good data on pension stocks and flows therefore requires a detailed, lengthy and expensive interview process. As regular pension statements become more common this may help data collection in the future.

■ Many people are unwilling to reveal wealth holdings, and it is likely that this unwillingness is skewed: richer people in particular may not wish to participate in wealth surveys. This is one explanation of the fact that surveys of individual saving do not aggregate up to national totals.

■ There are a number of problems related to capturing data on debt. Respondents may have a persistent tendency to under-report it. Tudela and Young (2003) suggest that this may be because people do not think of goods being paid for in instalments as debt. The coverage of debt also differs between surveys and official figures, making reconciliation difficult. Surveys tend to exclude balances not bearing interest but these tend to be included in the official figures.

■ If the selected respondent is not available for interview, a partner or other proxy respondent may have little, if any, knowledge of the details of the pensions and other assets of the individual in question. Even for their own assets, individuals may not always know the value of the assets they own. This may be particularly true for an asset like housing, which may be held over a long period of time and the value of which cannot be accurately determined until it is put on the market.

Main data sources: Table A.1 sets out the key features, advantages and deficiencies of the surveys and sources on which we have drawn. Key points to note are:

■ British Household Panel Survey (BHPS): This is a multi-purpose panel survey that has been following a representative sample of individuals over time since 1991. It collects information on topics such as labour market activity, health, education, personal finances and pension arrangements. Housing wealth information is collected annually and aggregate financial wealth and debt data has been collected in two waves in 1995 and 2000. The next wealth module is planned for 2005. The pension information covers details of membership as well as contributions to personal and occupational pensions, but not accumulated rights or funds. Its primary disadvantages are its low frequency and relatively small sample size which restricts some analyses.

■ Family Resources Survey (FRS): DWP survey is a major source of data on various sources of income. Its main focus is to collect information on income to help DWP forecast benefit entitlement and expenditure and so the breadth of the pensions information collected is limited. For wealth analysis it has a broad measure of aggregate savings, but no information on current debts, so a net financial position cannot be obtained. And we cannot calculate a measure of net housing wealth.

■ New Earnings Survey (NES): In this annual survey conducted by the ONS, questionnaires are sent to employers who respond on behalf of the specific employee(s) selected. Information is collected on membership of employer-sponsored pension schemes. Classification information on the company is also available for analysis. As the sample is based only on PAYE employees the levels of pension participation are likely to be overstated. Many low earners in small companies are not included in the sample as people earning less than the income tax personal allowance are intentionally excluded. These people are generally less likely than others to be members of pension schemes, so headline percentages of employees who are members of pension schemes may be inflated. In addition non-response may be biased towards small- and medium-sized companies, which are also less likely to offer pension benefits to their employees. The future grossing of the dataset, and other developments to the survey, should help to reduce these problems. And as the same employees are selected each year, longitudinal analysis is also a possibility.

■ General Household Survey (GHS): The survey presents a picture of households, families and people living in Great Britain, and pensions is only one of the many topics it covers. There is no information on other assets. The survey was established in 1971 and pension questions have been included for a number of years so time series information on participation is available.

■ MORI Financial Services Survey (MFS): In the interests of its primary users in the financial services sector MORI Financial Services conducts a monthly survey directed at investigating individuals' holdings of different financial products. The survey can be used to derive the values of net housing equity and aggregate non-pension financial assets, apart from life assurance, as well as personal loans and credit card debt. The values of other types of loans are available from 2004. The pension questions cover the types of current pension provision and questions on contributions have been included for the first time this year. It will, however, still not be possible to calculate accumulated pension wealth from this source. Similarly to other surveys of wealth and assets, the MFS survey appears to underestimate total financial wealth and debt while it appears to approximate housing wealth more closely. Another difficulty with using the MFS survey is that it does not apportion jointly held assets or provide much information on the household so that the coverage of wealth estimates is not clearly defined and cannot easily be inferred.

■ NOP World Financial Research Survey: This survey collects detailed information on the type of financial products people have, and there is information on the actual value of savings and investments in these products. But there is no data on the value of outstanding debts and so net financial assets cannot be calculated. A measure of net housing wealth is also not available. Pensions information is limited. New questions have been introduced on retirement planning.

Table A.1 Sources of Individual Wealth, Saving and Pensions Data

Issue	BHPS	FRS	NES	GHS
Main purpose of survey	Longitudinal survey of social and economic change.	Assess income available to individuals, families and households.	Collect information on the earnings of employees directly from employers.	The survey presents a picture of households, families and people living in Great Britain.
Population coverage	Households in GB, UK from 2001 onwards. (i.e. excluding communal residences, although sample members who move into communal establishments are eligible for interview.)	Private households in UK (previously only GB). (i.e. excluding communal residences)	Employees who are members of PAYE. (i.e. excluding those earning less than the income tax personal allowance)	Households in GB. (i.e. excluding communal residences)
Age coverage	16+	Adults and children	16+	16+
Sample size	Approx 5,000 households; approx 10,000 individuals per year, so analysis of detailed groups is limited.	Approx 25,000 households.	Around 160,000 individuals per year.	Achieved sample size in 2002/03 of 8,620 households and around 20,000 individuals.
Sample approach	Two-stage clustered probability design and systematic sampling for first stage. In subsequent stages interview all adults in all households containing at least 1 resident from a household interviewed in stage 1.	Stratified clustered probability sample.	Sample based on 1% sample of employees selected by NI number.	The survey uses a probability, stratified two-stage sample design.
Timeliness	Annual Wealth modules 1995 and 2000.	Annual.	Annual – fieldwork in April, results published in October.	Data collected throughout the year April-March. Annual publication.
Non-pension Wealth and Savings information available	Value of mortgage at time of arrangement. Personal estimate of current house value. Analysts need to estimate net housing wealth. Aggregate value of savings and investments. Value of savings per month. Value of debt.	Cannot get net housing wealth. Broad measure of aggregate savings, more detail for a subset. No information on debts.	None.	None
Pensions information available	Scheme membership by type of scheme. DB/DC split possible (but not sure of the quality) Some individual contributions information.	Scheme membership by type of scheme. Some individual contributions information. No DB/DC split.	Type of employer-sponsored pension. DB/DC split is available. Contracting-in or out information is available.	Current pension scheme membership, whether employer has a pension scheme, whether eligible to join. Some information on personal pensions for the self-employed.
	No data on value of accumulated pension stock.	No data on value of accumulated pension stock.	No data on value of accumulated pension stock.	No data on value of accumulated pension stock.

MORI-MFS	NOP	ELSA	EFS
Market research for financial services companies.	Market research for financial services companies.	Multi-purpose longitudinal survey focusing on ageing.	The main reason for conducting a regular survey on expenditure by households has been to provide information on spending patterns for the Retail Prices Index.
Individuals in GB; limited household data. (i.e. excluding those in communal residences)	Individuals in GB; limited household data. (i.e. excluding those in communal residences)	The first time people are interviewed they are only drawn from the household population in England. They will be followed (if possible) into institutions in subsequent waves.	Households in the UK. (i.e. excluding communal residences)
16+	16+	50+	16+, 7-15 year olds also keep a diary though it is not compulsory.
Target 48,000 individuals per year.	Target 60,000 individuals per year.	8,000 households, 12,000 individuals.	6,342 households in Great Britain took part in 2002-03.
Two-stage quota sampling design of parliamentary constituencies and then respondents.	Quota sample.	Eligible adults drawn from Health Survey for England which is stratified clustered probability sample of postcode sectors and then addresses.	Multi-stage stratified random sample with clustering.
New data every month.	New data every month.	Wave 1 initial results published December 2003.	Data for 2002-03 was published in June 2004.
Value of mortgage at time of arrangement, value of additional borrowing, personal estimate of current house value. Value of savings and investment products, aggregated to give total savings/investment holding. Value of outstanding credit card debt and value of personal loan at time taken out.	Values of house and mortgage only at time of arrangement. Asks what type of accounts/assets respondent has and the value held within these assets. Information on type of debts, but not the outstanding value.	The self-reported current value of the primary house and detailed mortgage information collected separately. Net housing wealth is defined as the current value of the primary house less any outstanding mortgage debt. Values for different financial assets asked separately. Values of credit card debt and loans from friends/family available separately with the rest of debt in aggregate.	The survey focuses on consumption rather than saving and wealth issues.
Whether currently have contributions paid into company scheme, personal pension, AVCs, FSAVCs or Stakeholder. Distinguishes whether company scheme is DB or DC. Questions on individuals' current pension contributions available from January 2004.	Whether currently contributing to a scheme, by type of scheme. No DB/DC split. Limited individual contributions data.	Very detailed information on pension type including DB/DC and details of scheme. Information on employee and employer contributions also requested. Data on past pensions available.	Some individual contributions information collected, but individual records are not available for use due to confidentiality issues. Payroll deductions for main pension and last contribution to pension outside of payroll.
No data on value of accumulated pension stock.	No data on value of accumulated pension stock.	Potential exists to calculate the value of accumulated stock from the data provided.	No data on value of accumulated pension stock.

■ English Longitudinal Study of Ageing (ELSA): When fully implemented this study will represent a major step forward in the adequacy of data because it is based on interviews detailed enough to allow estimates of the accumulated stock of pension rights/funds, and because it will give us longitudinal data, allowing a clear identification of true trends. Furthermore ELSA asks detailed questions on exact values of financial wealth, probing broader indications of value where the exact figure is not known. As a result ELSA finds more wealth than other household surveys. There are however three problems, one permanent, the others temporary:

  – It only covers people aged 50 or over.

  – It has only just been launched. The longitudinal data will therefore only emerge as the years pass.

  – The complicated processing of data to produce estimates of accumulated pension wealth has not yet been done, though it is hoped that it will be completed by early 2005.

■ Expenditure and Food Survey (EFS): Although we have not used the EFS to consider pensions data as such this is a useful survey in analysing patterns of consumption for different groups. The panel included in Chapter 4 used the data to consider changes in consumption patterns for different age groups as part of our work on pension adequacy. Analysis in this area could be improved if equivalised income analyses were available.

Planned and required data developments: Improvements in the quality of the data are therefore required to support more effective evidence-based policy making. Some improvements are already planned on the pensions side, but they will take some time to implement and produce results.

■ The FRS team is reviewing the current pensions module with the aim of introducing a new set of questions in 2006. They are conducting research to assess the feasibility of asking for more information on issues such as scheme membership, eligibility, the type of pension scheme and contributions made.

■ The NES team has piloted new questions asking about employer and employee contributions to pension schemes. The Pensions Commission hope that the pilot is successful so that this information can be collected in 2005.

■ In the area of individual non-pension wealth and savings data however no improvements are planned that will produce a major transformation of data available over the next year. Recommendations on pension policy in the Pensions Commission 2005 Report will therefore necessarily be based on the judgements from imperfect data which Chapters 3, 4 and 5 present.

Over the longer-term, however, a more significant improvement in official data on wealth and assets is a priority. The ONS is developing the specification for a Wealth and Assets Survey which would aim to collect comprehensive information on both the stock and flow of wealth and assets of all types, including pensions, for all age groups. The Pensions Commission believes that progress with this project should be a priority, and notes the following key improvements which such a survey should ideally seek to achieve.

- Longitudinal information would be useful to get a better picture of how individuals accumulate assets over time, and how savings patterns relate to major life events.

- Information on the accumulation of pension rights for younger age groups not covered by ELSA is vital for assessing future pension adequacy.

- Ideally the survey will also allow us to consider the impact of inheritance and bequests on savings accumulation.

- If the survey could link to National Insurance administrative sources this would allow analysis of the complete pensions picture, including the accumulation of state pension rights.

The Pensions Commission recognises that this is a challenging project and hope that the planned feasability work is successful and provides a clear way forward.

2. Other sources on pension provision, membership, and contribution rates

The previous section of this Appendix looked at the surveys from which we attempt to draw an integrated picture of individual wealth holdings spanning all wealth categories, including pensions. This section considers the other data sources which provide information on overall trends in pension scheme membership and contribution rates. Chapter 3's description of trends in UK pension provision drew on these data sources.

The ideal dataset: This would give us data over time on:

- Membership of each type of pension scheme: DB, DC, Group Personal Pension (GPP), individual personal pension and Stakeholder Pensions. Details of the schemes themselves are also useful.

- Data from employers (analysed by size and sector) on pension schemes provided, participation rates and contribution rates.

The sources for these types of data are in general better suited to evidence-based analysis than those for integrated individual wealth considered above. But there remain **some key gaps and data interpretation problems.**

■ It is difficult to establish a clear picture of the **individual** personal pension market (as distinct from GPP) from the range of sources available. Individuals may hold multiple individual pension policies, but they might not be currently contributing to all of them. Individuals moving money between different pensions can also affect interpretation of the data, since industry sources tend to identify these as "new premiums" even though they do not represent new savings.

■ There is a significant problem of timeliness of data, in particular when we are trying to assess the progress of a fast-moving trend such as the DB-DC shift.

Main data sources: Key data sources used for analysis under this heading are set out in Table A.2. Some key points are:

■ The GAD survey of occupational pension membership and contribution rates has the advantage of collecting scheme-based information from a sample drawn from the whole population of occupational schemes. The breadth of information collected on scheme characteristics is also beneficial. But its usefulness for analysis of recent trends in pension scheme membership is severely restricted by poor timeliness: the latest report published in 2003 is based on data for the year 2000. When assessing the scale of the DB-DC shift, the value of the GAD survey is limited. More fundamentally, however, the GAD survey will become less effective over time as more pensions are provided in a GPP form, rather than under the trustee-based occupational form, on which the GAD exclusively focuses.

■ The Employers' Pension Provision survey (EPP) is a very useful large-scale survey of private sector employers in Great Britain. In normal circumstances its timelines could be considered reasonable. The 2003 survey published in March 2004 was based on fieldwork in spring 2003. When assessing the scale of the DB-DC shift, however, data even just one year out of date can seriously mislead. Analysis of the latest trends therefore also has to draw on several less comprehensive, smaller scale, but more up-to-date surveys which were outlined in the panel on page 85 of the main Report.

■ Inland Revenue Pension Statistics: The Inland Revenue holds administrative data on aggregate contributions to personal and Stakeholder pensions. Contributions to GPPs are included amongst these. However, the whole time series is not available prior to 1989-90. Prior to April 2001, the self-employed claimed tax relief on their pension contributions through Self-Assessment and their details were not reported by personal pension providers. This results in a discontinuity in the aggregate personal pensions data at 2001 when the self-employed were included for the first time. Data is available on individual pension contributions through the administrative data source, Third Party Information. This is received from personal pension providers for each individual plan and is used for the compilation of National Statistics and compliance checking purposes. Along with details of contributions, the individual's National Insurance (NI) number and some of their characteristics, such as age, gender, address and economic activity status are available. The Inland Revenue have matched a sample of the Third Party Information cases to the Survey of Personal Incomes (SPI) by NI number in order to obtain corresponding earnings. However, the SPI and Third Party Information data which are matched refer to different years due to different timings of availability and there are presently no plans to re-match the data retrospectively.

Unlike for personal pensions, tax relief is granted at source on occupational pension contributions with the consequence that Inland Revenue does not hold administrative data on these contributions and there is no prospect of it being held in the near future.

- The Lifetime Labour Market Database (LLMDB2) holds a longitudinal 1% sample of records from the National Insurance Recording System (NIRS2) and is a fully representative sample of around 600,000 people who have made any NI contributions or been awarded NI credits since 1975. Amongst other information the database contains information on contribution histories and the type and duration of contracted-out second tier pension provision in which individuals participate. The database holds no private pension information on those individuals who are members of private pension schemes that are not contracted-out. The database also contains information on self-employment and employee earnings. In the future there could be the potential for linking the data to other sources based on NI number: this would increase the usefulness of the data.

- ABI Market Data: The Association of British Insurers collects a variety of data from insurance companies about premiums flowing into long-term savings including pensions. They collect data on "new business" for policies sold during the year, and also for "business-in-force" (including premiums for policies put in place in previous years). However, these statistics need to be interpreted carefully in order to develop a true picture of trends in pension saving since:

  (i) The "business-in-force" figures are broken down into "regular premiums" and "single premiums". While the latter include some real flows of new money from personal sector savers, they also include a large element of money transferred from existing pension policies with other providers. Adjustments to exclude these transfers can be made using other data available to the ABI.

  (ii) The "new business" figures may also include money being transferred from existing policies (though this can be identified separately). Even if this is not the case "new business" premiums may be matched by the cessation of payments to an existing policy.

Table A.2 Other Sources of Pensions Data

Issue	GAD	EPP
Main purpose of survey or dataset	Detailed view of the nature of occupational pension provision.	Investigate the extent and type of pension provision offered and/or contributed to by businesses in the private sector.
Population coverage	All occupational pension schemes.	Private sector employers in Great Britain.
Sample size	Around 2,000 schemes in the year 2000, and around 1,300 in 2004.	Around 2,000 completed interviews.
Sample approach	Sample stratified by size and type of scheme.	Sample stratified by size band.
Timeliness	Conducted every 4 or 5 years so far. But data can be published some time after the data was collected.	Conducted every 2 or 3 years so far. Fieldwork in the spring, aiming to publish results within a year.
Pensions information available	Details of types of scheme and their membership, benefits and contributions. Information about scheme finances and governance is also available.	Information on types of schemes employers offer, participation in those schemes, contributions made and other details.

Inland Revenue	LLMDB2	ABI
Administrative data on aggregate contributions to personal, Stakeholder and Group Personal Pensions as a product of the process of granting tax relief. Third Party Information on individual pension contributions for the purposes of compliance checking and National Statistics. A sample of the Third Party Information cases is matched to data from the Survey of Personal Incomes (SPI) in order to link earnings data to the contributions data.	It analyses people in the United Kingdom who are members, or have been members of, a contracted-out occupational pension, an Approved Personal Pension scheme or have contributed to the State Earnings Related Pension Scheme.	As an industry body the ABI collects information from its members about their business and this includes information about pension policies organised through insurance companies.
All contributions to personal, Stakeholder and Group Personal Pensions. Earnings data covers a sample of these across the UK.	Individuals who have contributed to National Insurance.	Member companies of the ABI.
Around 200 personal pension providers.	Around 600,000 people.	All members of the ABI. This is around 120 companies which account for 97% of long-term insurance business.
Administrative data. Matched sample to SPI.	1% sample of records from the National Insurance Recording System.	All members of the ABI.
Data is available around 18 months after the end of the relevant financial year. But the SPI to which the Third Party Information is matched relates to an earlier period.	The sample is taken 15 months after the end of the latest tax year to be analysed to allow for late returns by employers. Therefore the results may not be timely.	Quarterly survey results are available 8 weeks after the end of the period. Annual data is published 8 months after the end of the calendar year.
Minimum, employer and individual contributions; numbers of arrangements; average contributions and numbers of individuals by age, gender, region and earned income.	The database contains information on the type and duration of contracted-out second tier pension provision that individuals participate in. No information is held on individuals who are members of schemes that are not contracted-out.	Regular and single premium information on personal and insured schemes, together with payments data. The quarterly new business data give details on new policies taken out, and breaks down the amounts of business sold by distribution channel.

These data interpretation problems are severe because of the significant churn within the personal pension market, and became more severe in the late 1990s and 2000s with e.g. significant movement of funds out of Equitable Life into other providers, and significant new pension flows into Stakeholder Pensions which did not represent a true increase in aggregate pension contributions. Because the problems became more severe, the apparent trends can be misleading as well as levels.

Despite these numerous problems we believe it is possible from the available data to get a reasonably accurate picture of key trends. And one of the problems (the timeliness of data on the DB-DC shift), is particularly important today, but may cease to be a key issue once the pace of change declines. It would not therefore be appropriate to redesign ongoing data sources around today's specific problem.

Planned and required data developments: The following improvements would however aid analysis. Many of these are already planned, and others are proposed for consideration.

■ The next EPP survey is planned to start fieldwork in the beginning of 2005 with results planned for the end of the year. From an analytical point of view it would be preferable for this to be a regular survey conducted every other year as it is the only survey which collects detailed pension provision information from employers. A survey conducted every second year would enable trends in pension coverage from the employer perspective to be monitored more effectively.

■ The GAD has recently conducted a review of its survey and is now developing plans for the future. The review identified that the relatively low frequency of the survey, and the length of time taken to produce results, limited the usefulness of the data in monitoring changes to pension scheme provision. GAD is now conducting an annual survey within what is planned to be a three year cycle, collecting information each year on different pension-related topics. It is hoped that this approach will improve response rates, and also lead to more timely results being available: the results from the survey currently being carried out into the benefits offered by pension schemes as at 2004 should be available in the first half of 2005. The long-term future of the GAD survey depends on the development and role of the new Pensions Regulator. However, if there is an increase in membership in GPPs this will limit the usefulness of the GAD survey in the future. GAD and others therefore need to consider now if there is a practicable way to collect useful information on membership and contribution rates in GPPs.

■ The Pensions Bill provides for a new Pensions Regulator and the creation of the new Pension Protection Fund (PPF). The new regulator is expected to be more proactive than OPRA, the current pensions regulator, with new powers to enable it to achieve its statutory objectives. An important tool for the new regulator will be a scheme return which all but the smallest pension schemes will be required to complete annually. The information from scheme returns, along with other information gathered by the regulator, will enable it to assess the risks to pension scheme members' benefits at a scheme and industry-wide level. It will also provide, for the first time, a comprehensive and up-to-date overview of the membership and status of pension schemes in the UK. It is expected that the regulator will start to collect scheme returns during 2005 although it is expected to take over a year to have collected returns from all schemes. Because data will be held on individual schemes it should, in the longer term, be possible to undertake longitudinal analysis of pension schemes. The PPF will also be collecting information from pension schemes to facilitate its work, and this information could also be useful in policy making.

- Following the introduction of new data-sharing provisions in the Employment Act 2002 the DWP is able to receive more data on employment from the Inland Revenue. The DWP Longitudinal Study will enable DWP to link all benefits records it holds against all employment records from the Inland Revenue. The Pensions Bill includes data-sharing provisions that would allow DWP to receive individual pensions and financial savings information from the Inland Revenue to inform both private and state pensions policy. This dataset will be used to undertake a variety of analyses, and together with the pensions data in the Longitudinal Study would provide an important data source for monitoring pensions' developments in the future.

- A consistent time series of aggregate contributions to personal pensions would be highly desirable. This can be achieved if the Inland Revenue could include estimates of the self-employed contributions to personal pensions prior to 2001 and present the data from 1989-90 to now as a continuous series.

3. DWP modelling capabilities: Pensim2

To estimate the likely impact of different policy regimes on the long-run level and pattern of pensioners' incomes, the Pensions Commission will need access to an appropriate 'dynamic microsimulation' model. The DWP are currently in the final stages of the development of such a model, Pensim2.

When the Pensions Commission started its work in spring 2003, it was initially envisaged that we would be able to use Pensim2 to conduct modelling of the scale of "under-saving" by different demographic groups. In fact since Pensim2 is still under development, this has been impossible, and we have had to develop our own much simpler model of under-saving, the results of which are presented in Chapter 4 with the details described in Appendix G. The Commission recommends that the DWP works to ensure that it is available for use by, or on behalf of, the Pensions Commission by the end of February 2005, to help us develop and inform our conclusions for the Second Report.

4. Aggregate national data on pension contributions and benefits

The Pensions Commission was asked to assess the adequacy of existing private pension savings and the implications of trends in pension savings. The most fundamental facts we needed to know therefore, were the present level and recent trends of total private pension contributions. It became clear at an early stage of our analysis, however, that published aggregate national figures for pension contributions (and also for private pension benefits) were wrong by very large amounts, and that the trends were not at all as suggested by published figures in UK National Accounts (the "Blue Book").

The fact that there were problems with the data was already known when we started our work, since discrepancies between figures quoted by DWP for total pension contributions (drawing on ONS figures), and figures provided by Inland Revenue for total tax relief had been subject to some public discussion. What was not apparent until our analysis progressed, however, was that the Inland Revenue figures were also overestimates, since in relation to occupational pensions they drew on erroneous ONS data. Our current best estimates of the level of private pension contributions are presented in Figures A.1 and A.2, showing comparisons with the figures implicit within the ONS UK National Accounts and with the figures published by the Inland Revenue. Errors of a similar magnitude exist in Blue Book figures for private pension benefits paid, which we believe are about £40 billion in 2002 versus a Blue Book figure of £64 billion.

We have worked closely and co-operatively with ONS in analysing and resolving these deficiencies, and ONS have published new estimates in their July 2004 document *Private Pension Estimates and the National Accounts (Tily, Penneck, Forest, 2004)*. Steps are now being taken through the inter-departmental Pension Statistics Task Force to achieve a step-change in the quality of ONS pensions statistics. And we believe that the estimates we have now broadly agreed with ONS provide an adequately sound basis for policy development. But the current data deficiencies have considerably delayed our analysis, and they raise important questions about cross-government co-ordination, about high-level data validation, and about resource adequacy which need to be carefully considered.

The key problems in the data have been described in ONS's July 2004 document, which has also been published as an article in the August edition of Economic Trends. There have been three key categories of problem.

- **Imperfect removal of double-counts:** The essential data gathering problem is that some survey data on private pension contributions (whether in the ABI Statistics or in ONS's MQ5 survey) does not distinguish between genuinely new savings and transfers of existing pension funds from one provider to another. A transfer of an existing fund to a new provider is, in the raw data, counted as a benefit paid

Figure A.1 Total Pension Contributions to Funded Pensions in Nominal Prices: £ billion

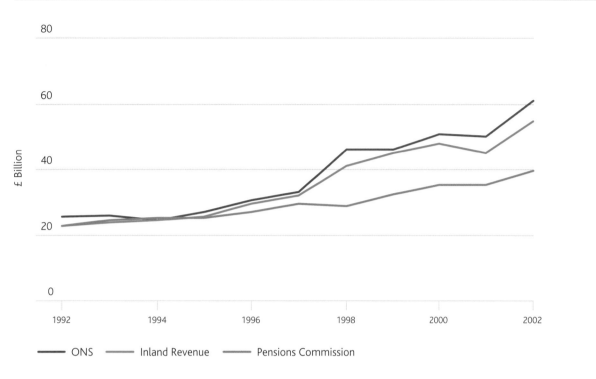

Source: ONS, Inland Revenue and Pensions Commission estimates

Figure A.2 Pension Contributions as a Percentage of GDP

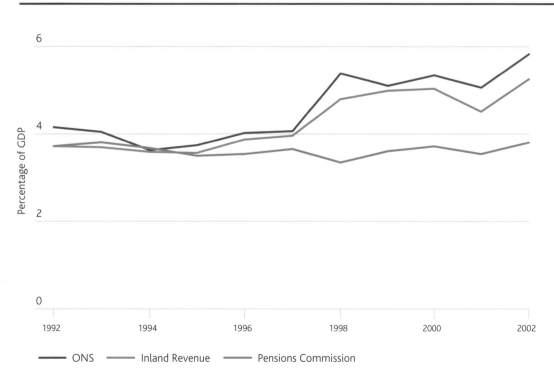

Source: ONS, Inland Revenue and Pensions Commission estimates

by the old provider and a contribution received by the new provider. This problem has been recognised for many years, and ONS have always taken steps to attempt to remove the double-count. But the data available from which to infer the scale of double-counting have been inadequate, and the assumptions made have not always reflected best understanding of industry dynamics. As a result a significant double-count remains in the figures and this double-count has grown substantially since the early 1990s as churn within the industry has increased, thus making apparent trends as well as levels hugely misleading.

Inland Revenue figures have provided a useful double-check against ONS figures for personal pensions, since Inland Revenue has a precise record of tax relief paid out for personal pensions. The fact that the gap between the Inland Revenue and ONS figures has widened since 1994 reflects the removal of the personal pensions double-count in the Inland Revenue figures but its incomplete removal in the ONS figures. But for occupational pensions, Inland Revenue have no independent estimate of tax relief granted (since the tax is never paid in the first place), but instead make their estimates of tax relief from ONS estimates of total contributions. Because the ONS estimates include unremoved double-counts, even the Inland Revenue estimates of total contributions are therefore still significantly too high. And, as a knock-on consequence, so too are Inland Revenue estimates of tax relief granted. We believe that the total tax relief on pensions is at least £4bn lower than the £13.9bn published figure for 2002/03.

■ **Significant coding and logic errors:** These data availability and interpretation problems have been made worse by some errors in the methodology used to produce the estimates in the National Accounts, which have also greatly slowed the task of arriving at a full understanding of the problem and at a new set of estimates. The tables used to produce the estimates have been set up in a way that has allowed errors to creep in (e.g. a memorandum item, intended to record the fact that it is already in an aggregate line, then added to the aggregate line). Understanding the logic of the calculations is a key step in identifying errors. This was impeded by the complex structure of the calculation tables, by an imperfect audit trail and by unclear labelling inherited from the past, creating a great reliance on individual experts.

■ **Imperfect understanding of pension types:** Finally, though this is a less important contribution to the errors than the two factors mentioned above, it is worth noting that communication between the industry and ONS is also confused by imperfect understanding of different categories of pensions and/or by imprecise categorisation of data. As Table A.3 shows, it is vital to understand the different and overlapping categorisations of pension types between Occupational versus Personal Contract, Employer provided versus Individually Bought, DB versus DC, and Self-administered versus Insurance Company managed. Confusion as to the appropriate categorisation of **Group** Personal Pensions, both in communication between the industry and ONS and possibly within insurance companies when filling in the MQ5 survey, have added an extra source of uncertainty about the meaning of some aggregate figures.

Major steps are now being taken by ONS, through the inter-departmental Pension Statistics Task Force, to put right these problems, and the Pensions Commission will continue to work closely with ONS in the resolution of the remaining issues, and looks forward to the improved data which should flow from the redesign of the crucial MQ5 survey. But we urge all the relevant wings of government (DWP, HM Treasury, Inland Revenue and ONS) to consider whether there are wider lessons to be learnt from these problems, which have resulted in figures appearing in UK National Accounts, the single most important document in national economic statistics, which are wrong by whole percentage points of GDP. In particular we pose the following questions:

■ How can cross-departmental co-ordination and flows of information and insight be improved? We found in our discussions with the Inland Revenue that they had concerns about one aspect of the ONS methodology going back to the early 1990s. However these concerns and their solution to the problem had not been shared with the ONS, which could have led to much earlier identification of some of these problems.

■ Should there be better processes for high level checking of the credibility

Table A.3 Types of Private Pension Provision

Occupational salary related	Occupational money purchase	Group personal pension	Individual personal pension
Occupational		Personal (contract based)	
Employer Sponsored			Not employer sponsored
DB	DC		

Occupational schemes can also be divided between self-administered and insurance managed. Most but not quite all DB schemes are self-administered.

Note: An occupational scheme is one with scheme trustees and governed by trust law. A personal pension (whether sponsored by an employer or not) has the legal form of a contract between an individual and a pension provider (usually an insurance company).
Individual personal pensions are most common among the self-employed and others who are not entitled to join occupational schemes such as those in partnerships.
Stakeholder pensions are a subset of personal pensions and can be either GPP or individual personal pension in form.

of major National Statistics figures? It should for instance be obvious to any well-informed user that the line in Table 6.1.4S of the Blue Book for 'Pensions by life companies' (D.622-QZBU) displays a trend which makes no sense, and seems likely to be wrong by many billions if not tens of billions of pounds. But there appears to be no mechanism for ensuring that such obvious order-of-magnitude credibility checks are made.

■ Does ONS have sufficient and appropriate resources to do its task effectively? Our analysis has revealed that many key calculation steps which go into the National Income and Accounts estimates are dependent on complex and inadequately documented legacy systems, and that there is significant 'key person' risk (i.e. very few people in a position to describe the underlying structure of calculations, which cannot be worked out without prior knowledge due to incomplete documentation and confusing labelling).

5. Other areas of analysis

This sub-section covers three other analytical areas not covered elsewhere in this Appendix.

■ **Healthy/unhealthy ageing debate:** Chapter 2 addresses the issue of how far average retirement ages can and should rise. It identified that a crucial issue was whether increased longevity, and in particular increased life expectancy at age 65, is resulting in more years of healthy active old age, or more years of ill-health, or what the balance of the two effects is. We have tried to identify existing analysis of this issue, but have found it surprisingly limited. Several published analyses draw on self-reported measures of health, but often without considering whether changes in expectations of health over time make time series analysis of this data open to misinterpretation. Conversely there are very few studies which have looked at objective measures of health (e.g. ability to perform basic physical tasks) over time. This data will become available as ELSA matures, but it will be 10-20 years before we can start drawing reasonably confident conclusions.

Given the importance of this issue across a wide range of public policy areas – health care, residential care, employment rights policy (e.g. the default age of retirement debate), and pensions – we flag this issue as an important priority for research, which the Medical Research Council (MRC) and the Economic and Social Research Council (ESRC) in particular may want to consider. We recommend that steps be taken to ensure that DWP and the Department of Health share data and insights on this issue.

■ **Consumption patterns in old age:** In our analyses of pension income adequacy in Chapter 4, we looked at expenditure patterns of pensioner households using information from the Expenditure and Food Survey. However, at present the data is only available on a household non-

Mile End Library

Queen Mary, University of London
Summer Vacation
9th June - 17th September

Extended Summer Vacation Loans
Ordinary Loans borrowed or renewed
from Saturday 12th May
will be due back on
Friday 28th September

One Week Loans borrowed or renewed
from Saturday 2nd June
will be due back on
Wednesday 26th September

Borrowed items 31/08/2012 11:19
XXXXXX7765

Item Title	Due Date
New developments in intern:	14/09/2012
International commercial arb	14/09/2012
* Pensions : challenges and	14/09/2012
* The politics of retirement ir	14/09/2012

* Indicates items borrowed today
PLEASE NOTE
If you still have overdue books on loan
you may have more fines to pay

PLEASE NOTE
Summer Vacation Loans will be recalled
if they are required by another reader
and must be returned
Please check or forward your e-mail
if you will be away from college

equivalised basis. This can exaggerate the decline in expenditure of older households relative to younger ones because of decreasing household size. The Commission welcomes ONS plans to look at the equivalisation issue shortly.

- **Surveys of attitudes and expectations:** It is vital to understand people's motives for saving, why many people save little, and people's expectations for retirement. Appropriate policy choices may differ according to the reasons for inadequate saving, for example whether it is seen as a low priority, whether it results from underestimates of the levels of saving required to secure adequate retirement income, or whether people are planning to retire later than previous generations. Appropriate policy, or the actual outcome from a laissez-faire approach, will also differ according to people's subjective definitions of pension adequacy, and according to their preference between the four different options (later average retirement, higher taxes, higher savings and poorer pensioners) outlined in Chapter 1. And assessment of the compulsion option should be informed by the best available evidence on the balance of opinion for and against, among individuals and among employers.

  For this report the Pensions Commission has drawn on a number of surveys of expectations and attitudes, but we have not systematically reviewed all available surveys and analyses. Over the coming year the Pensions Commission intends to commission research into attitudes and expectations, and will systematically review the existing survey data available. We encourage all interested parties to draw our attention to such survey data during the consultation period. In our 2005 Report we will make recommendations to government on whether official surveys should play a bigger role in developing a better understanding of attitudes and expectations.

6. Summary of recommendations on data improvements

This section summarises both likely developments already in hand which the Pensions Commission welcomes, and recommendations on further improvements which should be considered.

We welcome in particular:

- The work of the Pension Statistics Task Force to improve aggregate data.

- NES piloting of new questions on employer and employee contributions.

- The plans of the new Pensions Regulator to develop a regular detailed analysis of scheme returns.

- The better information likely to emerge from data sharing between DWP and Inland Revenue made possible by the current Pensions Bill.

- ONS plans to include equivalised income analyses within the Expenditure and Food Survey.

We make the following recommendations on priorities:

■ The ONS Wealth and Assets Survey should be a major priority, and should aim to support:

  – Effective longitudinal analysis.

  – Analysis of pension rights accumulation among all age groups.

  – Analysis of the impact of inheritance on asset accumulation.

  – Linkage to administrative records to allow a complete pension picture, including state pension rights.

  – Some analysis of expectations and attitudes that influence savings behaviour.

■ Completion of the development of Pensim2, and its availability for Pensions Commission analysis, is important. We hope to be able to use its modelling capability during the next year of our work: this requires that it is available for use by, or on behalf of, the Pensions Commission by the end of February 2005 to help us develop and inform our conclusions for the Second Report.

We make the following proposals for consideration:

■ It would be preferable for the Employers' Pension Provision (EPP) survey to be undertaken every two years.

■ Adequate information needs to be gathered on GPP schemes as well as on trustee-based occupational schemes. GAD and the new Pensions Regulator should give consideration to how such data can be gathered, and to the co-ordination of their data gathering efforts.

■ DWP and Department of Health should consider how best to share insights and co-ordinate research into the healthy/unhealthy ageing debate, which the relevant research councils (MRC and ESRC) should also note as a key issue for society.

■ HM Treasury, DWP, ONS and Inland Revenue should consider whether there are wider lessons to be learnt from the severe problems that have occurred in aggregate pension statistics, looking in particular at (i) cross-departmental co-ordination (ii) high-level credibility checks (iii) resource adequacy within ONS.

Macro-theory and Macro Modelling

This Appendix covers two subjects:

1   The macroeconomic theory of pensions and in particular the differences, but also the similarities, between funded and unfunded pension systems.[1]

2   A description of the macro model of pension contributions and pensioner incomes, the results of which were presented in Chapter 4.

THE MACROECONOMICS OF PENSIONS

A crucial choice in pension system design is whether to rely on an unfunded Pay As You Go (PAYG) system or to fund pensions via investments in marketable assets. There are important differences between these two approaches, but both entail a transfer of resources from the working population to pensioners and both therefore are affected by changing demography. This section sets out the key differences and similarities, dealing in turn with:

1   Demographic change and PAYG systems.

2   The theory of funded savings: what is different and what is not.

3   Demographic impacts on rates of return and asset prices: the theory.

4   Impacts on rates of return and asset prices: estimates of size.

5   Does overseas investment in global capital markets provide an escape from the demographic effect?

6   Housing as a pension asset.

[1] Note: This review of the theory is set out in more detail in Adair Turner's, "The MacroEconomics of Pensions", lecture to the Actuarial Profession, 2003.

1. Demographic change and PAYG systems

In a PAYG system it is clear that the current generation of pensioners is dependent on the taxes/social insurance contributions paid by the current generation of workers, and that the ratio of workers to pensioners determines the relationship between contribution rates as a percentage of earnings and pensions as a percentage of earnings. Thus in a simplified example, in which people work for 45 years and retire for 15 years, in which each generation is the same size, and in which all people earn the same, a tax/contribution rate of 20% on all earnings can support a pension equal to 60% of average earnings, because there are three times as many workers as pensioners.

Given this relationship it is easy to understand the impact of demographic change on a PAYG system.

■ If life expectancy increases but the retirement age does not, then the ratio of workers to pensioners falls and either (i) pensioners must accept a lower pension relative to average earnings or (ii) workers must pay a higher percentage of earnings in taxes/contributions. However if instead the retirement age rises to keep stable the proportion of adult life spent working (e.g. if an extra 4 years of adult life are divided between 3 years of extra work and 1 extra year of retirement) then no change in either the contribution rate nor in the generosity of pensions is required to keep the system in balance.

■ But if fertility falls the problems are more difficult to overcome. The ratio of workers to pensioners now falls even though life expectancy is unchanged: and an increase in the proportion of adult life spent working is now required if either higher contributions or less generous pensions are to be avoided. Thus in our simple example, if the next generation is 25% smaller (which would be the result of a fertility rate of 1.5 children per woman) the ratio of workers to pensioners falls from 3.0 to 2.25, and either the contribution rate has to rise by a third, or pensions have to fall by 25%, or the retirement age has to rise by 3 years despite unchanged life expectancy, cutting the number of years of retirement by 3 years. (There are then 4 years of work per year of retirement (48:12), but 3 workers per retiree because each generation is 25% smaller.)

The impact of falling fertility is thus more difficult to deal with than a rise in longevity. It is also worth noting that lower fertility reduces the implicit return which people receive on their PAYG pension contributions.

■ In a stable and non-redistributive PAYG system, with the contribution rate as a percentage of earnings stable and the level of pensions as a percentage of average earnings also stable, pension scheme members receive an effective rate of return equal to the rate of growth of the population plus the rate of productivity growth, which together equal the growth rate of the economy.[2]

[2]Note: For the classic presentation of these relationships see P Samuelson, "An exact consumption loan model of interest with and without the social contrivance of money". Journal of Political Economy 66. 1958.

■ Therefore if the population growth rate falls (or becomes negative) and if productivity rates are unchanged, the effective rate of return falls.

■ The returns effectively earned within PAYG systems during the second half of the 20th century were swollen by population growth: the relationship between contribution rate in and pensions out was only sustainable because each successive generation was larger than the one before. As population growth slows or reverses lower implicit rates of return in PAYG schemes are inevitable, whatever the trade-off chosen between higher contributions, lower pensions and higher retirement ages.

2. Funded savings: what is different and what is not

In funded systems, as much as in unfunded PAYG systems, there has to be a transfer of real resources from the working generation to the retired generation. If pensioners are to consume but not to produce, there have to be workers who consume less than they produce, and who in some way transfer resources to pensioners. The difference lies therefore not in the fact of resource transfer, but in the mechanism by which it is achieved. In funded systems workers put savings into funded pensions and by doing so they reduce their consumption. When they retire they then sell their accumulated assets to the next generation of workers/savers, and receive money with which to buy consumption goods which have been produced but not consumed by the next generation of workers. A resource transfer is achieved, but via the market for capital assets not via the tax system.

The fact that a resource transfer must still occur does not mean that a funded system has no advantages, but it does mean that funded systems are, like unfunded, affected by demographic factors and in an analogous way.

The potential advantages of a funded system can be considered at both the individual and at the aggregate level.

■ **Advantage at the individual level: a higher rate of return?** As explained above, a PAYG system on average delivers a return to members equal to the rate of growth of the economy. It therefore follows that if a funded system can deliver a return which is higher than the national economic growth rate, individual members can be better off in retirement. Appendix C sets out historical patterns of rates of return on equities and bonds, and explains the assumptions we have made looking forward. It stresses the high variability of past returns and the limited help which economic theory gives us in determining what rates of return are likely on average to be. But one finding of macroeconomic growth theory is that in an efficient economy the average rate of return on all productive assets (to which equities and bonds are indirect ownership claims) will be higher than the rate of growth. Provided that selling, administration and fund management costs are not too high therefore, individuals should on average be better off in funded schemes: and the assumptions we have made in our various models all assume average returns above the likely growth rate (e.g. 3-4% real after charges rather than the growth rate of about 2% real). We must note however that these higher rates of return cannot be secured without significant exposure to higher risk equity assets. Thus while **on average** individuals are likely to gain from a funded system, some may lose, while others may gain a great deal.

■ **Advantages at the aggregate level: a higher rate of saving?** When an individual saves in a funded pension scheme, the extra saving they make could either result in real investment in productive assets (in which case aggregate national savings and investment rise, while aggregate consumption at least initially falls), or the extra saving could be matched by someone else selling to the new saver an existing asset (in which case there is no change in aggregate savings, investment and consumption, with one person's decision to save and defer consumption offset by another's decision to dissave and bring forward consumption).

From the individual's point of view, it does not matter which is the case: all that matters is that the return achieved is above that implicit within the PAYG scheme. But at the aggregate level, a move from unfunded to funded pensions can only produce additional aggregate resources to support future pensioners if aggregate national savings are increased, and if additional future national income is generated, either via greater domestic capital investment and increased productivity (which increases GDP) or via investment abroad which generates increased future investment income (increasing GNP but not GDP).

There are therefore two important issues to be considered when assessing the merits of a move to a more funded system, and in particular when assessing any compulsory system of funded saving.

These are:

(i) Does the introduction of compulsory savings actually result in an increase in aggregate national savings, or are additional savings in pensions offset by lower savings or additional debt elsewhere? The available evidence we have on this issue is not extensive. But as Chapter 7 and Appendix D set out the best study of the most relevant country for UK comparison, i.e. Australia, does suggest that the offsets are not total and that a significant increase in aggregate retirement savings is achieved.[3]

---

[3]Note: The issue of whether the national savings rate increases if a compulsory savings scheme is introduced depends not only on the behaviour of individuals, but also on whether these compulsory savings are in addition to or instead of contributions to a prior existing PAYG scheme. If they are instead of, then the government will, everything else equal, need to borrow money to meet its obligations to the present generation of pensioners (who contributed to the PAYG scheme when they were workers) and this government borrowing will offset the increased private saving at the level of aggregate national saving . Only if people are required to save in addition to supporting the previous generation via PAYG contributions can compulsory savings raise the national savings rate.

(ii) If aggregate national savings do increase, will this inevitably mean that the rate of return achieved on savings decreases, and how does this vary according to whether the savings are invested in the home country or overseas? And are returns on savings affected by demographic factors, even in situations where aggregate national savings do not increase? This issue is considered in the next section of this Appendix.

Subject to the answers to these two questions, therefore, funded pension systems can have advantages over PAYG, and there can therefore be a macroeconomic case for including a funded element as well as a PAYG element within the compulsory part of a pension system. But equally it is worth noting that it is possible to design a compulsory funded scheme which delivers no benefits over PAYG either to individuals or to the aggregate economy. Thus:

■ If people are compelled to save and either are compelled to or choose to invest their money in government bonds; and

■ If the government issues more bonds to meet this demand and to fill the public finance gap created by the loss of PAYG contributions previously paid; and

■ If the rate of return on government bonds is equal to the rate of growth (which tends to be roughly the case in developed economies):

■ Then it can then be demonstrated that such a funded scheme is the precise economic equivalent of a PAYG scheme, in terms of aggregate savings, investment and consumption, and in terms of each individual's consumption levels in both working life and retirement. Nor is this just a hypothetical illustration. The Mexican system of compulsory funded pension systems, with a requirement for investment in government bonds, achieves essentially this effect, but with the disadvantage of administration costs well above those of a well-run PAYG scheme.

3. Demography, rates of return and asset prices: theory

Funding pensions can thus have the advantages set out above. But there is still an underlying resource transfer from current workers to current pensioners, and it is therefore inevitable that the stresses created within a PAYG system by a declining ratio of workers to pensioners are matched by analogous effects within funded systems. In a funded system, these stresses operate through the market for capital assets and the rates of return earned on those assets. And, just as for PAYG systems so for funded, there are subtly different implications when we consider first increased longevity and then reduced fertility.

■ **Increased life expectancy:** The impact of increased life expectancy on rates of return and asset prices depends on the behaviour of both the present generation and next generation.

– If life expectancy increases, and people do not accept an increase in retirement age, and if the savings rate during working life remains unchanged, pensioners will reach retirement with the same assets as before, but facing a longer retirement to fund and will therefore secure a lower annual pension income.

– If, however, faced with this prospect, people increase their savings rates and increase domestic investment, this produces an increase in the capital stock relative to an unchanged supply of labour, and economic theory suggests that this must imply a fall in the rate of return on capital, even if the next generation, also facing increasing longevity, has the same preference for higher saving over later retirement, and therefore chooses to buy the increased capital stock.

– If, however, the next generation makes a different choice and decides to retire later and to reduce its savings rate back to the original level, the current generation will face the additional problem that capital asset prices may then fall as it attempts to sell its accumulated capital stock to the next generation (since the next generation has a lower desired capital stock than that accumulated by the present generation).

Increased life expectancy can therefore create capital market return and price effects if a higher savings rate is chosen in preference to later retirement, and the severity of those effects depends not only on the savings behaviour of the current generation, but also on the savings behaviour of future generations.

But just as we saw with the PAYG system, so with the funded system, if the only demographic change we faced was increased longevity, and if the response was to accept a proportionate rise in the retirement age, all the problems would disappear. Thus if to repeat the simple example used earlier, longevity increased by 4 years and the retirement age increased by 3 years to keep stable the proportion of adult life spent working, then no increase in the savings rate is required to continue to secure the same retirement income, since the 3 years of extra work and of investment return fund (and indeed slightly more than fund) an extra year of retirement at the same annual pension income as before.[4] And while in this scenario the capital stock increases, so too does the supply of labour, leaving the capital/labour ratio unchanged, and the relative supply and demand for existing assets also unchanged. There is therefore no reason for change either in returns or in asset prices.

[4]Note: Provided that the rate of return earned is higher than the rate of growth, the impact of an extra year's compounding of investment return is such that the proportional rise in retirement age will, in the funded system, produce not only the equivalent pension, but actually a slightly larger one. Or, alternatively, the rise in the retirement age required to keep the system in equilibrium is, in a funded system, very slightly less than proportional. This is however a relatively minor second-order qualification to the close equivalence of the demographic challenge in funded and unfunded systems.

■ **Falling fertility:** However just as with PAYG systems so with funded, a proportional rise in retirement ages is not a sufficient solution if the demographic factor at work is falling fertility. If the current generation saves to fund its retirement, but is then followed by a smaller next generation, then the capital stock/labour supply ratio will increase, tending to reduce the rate of return. And as the current generation attempts to sell its accumulated assets to a smaller next generation, (which because smaller has in total a smaller asset accumulation requirement), capital asset prices will tend to fall.

It is this logic which lies behind concerns that the attempt of the baby boom generation to sell its accumulated pension assets will lead to falling asset prices, and, in the more sensational versions of the story, to an "asset price meltdown".

4. Impact on return and asset prices: possible size of the effects

As explained above there are good theoretical arguments for believing that demographic factors will affect asset returns and asset prices. There is general agreement among economists that these effects ought to be present, and the direction of change is clear. The crucial issue is how large the effects might be. Much theoretical and empirical work has been devoted to estimating them.

There are two separate though related effects we are trying to estimate.

■ **Changes in the rates of return earned on capital assets:** These changes derive from changes in the capital/labour ratio and should therefore be permanent effects if the demographic effects are permanent, e.g. an economy with a permanently falling population ought in perpetuity to have lower returns to capital than one with a growing population. And these changes would occur even in a theoretical world of totally efficient capital markets.

■ **Changes in the prices at which existing capital assets trade, e.g. at which equities (which are claims on capital assets) trade:** These changes are more transitional in nature, and would not occur in the theoretical world of perfect information and immediately adjusting markets. If new capital goods could be created immediately, and if old capital goods either become redundant immediately or could be converted into consumption goods, capital asset price fluctuations driven by demography would not occur because capital assets would always be valued at their replacement cost. And if equity markets efficiently processed all information, and if likely demographic changes were understood far in advance, abrupt changes in asset prices, driven by demography, would be impossible: if it were known for certain that equity prices were going to fall when the baby boom generation retires, in an efficient equity market they would have already fallen. In fact equity markets are not perfectly efficient and foresighted so future unanticipated falls are possible.

There are two possible ways of estimating these different effects. One is to develop complex equilibrium models, with multiple overlapping generations and assumptions about savings behaviours over the life-cycle which match real world experience, and to observe the different results that these models produce when we plug in likely future demographic changes.

The other is to use econometric techniques to measure whether past changes in returns or in asset prices have correlated with changes in demography.

The models tend to suggest small but non-trivial changes in underlying rates of return, and somewhat larger changes in asset prices (though with the latter results highly influenced by the specific assumptions made). Thus:

- ■ **Underlying rates of return: model results:** A Bank of England working paper by Garry Young shows that UK rates of return might fall by about 0.5% in the face of the three different demographic factors we face (increased longevity, a sustained fertility fall, and the one-off impact of the baby boom).[5] A study by Professor David Miles illustrates real returns falling from 4.6% to 4.2% in the face of the UK's possible demographic change, and to slightly below 4.0% if in addition a major shift from PAYG provision to funded saving was achieved.[6] Similar studies for the US produce similar order of magnitude effects.[7]

  These effects are modest but not trivial. They should not be compared with returns achieved only in the 1980s and 1990s and only on equities (e.g. 10-15% real) but with the likely long-term average return on all productive assets, and on all the claims on those assets (bonds and equities combined). This is more likely to be about the 4.0-4.5% real which Professor Miles illustrates, and which is slightly lower still once transaction costs are taken into account. Appendix C justifies the use of a 3.0-4.0% range for average real returns after transaction costs. Against these returns a demographic effect of say 0.5% is modest but not trivial.

- ■ **Asset prices: model results:** The results from models of asset prices are heavily dependent on the precise assumptions made, e.g. on the variability of the supply of capital goods, and on the degree of capital market foresight. But some models suggest the possibility of a baby-boom effect which first raises asset prices by between 15-35% above their base case (no demographic change) level, with this effect then unwinding and then generating falling prices as the baby boom generation retires.[8]

[5] Note: Garry Young, "The implications of an ageing population for the UK economy," Bank of England Working Paper.

[6] Note: David Miles, "Modelling the impact of demographic change in the economy," Economic Journal.

[7] Note: See e.g. Peter Yoo, "Age Distribution and Returns on Financial Assets," Federal Reserve Bank of St Louis Working Paper 94-002b. See the attachment to James Poterba's article cited in note 9 for a fuller set of references.

[8] Note: See Yoo op cit, and see Poterba, cited in Footnote 9, for the full range of literature.

The econometric evidence on whether these effects have actually been seen in the past has been summarised by Professor James Poterba in a recent paper.[9] The results at first sight appear confusing. It is not possible to find statistically significant correlations between past demographic patterns and past movements in real returns. But conversely some studies find evidence of demography-induced changes in asset prices which are considerably larger than the theoretical models suggest are likely, and which provide econometric support to the prima facie observation of a relationship between demographic developments and equity prices, which simple chart analysis appears to suggest [Figure B.I].

The empirical evidence is therefore frustratingly unclear. But this should not surprise us, given the limitations of econometric methodologies when there is a huge amount of noise and too few observations. Returns on equity over say 10 year periods are only marginally affected by underlying real developments during each period and hugely by the extent to which developments were foreseen at the beginning of the period, and by swings of sometimes irrational exuberance and despondency. And the available historical record of liquid capital markets only includes one period of fertility increase (the post-war baby boom) and one of fertility decline. There are simply not enough data points in the history of stock market capitalism for us to be able to discern clear patterns.

Frustrating though it is therefore, we have to face the limitation of empirical analysis and accept, as Professor Poterba says, that "the theoretical models should be accorded substantial weight in evaluating the potential impact of demographic shifts."[10]

Figure B.1 Real S&P500 Price Index and Percentage of 40-64 Year Olds Among Total U.S. Population, 1950-2003

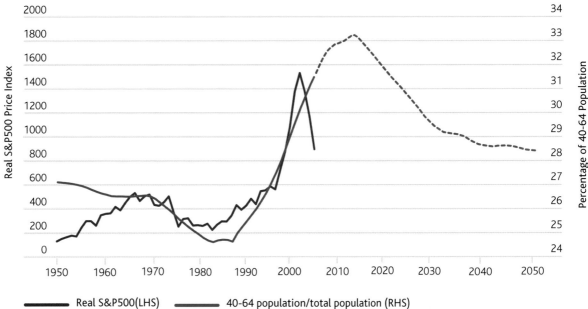

Real S&P500(LHS)   40-64 population/total population (RHS)

Source: Poterba (2004)

[9] Note: James Poterba. "Population Ageing and Financial Markets", paper presented to Federal Reserve Bank of Kansas Jackson Hole Economic Symposium, August 2004.

[10] See 9

What those theoretical models tell us is that demographic change is likely to have a mildly depressive effect on underlying rates of return, and that there may also be transitional demographic effects on asset prices (both up and down) which are extremely difficult to predict, but which introduce an added element of risk into equity market investment. These demographic effects then need to be considered alongside other analyses of likely returns.

As Appendix C sets out, estimating future returns, and in particular equity return, would be extremely difficult even if there were no demographic effects at work. Past returns over 10, 20, and 30 year periods have been very highly volatile, and there are in any case major theoretical issues over whether the past record carries any clear implications for future performance. But what is clear is that the equity returns of the 1980s and 1990s were exceptionally high. Demographic factors provide simply one additional reason for believing that these returns are extremely unlikely to be repeated over the long-term.

For **our projections of future equity returns**, explained in Appendix C, we therefore take the longest-term possible historic averages as the best but imperfect guide to future possible returns, but note that these assumptions are likely to be slightly too optimistic if demographic factors do produce effects in line with what the models predict.

5. Does the option of overseas investment change the picture?

As discussed above, one of the ways to estimate the impact of demographic change on returns and asset prices is to build complex models. These models tend to assume a closed economy, i.e. one in which increased savings must mean increased domestic investment, and in which resource transfers to future pensioners have to be from workers in the same country. And while the alternative estimating approach (using econometric analysis) makes no assumptions, but simply analyses whether past correlations can be identified given whatever mix of domestic and overseas investment actually pertained during the period analysed, it may be that the extent of overseas investment has increased over time with globalisation and has the potential to increase further. The question therefore arises whether increased overseas investment is a way round demographic effects, i.e. whether developed world savers can avoid declining return and asset price effects by investing overseas, creating increased capital stock in developing countries which still have expanding labour forces.

This issue has been extensively debated. The growing consensus suggests that overseas investment can make some difference, particularly for small countries, but that it does not entirely remove the impact of demographic effects, since these are increasingly global in nature.

■ Small countries are more likely to be able to benefit from an overseas investment approach, simply because a greater proportion of their increased saving can feasibly flow overseas. In an economy the size of the U.S., however, a significant part of increased savings is likely to result in increased domestic investment, given in particular the "home country" bias documented in several studies.[11]

■ But the more fundamental point is that the demographic trends towards increasing longevity and falling fertility are spreading to all economically successful developing countries far faster than demographers originally assumed. Fertility rates are forecast, on the United National Medium Variant, to fall below replacement level within 10-15 years in countries as diverse as Brazil, Turkey and Iran and in the five most economically successful states of India. They are already well below replacement level, and among the lowest rates in the world throughout East Asia: in China, South Korea, Hong Kong and Singapore, as well as Japan. The biggest demographic and pension challenges in the next 50 years indeed will arise not in developed countries but in currently low or middle income countries such as China and South Korea. The latter currently has 9.0 people aged 20-65 for every person over 65. By 2050 this is forecast to fall to 1.7 [Table B.1].

Table B.1 Ratio of 20-64 Year Olds to 65+

	2000	2050
UK	3.7	2.1
Italy	3.4	1.4
USA	4.8	2.8
China	8.8	2.4
Korea	9.0	1.7
World	7.8	3.6

Source: United Nations, Medium Variant

[11] Note: See Feldstein and Horioka, "Domestic Savings and International Capital Flows", Economic Journal 90, 1980.

Some of these developing countries are therefore already debating whether they need to invest overseas to support their future pensioners, not planning that their future workers will support western pensioners. And as demographic trends become increasingly global, the rate of return implications predicted by the models will apply at the level of the global capital market.[12]

The possibility of overseas investment through the global capital market therefore ameliorates slightly but does not remove the potential return and asset price effects of demographic change. It reduces further the already very slight risk of sensational "asset price meltdown" scenarios, since the different timing of demographic changes in different markets will help generate smooth rather than sudden equity market adjustments. But it leaves unchanged our modelling assumption. We assume equity market returns in line with very long-term averages, but we note the possibility that this may be slightly on the optimistic side in an era of lower fertility, particularly if the percentage of adult life spent in retirement increases as longevity rises.

6. Houses as pension assets: are they different?

As Chapter 5 of the Report illustrates, owner-occupied residential housing assets form a more important element of UK household wealth than either pensions or other financial assets. Total assets held via pension funds were around £1,300 billion at end 2003, other financial assets about £1,150 billion excluding unquoted equity, while the gross value of houses was about £3,000 billion, and even after mortgage debt of £750 billion, net housing wealth is about £2,250 billion. There is moreover at least anecdotal evidence that a growing number of people consider housing wealth to be a potential pension asset.

There is no reason in principle why they should not do so. In theory a funded pension system could be constructed entirely around the purchase and sale of houses, and much of the macroeconomic theory of funded pensions, and the assessment of the potential advantages of funded pensions versus PAYG, applies to housing assets in exactly the same way as to any other asset class. But the demographic risks also apply, and indeed may be exacerbated by some specific characteristics of the housing market, particularly in densely populated regions where there are tight controls on the supply of building land.

---

[12] Note: It is of course the case that some countries, particularly in Western Asia (e.g., Pakistan and Afghanistan), the Middle East and Africa still have rapidly expanding working populations and are likely to have them until at least the second half of the twenty-first century. But these countries also include a high proportion where political and economic instability undermine their attractiveness as investment destinations. The "Catch 22" of the argument that overseas investment in countries with expanding populations provides an escape from demographic effects, is that whenever countries become economically successful enough to be attractive investment destinations that economic success in itself means that they experience rapid birth rate decline.

Thus:

■ It is quite possible to envisage a hypothetical economy in which the transfer of consumption resources from workers to pensioners is effected entirely via the purchase and sale of houses. This could operate in one of two ways.

  – Current workers could steadily during their working lives purchase houses and then as pensioners could, via equity release style products, gradually sell off their homes, leaving no housing assets to bequeath. At present this happens only to a minimal extent. Broadly speaking, most current ownership of non-housing assets is via pension funds and is "life-cycle self-liquidating" in nature i.e. accumulated during working life and decumulated as pension receipts during retirement.[13] Most housing assets conversely are not liquidated during retirement, but held till death and bequeathed. There is however no theoretical reason why this pattern should not be reversed, with housing assets liquidated during retirement, and a much higher proportion of financial assets held till death and bequeathed.

  – Alternatively, each generation of workers could purchase a home during working life, and could keep ownership throughout retirement, bequeathing it to the next generation of workers (then likely to be approaching retirement) who, since already owners of one house each, would sell this house on to the subsequent generation.

■ The conditions required for such a system to be advantageous to the individual, when compared to PAYG scheme membership, are moreover exactly those which apply if a funded scheme is invested in any other asset class. If the total return on housing assets (combining price appreciation and the "implicit rent" benefit of rent-free accommodation) exceeds the national economic growth rate, the individual gains, and if it is less they lose.

■ And the conditions which need to apply if saving in housing is to help meet the demographic challenge at the aggregate level are also the same as for other assets: there has to be an increase in aggregate national savings and thus in future GDP. Thus if extra savings in housing produces an increase in aggregate national **investment** in housing (i.e. real new house building and house improvement) and if the "housing services" delivered by that increased asset are valued by the next generation, then an increase in real GDP has occurred which helps provide real resources to support future pensioners.

The specific nature of housing assets, however, is shown by the fact that it appears that housing might provide the basis for an increased level of

[13] Note: See Chapter 5 for empirical analysis of how far different categories are actually run down in retirement versus bequeathed.

transfer from workers to pensioners even if aggregate national saving and investment does not increase. If, even without new investment in home improvements, house prices keep rising above the rate of growth of the economy, (i.e. keep rising relative to average earnings) then each new generation of workers would have to save an increasing proportion of income during working life to buy one house, and this could support an increasing percentage of GDP transferred to pensioners and thus allow an increasing number of pensioners to receive incomes rising with average earnings. And it is at least possible that house prices could rise faster than GDP, and thus faster than average earnings, if not in perpetuity, at least for many decades, if a large element of the house price reflects not the replacement building cost, but land prices.

This can occur if land is in general in scarce supply, and/or if house prices reflect the very specific characteristics of the land on which the house sits i.e. the specific attractiveness of a specific location. The more that housing is a scarce supply "positional" good, rather than a capital good whose value bears some relationship to replacement cost, the more that it might under some specific circumstances support increased transfer of resources from workers to pensioners even if no real new investment in housing assets was occurring.

But the more too its price will be exposed to the demographic risks discussed above in relation to asset prices in general. It was noted in that discussion that no demographic effect would be anticipated if capital goods could be produced instantaneously or if they become redundant (i.e. fully depreciated) very rapidly, since in those circumstances existing capital asset prices are always equal to replacement cost. The longer the life of an asset, and the longer the time it takes for new supply to respond to higher prices, the greater the extent to which the asset price rather than the volume of supply will change if the balance of buyers and sellers changes, for instance as a result of demographic change. Housing is a very long-life asset, and in a densely populated region with tight planning rules, an asset whose new supply is less elastic than almost any non-housing capital asset. And because in housing there is a huge "home country bias", i.e. almost all UK housing is owned by UK workers/pensioners, the ameliorative effects of diversification via the global capital market is minimal.

It is therefore likely that any demographic effects on asset prices (the possibility that the baby-boom generation could generate first an upward surge in asset prices and then a fall as they retire) is more likely to be seen in house prices than in any other asset category. Whether it will occur and its implications for house prices from today's starting point, depends upon a number of other highly uncertain factors, e.g. whether the present level of house prices is at an equilibrium, or at an irrationally higher peak, and whether immigration will underpin house prices even as fertility falls.

But the fundamental point is clear: housing assets can be used as self-liquidating life-cycle assets, i.e. as pension funds, but the demographic risks to house prices are probably even greater than those that apply to equities, at least in a country like the UK where the supply of new housing is highly inelastic.

MACRO MODEL

This section describes our macro model. The purpose of this model is to estimate the level of future pensioner income from private pension savings, given current contribution rates and reasonable assumptions on rates of return. This informs our conclusions on whether current savings behaviour is adequate to meet the demographic challenges, given the declining role of the state in pension provision. Key results of the model are presented in Chapter 4.

We set out below:

1   Key features of the model structure and assumptions.

2   Some key mathematical relationships.

3   The theoretical impact of increased longevity and declining fertility.

4   Results with order of magnitude UK values and demographic trends.

5   Reconciling results to current funded pension incomes.

6   A crucial issue: reduced "leakage" to early retirees?

7   The impact of an increased retirement age.

8   Sensitivities given different contribution rate and investment return assumptions.

1. Model structure

In the model, workers make cash contributions from their earnings. Employer contributions are not explicitly modelled but can be considered as increasing workers' earnings. These pension contributions are invested and the investment income is capitalised each year to produce a fund at retirement. The fund is then used to buy an annuity. In effect, this income flow in retirement stems partly from the sale of capital and partly from investment return on the declining fund. The annuity is assumed to be fair so that the fund is exhausted when a worker dies, after having lived for the average life expectancy post-retirement.

Several simplifying assumptions are being made in the model.

■   Pension savings are the only savings so that there are no other owners of capital in the domestic economy. An additional sector of "other capital" and "other return" could however be added without invalidating our results.

■ The economy is assumed to be "open". As a result the rate of return on investments and wages are exogenously determined and are not affected by changes to the savings rate or the capital: labour ratio. We do not therefore allow for any of the possible negative demographic impacts on rates of return which were considered in the macroeconomic theory section of this Appendix.

■ There is no explicitly modelled corporate sector. Workers are implicitly sole proprietors with capital expenditure a deduction from gross income.

■ There is also no government sector.

Over one hundred overlapping single year cohorts enter the simulation, each adopting the pattern of pension fund accumulation and decumulation described above. Each cohort is assumed to start working and contributing to a pension at the age of 25. In the base case 40 years are spent in work and contributing to a pension: retirement is at 65, at which point life expectancy is assumed to be 20 years so that each cohort dies at age 84, having exhausted their pension funds. The base case assumes that each cohort is the same size.

The overlapping cohorts build up to a steady state in the year the first cohort dies. This can be straightforwardly explained in the base case because from this point, the total numbers of workers and pensioners remain constant. In each year after this point the pensioners in one cohort will die, the workers in the cohort 20 years behind will retire, while the cohort 60 years behind will start working and saving towards a pension.

The outputs we are interested in are the amounts of pension contributions, pension incomes, capital stock, investment income and earnings over all the living cohorts. These aggregates expressed as a percentage of GDP also achieve steady states once the first cohort in the model has died. Our analysis focuses on the aggregates in steady state, i.e. looking at a private pension system in maturity. We can define maturity as a state where all living cohorts contribute and have contributed to their pensions at the steady state rate for the whole of their working life to date.

Apart from retirement age and life expectancy at retirement, other variable inputs to the model are the rate at which earnings grow, the rate of cash contributions, the rate of investment return on the workers' funds during accumulation and the rate of return on pensioners' funds during decumulation. The size of each cohort can also be varied so that assumptions can be made about fertility.

2. Key mathematical relationships

Results from the model confirm the relationships between pension savings and pensioner incomes which theory would suggest: these are summarized in Figure B.2. As described above, workers' savings consist of contributions from their earnings and re-invested investment returns. Pension income flows in retirement stem partly from the sale of the capital in the pension fund and partly from investment income on the declining fund. The pensioners' capital is purchased by workers as part of their accumulation of a pension fund for retirement. The remainder of workers' pension savings is used to buy new capital. Thus the excess of workers' contributions, from earnings and investment income, over the sale of capital by pensioners accounts for growth in the capital stock. And on the bottom line of the table we can see how pensioners' incomes are increased if the term r-g is positive, i.e. if the return earned is higher than the growth rate, which we noted in the theory section above as the key condition required if pensioners are to be better off in a funded system than a PAYG system.

3. Theoretical impacts of increased longevity and declining fertility

Having developed the model, we first used it to test the impact of some simple "pure play" demographic scenarios. These illustrate the interesting fact that an increase in longevity, if turned into longer retirement rather than increased working life, results almost entirely in a fall in pension income per person, while a fall in fertility does not, the automatic dynamics of the relationships tending to produce an increase in the percentage of GDP transferred to pensioners.

Impact of longer life and retirement: To determine the impact of increasing life expectancy on pensioner incomes, the model was run again with every cohort having a life expectancy of 25 years at retirement (rather than 20) while all the other inputs stayed the same as in the base case. The steady state aggregates under the two scenarios were then compared. The inputs to and outputs from the two scenarios are shown in Table B.2.

Figure B.2 Relationship between Pension Savings and Pensioner Incomes

Pensions $=$ Investment income $+$ Capital sales
of pensioners   by pensioners

$=$ Investment income $+$ $\big[$ Savings of workers $-$ Net Capital $\big]$
of pensioners   Expenditure

$=$ Investment income $+$ $\big[$ Cash contributions $+$ Reinvested investment $-$ Net Capital $\big]$
of pensioners   income of workers   Expenditure

$=$ Cash contributions $+$ Investment income $+$ Investment income $-$ Net Capital
of workers   of pensioners   Expenditure

$=$ Cash contributions $+$ r_w X Capital Stock $+$ r_p X Capital Stock $-$ Net Capital
owned by   owned by   Expenditure
workers   pensioners

$=$ Cash contributions $+$ r X Capital Stock $-$ g X Capital
Stock

Thus
Pensions
as %
of GDP $=$ Cash Contributions $+$ r x k/GDP $-$ g x k/GDP
as % GDP

$=$ Cash Contributions $+$ $\big[\ r\ -\ g\ \big]$ x k/GDP
/GDP

where r_w = rate of return to workers during accumulation

r_p = rate of return to pensioners during decumulation

r = average rate of return to workers and pensioners

g = rate of growth

k = Capital stock

Note: As our model assumes that the economy is open it generates aggregates as a percentage of GNP rather than GDP, whereas the real UK economy aggregates with which we compare the model outputs are expressed as a percentage of GDP.

Table B.2 The Impact of Longer Life and Retirement on Pensioner Incomes as a percentage of GDP

Assumptions

Rate of cash contributions (% earnings)	3.5%
Rate of growth	2.0%
Rate of return during accumulation	4.0%
Rate of return during decumulation	4.0%
Years of working life	40

Model Results: Relationships between Pensioner Incomes and Pension Savings with Longer Retirement

	K/GDP	Pensioner income as % GDP	=	Cash contributions as % GDP	+ rK/GDP	−	gK/GDP
20 years of retirement	135.46%	5.97	=	3.31	+ 5.31	−	2.66
25 years of retirement	146.57%	6.17	=	3.30	+ 5.75	−	2.87

Comparison of longer retirement against base case

Percentage change in absolute pensioner income	+3.87%
Percentage change in per capita pensioner income	-16.90%
Percentage change in number of pensioners	+25.00%

With greater life expectancy but a fixed retirement age and working life, the same size pension fund has to generate income over a longer period of time. This results is a lower annuity and thus poorer pensioners. There is a 25% increase is the number of pensioners but total pensions as a percentage of GDP changes only by a small second order amount (from 5.97%-6.17%) (which is determined by the size of investment returns relative to the rate of growth). Figure B.3 shows that pensions fall far short of the increase required to maintain pensioner incomes relative to average net incomes. Hence if pension savings rates and the length of working life remain unchanged, the burden of longer life will be borne by pensioners.

It can also be noted in Table B.2 that in this scenario the capital output ratio (K/GDP) has increased slightly and it is useful to understand this dynamic. It arises because a pension annuity represents both an ongoing though declining stream of investment income plus sale of capital. Lower annuities over a longer period imply a slower sale of capital but greater investment income for pensioners because the capital is running down at a slower pace. This can be seen in Figure B.4. As pensioners sell their pension capital more slowly, there must be a slower purchase of existing capital stock by workers saving for their pensions. But workers' savings are assumed to remain unchanged: more of that saving therefore takes the form of new capital expenditure. This results in higher capital stock at the whole economy level and a higher capital output ratio. Thus the capital stock can increase in the face of increased longevity even if workers do not increase their rate of savings. This increase in the capital stock and of the capital output ratio raises the issue (discussed in the theory section) of whether investment returns will as a result fall. In this model however we assume that the increase does not lead to a fall in the rate of return, which is exogenously given.

Impact of lower fertility: To investigate the effect of lower fertility on pensioner incomes, the model was run with an assumed fertility rate of 1.7. If the average child-bearing age is taken to be 30, this leads to a generational replacement rate of 85% and each year's cohort will be 0.54% smaller than the previous one. A comparison of the results with the base case, which assumes a fertility rate of two, is contained in Table B.3.

Figure B.3 Increase in Private Pension Income as a Percentage of GDP in Longer Life and Unchanged Retirement Age Scenario

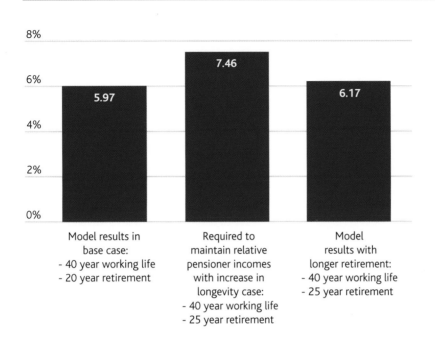

Figure B.4 Variation in Pension Income Sources through Retirement for Longer Retirement

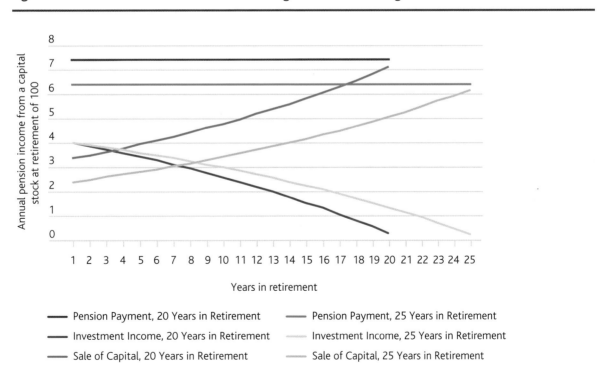

Pensioners' per capita incomes are unaffected by a fall in fertility as each individual works, saves and is retired for the same period. However, the decline in the number of workers leads to a fall in GDP: pensions as a percentage of GDP therefore increase proportionally to the rise in the dependency ratio. Figure B.5 illustrates that changes in fertility lead to automatic adjustments to pensions as a percentage of GDP such that pensioner incomes are maintained relative to average net incomes.

The mechanism by which this occurs is a decrease in new capital investment, as is clear in Table B.3. More of the capital purchased by workers is met by sales from pensioners so that less goes into new capital expenditure. Essentially what is happening is that whereas pensioners are becoming more of a burden on workers when measured in terms of the percentage of GDP transferred, this effect is offset by the fact that workers have been endowed with a larger capital stock (relative to need) than previous generations and thus have less need to make new capital investments. (This however will only be a real world effect if capital asset lives can be extended: if productivity growth depends on the scrapping of old capital and investment in new, the benefit of this effect will be offset by a higher level of depreciation as a percentage of GDP.) Despite this fall in capital expenditure, the capital output ratio increases because GDP falls further than the capital stock, but we assume that this does not result in a fall in the rate of return.

Figure B.5 Increase in Private Pension Income as a Percentage of GDP in Lower Fertility Scenario

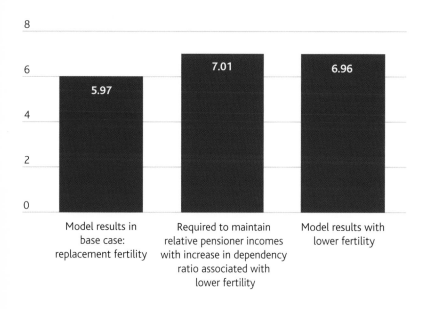

Table B.3 The Impact of Lower Fertility on Pensioner Incomes as a Percentage of GDP

Assumptions

Rate of cash contributions (% earnings)	3.5%
Rate of growth	2.0%
Rate of return during accumulation	4.0%
Rate of return during decumulation	4.0%
Years of working life	40
Years of retirement	20

Model Results: Relationships between Pensioner Incomes and Pension Savings with Lower Fertility

	K/GDP	Pensioner income as % GDP	=	Cash contributions as % GDP	+ rK/GDP	–	gK/GDP
Fertility rate of 2	135.46%	5.97	=	3.31	+ 5.31	–	2.66
Fertility rate of 1.7	145.47%	6.96	=	3.30	+ 5.74	–	2.08

Comparison of longer fertility against base case

Year	85	88
Percentage change in absolute pensioner income	-17.30%	-18.63%
Percentage change in per capita pensioner income	0.00%	0.00%
Percentage increase in number of pensioners	-17.01%	-18.34%

Note: The changes in absolute pensioner income and in the number of pensioners are given for a selection of years once the model has reached steady state. The values grow over time due to the decreasing sizes of successive generations. The two values grow roughly in proportion to each other.

In summary the hypothetical results are that:

■ If people live a longer proportion of total adult life in retirement:

  – They receive smaller pensions per pensioner;

  – And pensions as a percentage of GDP change by only a small second-order amount, which is far less than the increase in the number of pensioners.

■ If fertility falls:

  – Pensioners' incomes per person are unaffected;

  – Pensions as a percentage of GDP increase proportionally to the rise in the dependency ratio;

  – More of the capital purchased by workers is matched by sales from pensioners so that less goes into new capital investment.

4. Results with UK order of magnitude values and demographic trends

Finally the model was run with real UK fertility and economic values. As life expectancy was found, in the hypothetical scenarios above, to have only a second-order effect on pensioner incomes as a percentage of GDP, changes in real UK life expectancy were not taken into account.

The following assumptions were made:

■ Growth rate of the economy: 2%.

■ Rates of return during accumulation (after all costs): a range of 3% to 4%. [See Appendix C for details.]

■ Rates of return during decumulation: 1.3% real. This is in line with rates implicit within current annuity pricing.

■ Cash contributions: 2.9% of GDP. This reflects our calculations of contribution levels (3.8%) and our estimates of the impact of the DB-DC shift. [See Chapter 3, Figure 3.51 for details.]

■ Retirement age: 65, after 40 years of work.

■ Life expectancy at 65: 20 years.

■ Fertility trends: we input the number of 25 year olds in each year from 1942 onwards, using Pensions Commission estimates for years 1942-1970 (derived from ONS population estimates for the equivalent single year cohorts after 1971), actual data from 1971-2002, and GAD principal projection forecasts for 2003 onwards.

The outputs of the model are shown in Figure B.6. The figure illustrates how, in a simple stylized world, changes in pensions as a percentage of GDP reflect the pattern of net capital expenditure, which in turn reflects fertility trends. Over the next 40 years there will tend to be some automatic increase in pensioner incomes as a percentage of GDP, as more of workers' savings goes into the purchase of assets from pensioners and less into capital investment. This is particularly striking around the peaks in pensions in approximately 2035 as well as 2065, when baby-boomers and the children of baby-boomers will be retiring respectively.

But even with the benefit of this automatic fertility induced effect, pensioners' income will fall short of that required to maintain relative pensioner incomes, as Figure B.7 shows. Our best estimate is that the continuation of current levels of pension savings is likely to produce funded pensioner income of at very most 3.4-4.2% of GDP while 6.2% would be required in 2050 to maintain current pensioner living standards relative to average net incomes given current state system plans and if retirement ages remain unchanged (apart from the equalizing of male and female average retirement ages by 2020).

Figure B.6 Model Output in Steady State Years with UK Fertility

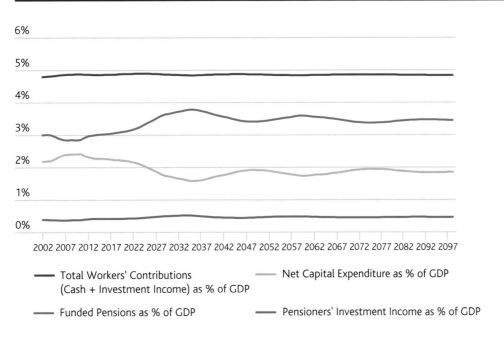

Note: This Figure uses a rate of return during accumulation of 3%
        See section 5 "Reconciling results to current pension income levels" for correct interpretation of these results.

5. Reconciling result to current pension income levels

As can be seen from Figure B.7, our estimated range for funded pension income as a percentage of GDP on 2050 is 3.4-4.2% compared with a current transfer of funded pension income to normal age retirees of 2.2%. The total funded pension income flowing to all retirees is currently 3.8%, with 1.6% flowing to early retirees. Thus the total future flow of funded pension income is forecast to be similar to today's. But it is important to understand that this similar result is the product of three offsetting factors.

■ Future cash contributions as a percentage of GDP below that of the last 10 years and well below the levels of the late 1970s and early 1980s illustrated in Figure 3.41.

■ A considerably lower average rate of return than has been achieved in the 1980s and 1990s, when equity and bond returns were far above long-term historical averages.

■ But offsetting these, the natural fertility effect discussed above, which, by decreasing the ratio of workers to pensioners, increases the proportion of cash contributions devoted to pensioner consumption rather than to net capital investment.

It is because the first of these two factors are at work as well as the third, that the figure for pensioner income in Figure B.6 for 2004 does not reconcile to the present actual figure. The figure for 2004 in Figure B.6 is what today's pension income would have been if contribution rates and rates of return had always been what we now anticipate looking forward. As a forecast of actual likely pension income as a percentage of GDP, Figure B.6 becomes steadily more realistic as we move from today forward.

6. A crucial assumption: reduced "leakage" to early retirees

Figure B.7 also illustrates the important point that while funded pension income as a percentage of GDP is now about 3.8%, only 2.2% of this flows to people of retirement age (as defined by the DWP's "Pensioner Benefit Unit" definition). In assessing the adequacy of future funded pension income, relative to the demographic challenge, we therefore need to make an assumption about how much of that income will in future flow to normal retirement age retirees.

Figure B.7 shows different scenarios. In one the proportion of funded pension income flowing to retirees stays as today: funded pension income flowing to over 65 year olds is then 2.1-2.6%, scarcely above today's 2.2%. In the other scenario all of funded pension income flows to above 65 year olds: the transfer to this group therefore increases from 2.2% to 3.4-4.2% with the increase almost entirely explained by this "no leakage" assumption.

There is a sound case for believing that "leakage" to early retirees will significantly reduce. Labour market participation rates prior to SPA are now increasing, and the generous early retirement packages which were made available by many DB schemes in the 1980s and 1990s are unlikely to be offered in future, given the disappearance of pension fund surpluses. But the assumption that there is no leakage of funded pension income to early retirees is an extreme one.

Figure B.7 The Implications of Current Private Savings Behaviour for Future Pension Incomes as a Percentage of GDP

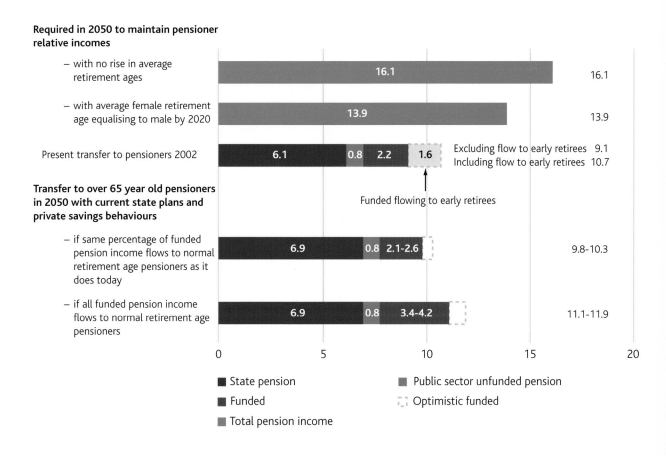

Note: In the absence of forecasts, we are assuming that the percentage of GDP transferred via unfunded public sector pensions does not change.

7. The impact of an increased retirement age

In response to the forecast shortfall in pensions as a percentage of GDP, one option is to delay the retirement age. Figure B.8 shows model outputs for two scenarios; one with a retirement age of 65 (40 years of work) and the other with a retirement age of 68 (43 years of work). Also shown are target levels of future pensions required to maintain relative pensioner incomes, given various assumptions about retirement ages.

Extending working life makes little difference to the actual percentage of GDP transferred (because the increased transfer is offset by increased GDP) but reduces to a more easily attainable level the target transfer required to maintain pensioners' relative incomes. This is because the higher retirement age means that the transfer is spread over fewer pensioners so each can receive the same relative pensioner income, despite a lower percentage of GDP transferred.

8. Sensitivities to contribution rate and return assumptions

Table B.4 shows how funded pension income as a percentage of GDP in 2050 varies with different assumptions about cash contribution rates and about rates of return.

- If the cash contribution rate did not fall from the current level, but instead rose slightly from 3.8% to 4%, and if the real rate of return after all costs was 5%, then pension income rises to 7.1%. At the aggregate level this would be sufficient to keep pensioners **on average** as well off as today, but would still leave many specific savings gaps for individual people. It would however require the total reversal of the impact of the DB-DC shift, plus additional saving on top, and a real return of 5% after costs which could only be achieved with almost 100% of funds invested in equities.

- If cash contributions fell further to 2% of GDP (e.g. through a continuation of the DB-DC shift and erosion of private pension saving) and if real rates of return achieved after costs were only 2% (which could result if people chose close to 100% bond investments) then the transfer of future GDP to post-retirement age pensioners would be only 1.9%, less than today's level even if we assume that "leakage" to early retirees is eliminated entirely.

Figure B.8 Funded Pension Transfers as a Percentage of GDP with Increase in Retirement Age

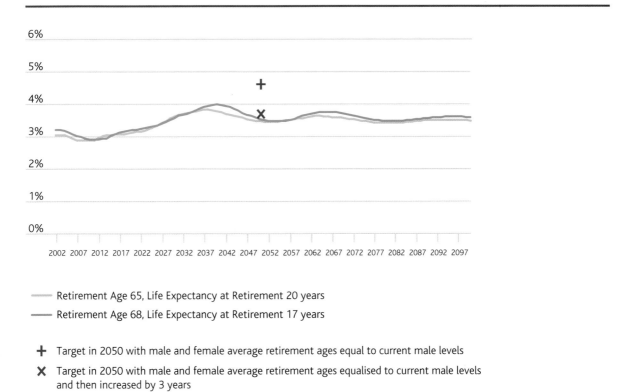

———— Retirement Age 65, Life Expectancy at Retirement 20 years

———— Retirement Age 68, Life Expectancy at Retirement 17 years

+ Target in 2050 with male and female average retirement ages equal to current male levels

✗ Target in 2050 with male and female average retirement ages equalised to current male levels and then increased by 3 years

Note: The target pension transfers in 2050 are derived from the level of funded pension transfers output by the model in 2002 with retirement at 65 and life expectancy of 20 years at retirement.

Table B.4 Private Funded Pension Income as a Percentage of GDP: Sensitivities

Contribution rate as % of GDP	Rate of return assumption			
	2%	3%	4%	5%
2.0%	1.9%	2.3%	2.9%	3.6%
2.9%	2.8%	3.4%	4.2%	5.2%
4.0%	3.8%	4.7%	5.8%	7.1%

6.2% is the level of private funded pension income as a percentage of GDP required to maintain relative pensioner incomes without changing average retirement age beyond equalisation to the current average for men.

▓ Presented as our base case

Rates of return before and after costs, tax and means-testing

This Appendix covers four subjects:

1 Rates of return received in the past on different classes of assets. These historical patterns can help inform reasonable estimates of future rates of return but are not certain predictors of future returns. They clearly illustrate, however, that the returns achieved on bonds and equities in the 1980s and 1990s were exceptional, and that any reasonable expectation of future returns will be much lower.

2 The costs involved in investing i.e. the extent to which costs incurred in trading, fund management, and in the sale and processing of retail financial products, reduce returns to the individual investor below the returns calculated from wholesale market data.

3 The overall post-cost rate of return used in the Pensions Commission's "Macro Model", and in our "Group Modelling", given in addition assumptions about asset allocation mix.

4 The effective rates of return which different categories of individual investor might receive, when we in addition consider the impact of taxes and benefits.

1. Historical rates of return on different asset classes

This section examines the rate of return achieved in the past on different classes of assets. It covers equities, bonds (nominal and index-linked), residential property and commercial property. It also considers briefly "alternative asset classes" such as hedge funds and private equity.

The returns on bonds, equities, and commercial property are all calculated on an income-reinvested basis. For residential property, returns need to be adjusted for implicit rental income and for maintenance costs. All returns are shown in real terms, removing the impact of inflation.

Bonds

To consider possible future returns on bonds, we look first at nominal government bonds, then at real index-linked government bonds, and finally corporate bonds.

Nominal UK gilts and US Treasuries: Government fixed-rate bonds are often described as a low-risk, low-return asset class, but over the last century they have not been low-risk. This is because the return actually achieved on nominal bonds, as against that which was anticipated, has been almost entirely driven by unanticipated accelerations and decelerations in inflation, with changes in underlying real rates of interest playing only a minor role.

Figure C.1 shows time series of returns on UK gilts held for one year, five year and 20 year periods. Figure C.2 shows the distribution of the returns earned in all five year periods, while Figure C.3 shows the distribution for 20 year periods. Even for 20 year periods, the distribution is very wide, with many periods of negative returns (concentrated during the sustained inflation acceleration of the 1950s to 1970s) but also periods of extremely attractive real return. These are concentrated in the 1980s and 1990s which saw a sustained deceleration of inflation.

Returns on nominal fixed-rate US Treasuries [Figures C.4-C.6] show a very similar pattern, with a slightly smaller tail of highly negative results, simply because US inflation did not accelerate quite as much as the UK's in the 1960s and 1970s.

Given the dominance of the impact of inflation on these returns, it is not possible to infer anything useful about the future from the average returns achieved over the long-term. We therefore derive our base case for future bond returns not from these figures but from the current yield on real index-linked bonds. One conclusion can however be drawn from this historical data: the rates of return earned on nominal bonds in the 1980s and 1990s were exceptional, caused by an unanticipated decline in inflation, and cannot be expected to repeat in the future. (Only if there were major price deflation, i.e. actual falls in the price index, could returns of this size be repeated, given the start point of already low inflation).

Figure C.1 Annual Real Rate of Return on UK Gilts held for 1, 5 and 20 Year Periods: 1899-2003

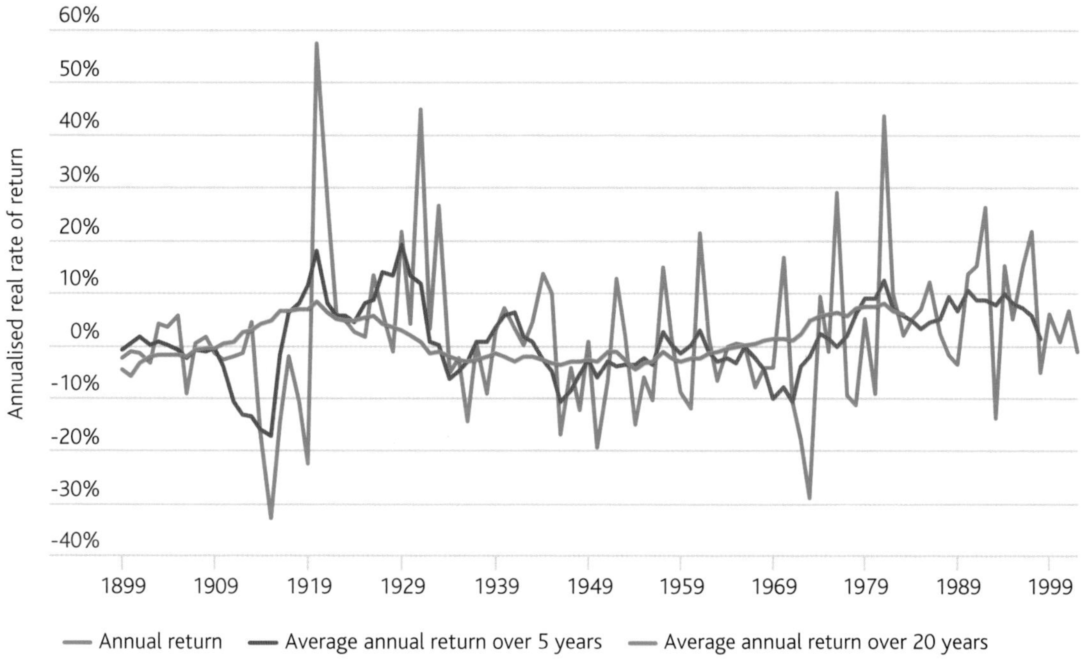

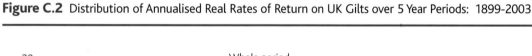

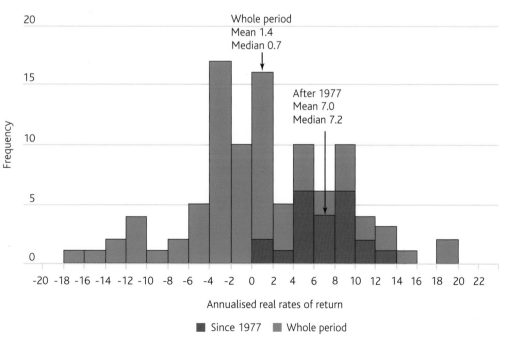

Source: Barclays Equity Gilt Study 2004

Figure C.2 Distribution of Annualised Real Rates of Return on UK Gilts over 5 Year Periods: 1899-2003

Source: Barclays Equity Gilt Study 2004

Figure C.3 Distribution of Annualised Real Rates of Return on UK Gilts over 20 Year Periods: 1899-2003

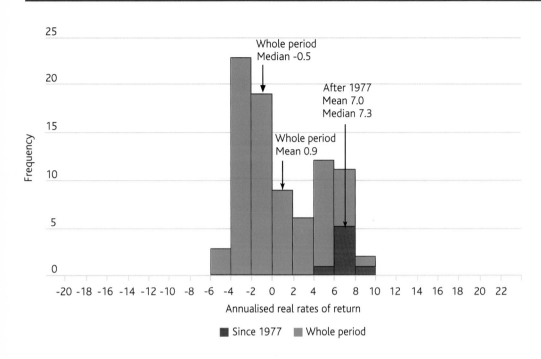

Source: Barclays Equity Gilt Study 2004

Figure C.4 Annual Real Rates of Return on US Treasuries over 1, 5 and 20 Year Periods: 1925-2003

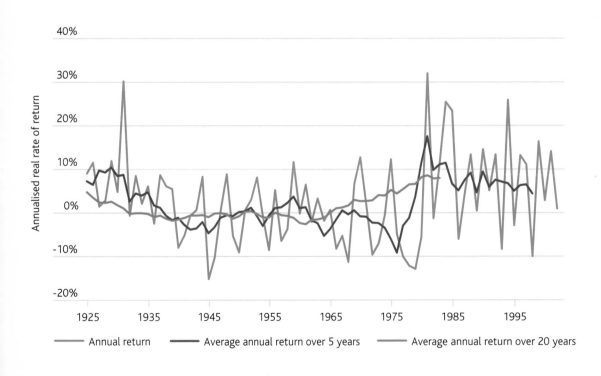

Source: Barclays Equity Gilt Study 2004

Figure C.5 Distribution of Annualised Real Rates of Return on US Treasuries over 5 Year Periods: 1925-2003

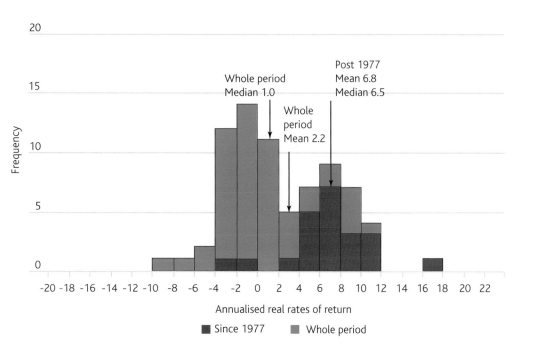

Source: Barclays Equity Gilt Study 2004

Figure C.6 Distribution of Annualised Real Rates of Return on US Treasuries over 20 Year Periods: 1925-2003

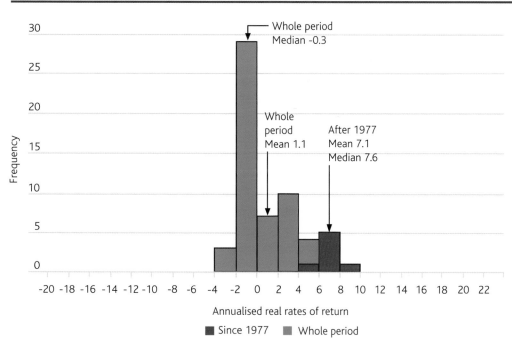

Source: Barclays Equity Gilt Study 2004

Index-linked gilts: Index-linked gilts, rather than nominal gilts, represent the true low-risk, low-return investment option. They can, under certain circumstances, deliver highly positive or negative returns if bought and sold before maturity (due to movements in the real yield). But if they are bought and held to maturity, they will give an absolutely certain real return equal to the current yield to maturity. The best benchmark for low-return, low-risk investment is therefore not the post-facto returns earned in the past on index-linked gilts, but their yield to maturity at the current time.

Index-linked gilts have only existed in the UK since 1981 and in the US since 1997, and it is therefore not possible to set out trends in real interest rates over a longer time period. But Figure C.7 sets out the data which is available for the UK for the last 18 years.

For 12 of these years (1986-98) real yields on 20 year bonds moved in a range of 3.5-4.5%. But since 1998, yields have fallen to around 2%. In the context of assessing pension saving adequacy, this is a very major difference. The position of Defined Contribution (DC) pension savers would be greatly improved if it were possible to achieve long-term risk-free real returns of say 3.5%.[1] It is therefore important to consider whether the real rate now pertaining is likely to sustain in future, or whether any return to higher levels is possible.

Unfortunately, economic theory provides us with no definitive understanding of what the long-term equilibrium real rate of interest should be. Nor are there definitive explanations of why the significant fall in real yields occurred between 1998 and 2000, though there are some technical explanations of why the fall was particularly pronounced for UK real gilts.[2] And as mentioned already, we cannot even work out with certainty what the expected real return on gilts has been over longer time periods. But today's 2% real yield certainly reflects the market's best estimate of what real interest rates will be over the next 20 to 30 years, so that if we believe that market prices efficiently reflect available information, today's rate is by definition the best estimate to assume for the future.

In our modelling assumptions, we have therefore assumed that the real risk-free rate of return available on index-linked government bonds throughout our projection period is 2%. We also assume that this 2% real return will apply to nominal fixed rate bonds. This assumption will only hold if

[1] Note: So too would be the measured adequacy of Defined Benefit (DB) funds, since the present value of liabilities is calculated (under accounting standard FRS 17) by discounting future pension payments using a long-dated bond yield combined with assumptions about future inflation rates. As a result the value of the liability rises if real interest rates fall. The fall in real interest rates since 1998 has been as big a driver of increased pension fund deficits as increasing life expectancy and the fall in equity prices.

[2] Note: The Minimum Funding Requirement regulations forces schemes under certain circumstances to invest in UK gilts. But there is a limited supply of UK gilts, particularly at the long-end, and particularly of index-linked. In addition, Bank of England rules on eligible assets for discounting increase the demand for UK gilts, increasing the price and depressing the yield. It is possible to argue as a result that the yield on UK gilts is in some sense below the "true" risk-free rate. This is reflected in the fact that corporate bond spreads above the government rate are higher in pounds than e.g. in Euros, where the same specific conditions do not apply.

monetary authorities are successful at maintaining inflation steady, in line with current market expectations. If there is an unanticipated acceleration or deceleration of inflation, real returns on nominal government bonds will be either lower or higher than our base case assumption.

To sum up therefore:

■ Index-linked bonds are assumed to have a mean expected real return of 2% with little or no risk.

■ Nominal bonds have the same expected return, but are subject to the risk of unanticipated changes in inflation.

Corporate bonds: Corporate bonds (almost all of which are currently nominal rather than index-linked) deliver a spread over government bonds to reflect credit risk. The spreads vary with the credit rating of the bonds, from as low as 0.1% for some AAA credits to 3% or more for sub-investment grade debt.

For the purposes of modelling we have assumed that on average corporate bonds achieve a net yield uplift above gilts or US Treasuries of 0.7% (70 basis points). This would be consistent with a slightly higher gross spread and a small average default rate.

The assumed rate of return on corporate bonds is therefore 2.7% real.

Figure C.7 Real Yields to Maturity on UK Index-Linked Gilts: 1986-2004

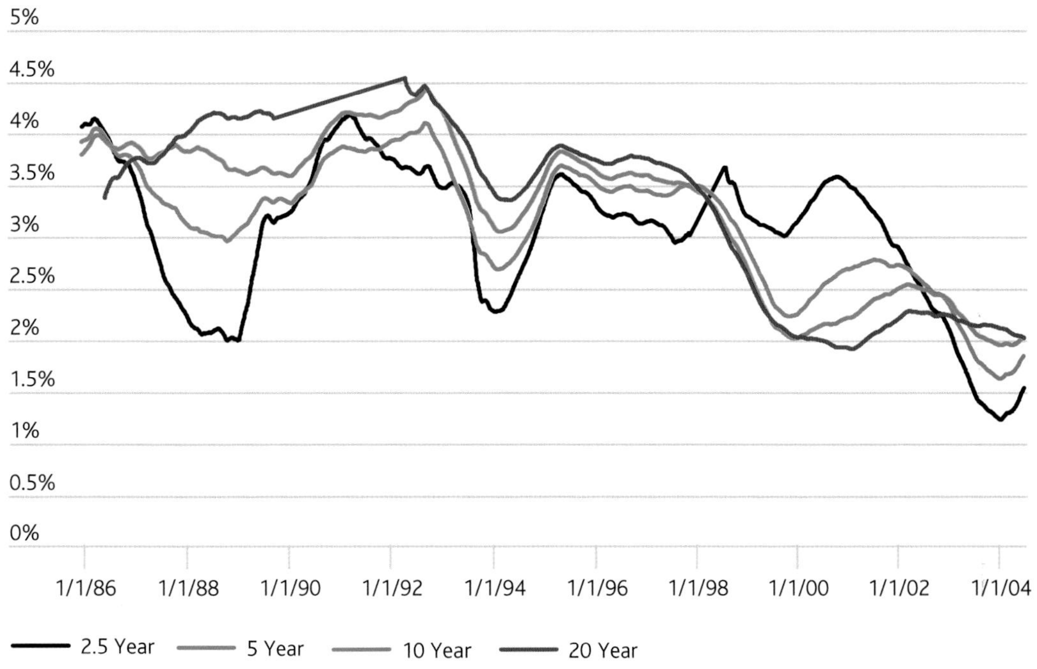

Source: Bank of England

Equities

This section looks at real equity returns in the UK since 1899 and in the US since 1925, and considers what implications if any can be drawn for future rates of return on equity investment.

Over the short term (e.g. one year) equity returns are hugely volatile. But the volatility reduces the longer the time period considered. Figure C.8 shows time series of real returns on UK equities from 1899-2003 for one year, five year, and 20 year holding periods. Figure C.9 shows the distribution of returns over five year periods, and Figure C.10 over 20 year periods. The longer the time period chosen, the less the spread of return, but even for 20 year periods (i.e. the period which might be relevant for a 45 year-old saving in a DC pension with a prospective age of retirement at 65), the variation has been very large with some experience of negative real returns. Only if we look at 50 year periods [Figure C.11] do we get a fairly tight distribution, but this result should be interpreted with extreme caution because of the small number of independent observations (each of the 50 year periods includes returns for specific years which are also present in many other 50 year periods). There are simply not enough independent observations in the history of stock market capitalism to make robust conclusions on the variance of return over very long periods.

Figures C.12 to C.14 show the equivalent figures for the US from 1925-2003. The variability of returns over 20 year periods is similar, but the mean return is higher, 7.3% versus 5.5% in the UK for the period 1899-2003, and versus 6.3% in the UK for the period 1925-2003.

Figure C.8 Annual Real Rates of Return on UK Equities over 1, 5 and 20 Year Periods: 1899-2003

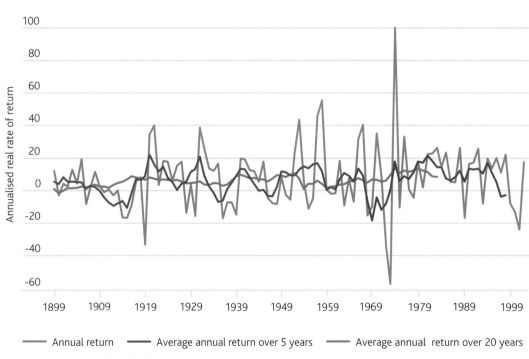

Source: Barclays Equity Gilt Study 2004

Figure C.9 Distribution of Annualised Real Rates of Return on UK Equities over 5 Year Periods: 1899-2003

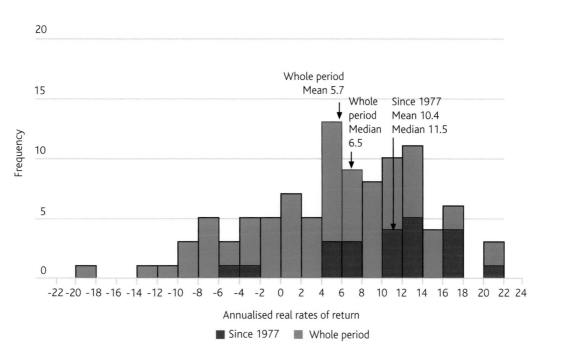

Source: Barclays Equity Gilt Study 2004

Figure C.10 Distribution of Annualised Real Rates of Return on UK Equities over 20 Year Periods: 1899-2003

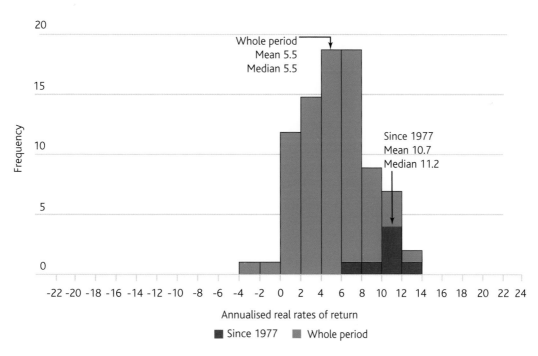

Source: Barclays Equity Gilt Study 2004

Figure C.11 Distribution of Annualised Real Rates of Return on UK Equities over 50 Year Periods: 1899-2003

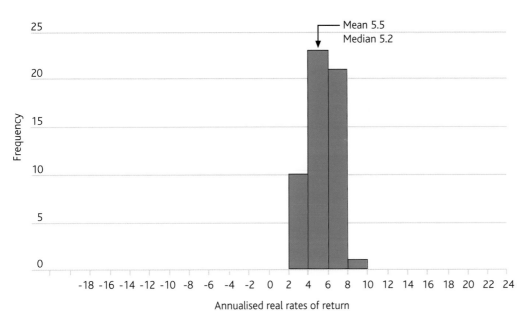

Source: Barclays Equity Gilt Study 2004

Figure C.12 Annual Real Rates of Return on US Equities held for 1, 5 and 20 Year Periods: 1925-2003

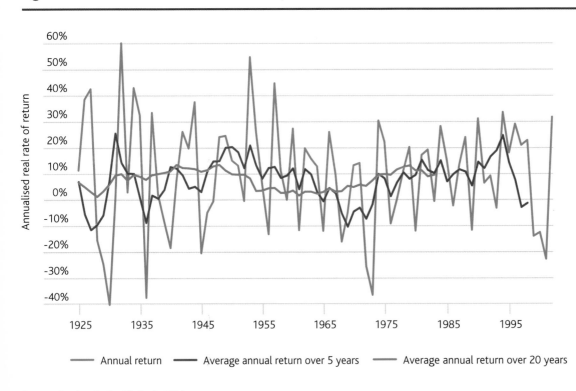

Source: Barclays Equity Gilt Study 2004

Figure C.13 Distribution of Annualised Real Rates of Return on US Equities over 5 Year Periods: 1925-2003

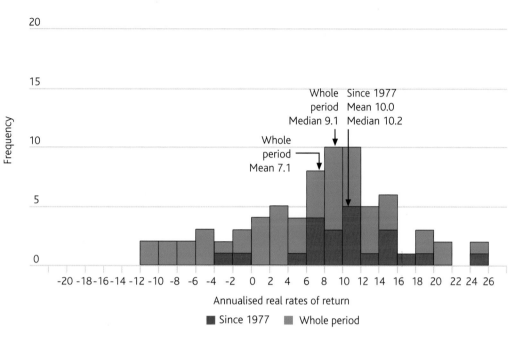

Source: Barclays Equity Gilt Study 2004

Figure C.14 Distribution of Annualised Real Rates of Return on US Equities over 20 Year Periods: 1925-2003

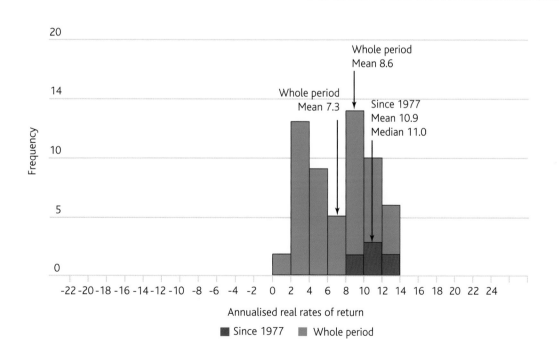

Source: Barclays Equity Gilt Study 2004

The key issue is what we can infer from these figures for future rates of return. One conclusion is clear. Just as with nominal bonds, so for equities, the 1980s and 1990s were periods of exceptional return, which cannot be expected to pertain in the future. If the historic record gives us any clues to the future, average returns earned over the longest observable period are a better guide.

This is however a lively debate in economic literature on whether the equity returns of the past do give us information relevant to assessing returns looking forward.

Key points are:

■ There are robust theoretical grounds for believing that the total average returns on capital (bonds and equities combined) in an efficient market economy should exceed the rate of growth of the economy. And good grounds also for assuming that equity should be expected to earn a risk-premium over risk-free government index-linked bonds, to reflect their greater riskiness. Beyond these rather broad guidelines, however, economic theory does not help define what precise rates of return to expect.

■ Measured as the difference between nominal equity returns and nominal gilt returns, the UK equity risk premium has averaged 4.3% since 1899: the average in the US has been 5.2% since 1925. But there are major conceptual and methodological uncertainties involved in defining and measuring these risk premia. Some economists, moreover, have argued that the equity risk premium during the 20th century was higher than we would logically expect given the inherent relative riskiness of bonds and equities.[3] It is possible indeed that the high returns on equity from 1980 onwards (which were well above long-term averages even if we include the years 2000-2004) reflect a fall in perceptions of the riskiness of equities and thus a fall in the required and anticipated return on equities looking forward from now on.[4]

■ It is also at least possible that equity returns looking forward should be less than those observed during the 20th century because of changing demographics, which can change the relative demand for capital and labour and thus equilibrium rates of return [as discussed in Appendix B].

[3]Note: Mehra and Prescott, "The Equity Risk Premium: A Puzzle" Journal of Monetary Economics, 1985.

[4]Note: This illustrates the severe conceptual problems involved in using historic equity returns or equity risk premia to forecast future returns or premia. If for some reason investors perceive that equity investment has become less risky, and demand a lower risk premium, there will be a one-off rise in the price of equities, to the extent required to bring future expectations of return down in line with the lower risk premium. But this price rise will mean that measurements of the long-term historical risk premium will increase. If an actual fall in risk premium looking forward produces a rise in the premium estimated from the historical data, then clearly we cannot use historical data to infer the future premium or future returns.

■ Finally any attempt to forecast equity returns from today, depends crucially on one's assumption as to whether the current market value is at, above or below its equilibrium level.

Any assumption on future equity returns is therefore a matter of judgment not science. For the purposes of modelling we assume average real returns to equity of 6%, slightly above the long-term UK average (5.5%), slightly below the US (7.3%). These expected returns are however combined with significant risk over periods relevant to pension investment.

Alternative investments: hedge funds and private equity

The vast majority of investment by pension funds is either in quoted bonds and quoted equity or in commercial property (considered below). But over the last several decades there has been an increasing flow of investment funds into private equity, and over the last 5 to 10 years into hedge funds (a generic term covering a wide variety of position-taking and arbitrage strategies).

On average private equity investment has delivered returns superior to public quoted equity, but with high variance. On average hedge funds seem to have delivered an attractive risk-return combination, with mean returns closer to equities than bonds, but with much lower variance than equities.

The question therefore arises whether greater investment in private equity and hedge funds could allow pension savers to achieve a better risk-return combination than is available from any mix of bonds and equities. The answer is "yes possibly" for individual investors, but "no" for all investors considered together. This is clearly the case for hedge funds, and largely true also for private equity.

■ Hedge funds are a position-taking and arbitrage activity. If successful, the hedge fund investors do better than the public market indices. But this return must come from somewhere, and in fact comes from a slight reduction in the return enjoyed by all non-hedge fund investors. The more money is invested in hedge funds, however, the fewer the opportunities to outperform the risk-return combination of the rest of the market. If everybody invested entirely in hedge funds, hedge funds would return the market combination of risk and return. Hedge fund investing cannot possibly increase the total risk return combination available to all investors considered together.

■ Private equity is also to a degree a price arbitrage activity. Some of its return is generated by buying and selling assets well, the flipside of selling and buying assets badly by public companies. To some extent therefore superior return on private equity must be at the expense of returns on public equities, and cannot increase total returns available to all investors. Only to the extent that private equity investment produces a real increase in the efficiency of actual business operations, and thus in the overall rate of return and rate of growth within an economy, does it improve the risk return combination available to all investors considered together. This effect may be present to some extent, but its total impact on overall returns across the entire economy is likely to be limited.

We have not therefore included in our modelling any assumption that alternative asset classes can improve returns for pension savers in general.

Residential property

Figure C.15 shows the real return which homeowner would have received as a result of changes in the price of houses, over all five year periods between 1930 and 2003. Figure C.16 shows the same for all 20 year periods. The source for the house price data is The Office of the Deputy Prime Minister long-run series on house prices which splices together series going back to 1930. The average mean return of 2.05% is considerably less than that on equity investment, but the variance is much lower.

These figures however understate the attractiveness of residential property because they omit the benefit which the homeowner gets from rent-free accommodation. To measure correctly the return on investment in housing we have to add the running rental yield: the implicit rental which the occupier notionally pays to the homeowner even if, for owner-occupied houses, these are one and the same person. This is the housing equivalent of dividend yield for equities, or interest income for bonds. But we also need to deduct the cost of maintaining property, since the house price appreciation would be less if this maintenance expenditure were not spent.

Figure C.15 Distribution of Real Returns from Residential Property Price Appreciation over 5 Year
Periods: 1930-2003

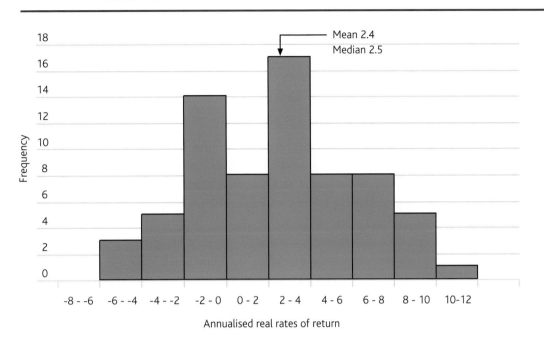

Source: Pensions Commission calculations based on ODPM house price series

Figure C.16 Distribution of Real Returns on Residential Property Price Appreciation over 20 Year Periods:
1930-2002

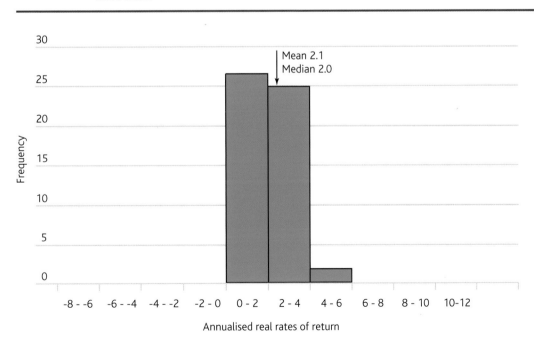

Source: Pensions Commission calculations based on ODPM house price series

Table C.1 shows ONS national totals of housing rent (implicit or actual) and house maintenance expenditure over the last 10 years, expressed as a percentage of the value of all houses. Taking the 10 year average implies that the return on housing is understated by about 3.5% when we look only at houseprice appreciation. Adjusting for this 3.5% produces the distribution of 20 year returns shown in Figure C.17. On this basis residential housing has displayed an extremely attractive risk return combination, with mean return similar to equities, but with much lower variance.

There is however one further adjustment which should ideally be made, but which we have not yet been able to do as this long-run price series is based on a simple average. This would be to calculate how much of house price appreciation has been due to capital investment in existing houses either by increasing the number of rooms or improving the quality of the house without increasing the number of rooms, for example the kitchen of the year 2004 is on average very different from that of say 1970.

We have not yet identified sources of information which estimate this capital investment, nor clarified whether some of the capital investment is implicitly included within ONS estimates of house maintenance expenditure. We will conduct further analyses of this issue over the next year. It is likely however that once this adjustment is made it will result in estimates of returns on housing slightly lower than suggested by Figure C.17.

Figure C.17 Distribution of Real Returns on Residential Property over 5 Year Periods adjusted for Rent and Maintenance Costs: 1930-2003

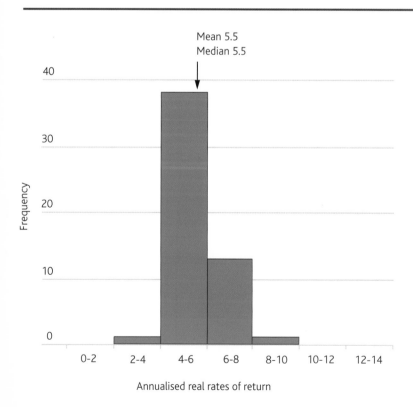

Source: Pensions Commission calculations based on ODPM house price series and ONS Blue Book

Table C.1 Aggregate Rent and Maintenance Cost from the Blue Book

£ billion	1994	1995	1996	1997	1998	1999	2000	2001	2002	2003	1995-2003 average
Gross housing value	1,206	1,205	1,319	1,422	1,634	1,848	2,107	2,268	2,737	3,045	1,954
Actual rent	24	25	25	25	25	25	25	25	25	25	25
Imputed rent	48	53	54	55	57	58	58	59	60	61	57
Maintenance and repair	0	8	8	9	9	9	9	10	10	11	9
Routine household maintenance	5	5	5	5	5	5	5	6	6	6	5
Actual and imputed rent as percentage of gross housing value	5.9%	6.5%	6.0%	5.6%	5.0%	4.5%	4.0%	3.7%	3.1%	2.8%	4.2%
Maintenance and repair as percentage of gross housing value	0.4%	1.1%	1.0%	1.0%	0.9%	0.8%	0.7%	0.7%	0.6%	0.6%	0.8%
Difference percentage of gross housing value	5.5%	5.4%	5.0%	4.6%	4.1%	3.7%	3.3%	3.0%	2.5%	2.3%	3.5%

Source: ONS

Commercial property

The return on commercial property investment is a combination of the running yield and the capital appreciation. With rental income reinvested, the distribution of five year returns between 1920 and 2000 is shown in Figure C.18, and 20 year periods in Figure C.19.

The 20 year period distribution suggests that UK commercial property has yielded on average a slightly lower return than UK equities, but with lower variance.

Overview of pre-cost risk return and summary of assumptions for modelling

The historic experience of different asset classes in the UK over periods relevant to pension investing can be summarised as per figure C.20, which compares mean 20 year returns with the variability (standard deviation) of these 20 year returns. Historic returns for 1930-2002 are shown for equities, nominal gilts, residential property (adjusted and unadjusted) and commercial property. The current yield to maturity of a long-term index-linked gilt is also shown at 2%, with a variance of zero. This is the variance which applies if the bond is held to redemption.

Figure C.18 Distribution of Real Returns on Commerical Property over 5 Year Periods: 1920-2002

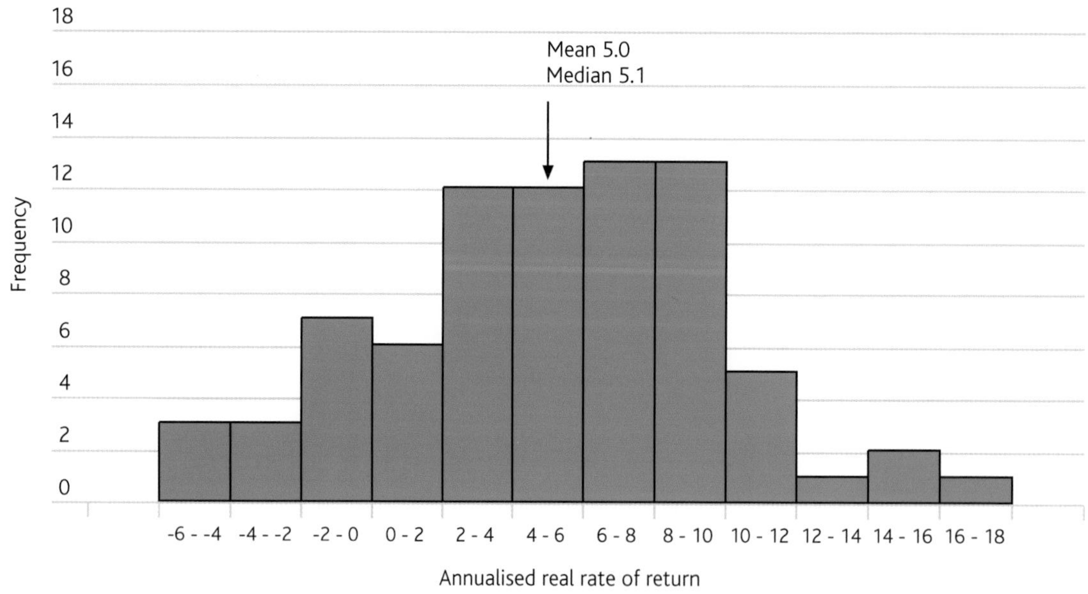

Mean 5.0
Median 5.1

Source: Credit Suisse First Boston

Figure C.19 Distribution of Real Returns on Commerical Property over 20 Year Periods: 1920-2002

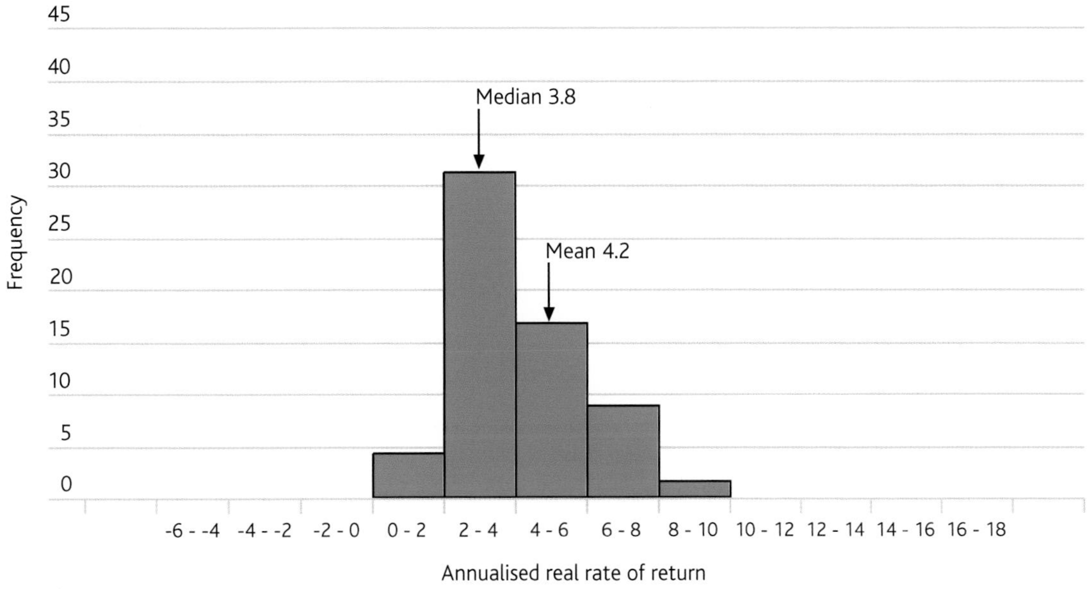

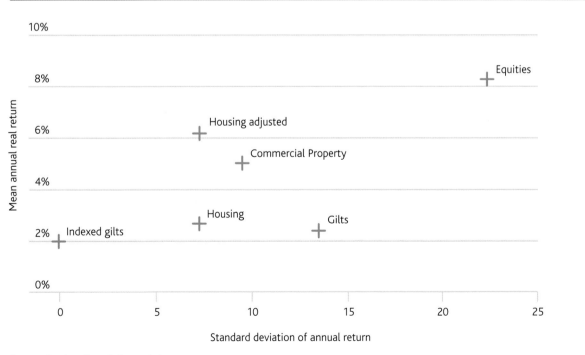

Source: Credit Suisse First Boston

Figure C.20 Annual Real Returns and Standard Deviations for Different UK Asset Classes: 1930-2002

Source: Pensions Commission analysis

With the exception of nominal gilts, where the 20th century experience is distorted by the impact of unanticipated charges in inflation, the risk return relationship is broadly as suggested by finance theory: higher average return can be achieved if higher risk is accepted.

The vast majority of pension funds in the UK are invested in equities and bonds. In summary our assumptions on these for the purposes of modelling are:

- Equities: 6% real return.

- Gilts: 2% real return.

- Corporate bonds: 2.7% real return.

These returns are however at the pre-cost and pre-tax level. To calculate returns to investors we therefore have first to consider the trading, fund management, selling and administration costs which are taken out of gross return.

2. The cost of investing

Some of the costs involved in investing are fairly clear, and indeed some are required to be by regulation. Personal pension products are required by regulation to reveal the Reduction in Yield (RIY) which results from the price charged by the provider to cover costs of selling, administration and fund management. Equivalent figures can de derived for the explicit cost of occupational pension schemes.

But even if these explicit costs were zero, investors would not receive the full market return calculated from market prices and dividend yields. This is because there are, in addition, trading costs, which are sometimes called implicit costs because their impact is not explicitly revealed, but rather reduces the return to investment before explicit costs are deducted.

In the sections below we first consider implicit costs, since these are the same for all investors in the same asset class, and then explicit costs, which vary by type of product, size of premium, or size of scheme.

Implicit costs

Estimating the implicit costs is difficult but vital if, as seems likely, the implicit costs are for some investors as significant as explicit costs.

In February 2000, the Financial Services Authority (FSA) published an occasional paper *The price of retail investing in the UK* authored by Kevin James, which is believed to be one of the most detailed studies of implicit cost.[5] The paper is not specifically focused on pensions, but on retail investments such as unit trusts, but its findings are likely to be broadly

[5] The price of retail investing in the UK, FSA occasional paper 6 (February 2000)

applicable to pension investment as well.
James considers two issues:

■ What are the inherent implicit costs of each specific trade, and what therefore are the annual costs of trading for any given fund turnover in a year?

■ What is the observed difference between gross returns in the market and net returns to investments (but before explicit costs)? This difference is the actual implicit cost given actual levels of fund turnover.

Implicit costs per trade: James estimates the cost of a two-way trade, i.e. the cost of buying one equity and selling another. In the London equity market he estimates the elements of this to be:

Broker Commission	30 b.p.[6] (i.e. 15 b.p. on both buy and sell side)
Bid-offer spread (the difference between the quoted price to buyers and to sellers)	75 b.p. (i.e 37.5 b.p. on each side)
Price impact (reflecting the fact that buying can move the price up and selling move the price down)	25 b.p. (i.e. 12.5b.p. on each side)
Stamp Duty	50 b.p. (only charged on the buy side)
Total	**180 b.p.**

These costs per trade, multiplied by the turnover of a fund, would give the total annual RIY. Thus if a fund turned over 200% (i.e 100% sold plus 100% bought) in the London market, an RIY from implicit costs of 1.8% would be expected.

These estimates do not feed into James's estimates of actual observed implicit costs (explained below). But it is useful to compare them with recent estimates of cost per trade to gauge whether costs may have changed since James's analysis.

---

[6] A Basis Point (b.p) is one-one hundreth of a percentage point.

Pensions Commission discussions with industry experts suggest present day estimates of 28 b.p. commission for a round trip trade (close to James's figures) but 70 b.p. for the cost of trading (combining the bid-offer spread and price-impact) compared with James's 100 b.p. This may reflect the fact that bid-offer spreads have come down, slightly for FTSE 100 stocks and significantly for FTSE 250 stocks, partly as a result of changes in the London stock exchange system for the matching of buy and sell orders.

Including the 50 b.p. for stamp duty these alternative estimates would suggest a round trip cost of 148 b.p. versus James's 180 b.p. This suggests that estimates of implicit costs drawn from late 1990s data might somewhat overstate present costs, but not dramatically so.

Estimates of actual implicit costs: James's estimates of what implicit costs actually were is derived by looking at the difference between market returns and the returns actually achieved by funds before explicit costs were charged. He draws on a large sample of funds from the Micropal database, and makes some complex econometric adjustments to allow for the different investment style of different funds.

His estimates are shown in Figure C.21, with UK active funds showing an implicit cost of 1.3% per year, UK trackers 0.88% per year, US actives 0.9% per year, and US trackers 0.4% per year. The lower levels for the US are to a significant extent explained by the absence of stamp duty, which if turnover were, say 100% (combining buy and sell orders), adds 0.25% per annum costs in the UK.

Assessment and assumptions for modelling: The FSA paper's analysis of costs as they were in the late 1990s appears methodologically robust and it is clear that implicit costs can be high, particularly for actively managed funds. The results, however, appear to some industry experts to be surprisingly high for UK trackers, and may not reflect the recent growth in importance of the tracker funds, which along with the decline in the bid-offer spread, may have resulted in reduced costs. And an alternative check can be made by looking at the actual level of stamp duty paid and then grossing up for other costs. In 2002/03 UK stamp duty paid on shares was £2.5bn, equivalent to 22 b.p. on the stock market value at the end of 2002. Our latest industry estimates suggest that stamp duty accounts for 50 b.p. out of 148 b.p. for a combined sale and buy round trip i.e. for about 33% of all trading costs. This implies total trading costs of 66 b.p. of fund values.

Balancing these different considerations, the Pensions Commission has decided to assume 65 b.p. implicit costs for equity investment on average (consistent with a lower rate for tracker funds and a higher one for active). Implicit costs for bond funds should be much less, but the Commission has not discovered an existing analysis of this issue. For now we use 25 b.p. for corporate bonds and 10 b.p. for government bonds in our modelling.

Combining these two assumptions would suggest about 40-50 b.p. for a balanced bond and equity portfolio. This double-checks well with an estimate of about 50 b.p. given to us by a major pension fund manager for total implicit costs across all their funds under management.

During the consultation period we would like to hear views on whether our current assumptions appear too high or too low. We intend to conduct further research and to request information from fund managers on this issue.

Figure C.21 Estimated Annual Percentage Reduction in Yield resulting from Implicit Costs: from Kevin James's Paper

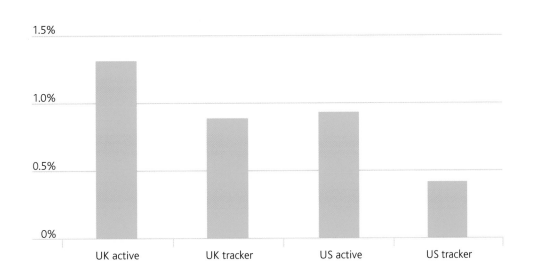

Source: FSA

Explicit costs

Explicit costs encompass the costs of selling, processing and administering pension products, and the explicit charges paid to fund managers. They are significantly higher for people purchasing personal pensions on an individual basis than for people gaining the benefits of employer bulk purchasing via occupational schemes or Group Personal Pensions.

Personal Pensions: FSA regulation requires that explicit costs involved in personal pensions are revealed as combined RIY figures. RIY captures the percentage reduction in return arising from whatever the combination of up-front charges and annual charges in the product pricing. FSA published data, drawn from these required disclosures, therefore provide a fairly clear picture of explicit personal pension costs.

- Between 1995-2002, and particularly after 1999, average RIYs fell significantly [Figure C.22]. This to a significant extent reflects the introduction of the Stakeholder Pension charge cap, set at 1% AMC (equivalent to 1.1% RIY) in 2001, and regulatory guidance from the FSA which has meant that financial advisers could not recommend products with charges significantly above this price cap.

- There remains, however, significant dispersion of prices in the market. Figure C.23 shows minimum, maximum, and median RIYs for products offered in June 2004, with the dispersion suggesting that many people do not shop around aggressively for the best deal. The figures also suggest some, but surprisingly little, fall in RIYs as monthly premium size increases. The median person paying a monthly premium of £500 incurs an RIY of 0.95% versus 1.1% for the median person paying £20 per month, despite the fact that the vast majority of selling and processing costs are fixed per contract and therefore fall with premium size. This reflects both the unsophisticated nature of customer choice in this market, even at relatively high income levels, but also the impact of the price cap at low premium levels. This price cap, however, has made the sale of small premium contracts economically unattractive to the financial services industry. Products are apparently on offer at a 1% RIY for the customer paying £20 per month, but almost no sales effort is being put into selling such products, and very few are therefore sold.

- Responding to this problem, HM Treasury therefore agreed in June 2004, following its review of the charge cap regime, to increase the cap to a 1.5% AMC over the first 10 years of a contract falling to 1% from year 11 onwards. This would be equivalent to an RIY of 1.2% for a 20 year contract held to maturity, but to an RIY of 1.56% for contracts which currently lapse before 10 years. The change in regime will therefore certainly increase median RIYs at small premium levels. Its likely impact on larger premium contracts is unclear, but some increase is possible in a highly imperfect market.

Figure C.22 Reduction in Yield for the Average Personal Pension Contract Held for 25 Years

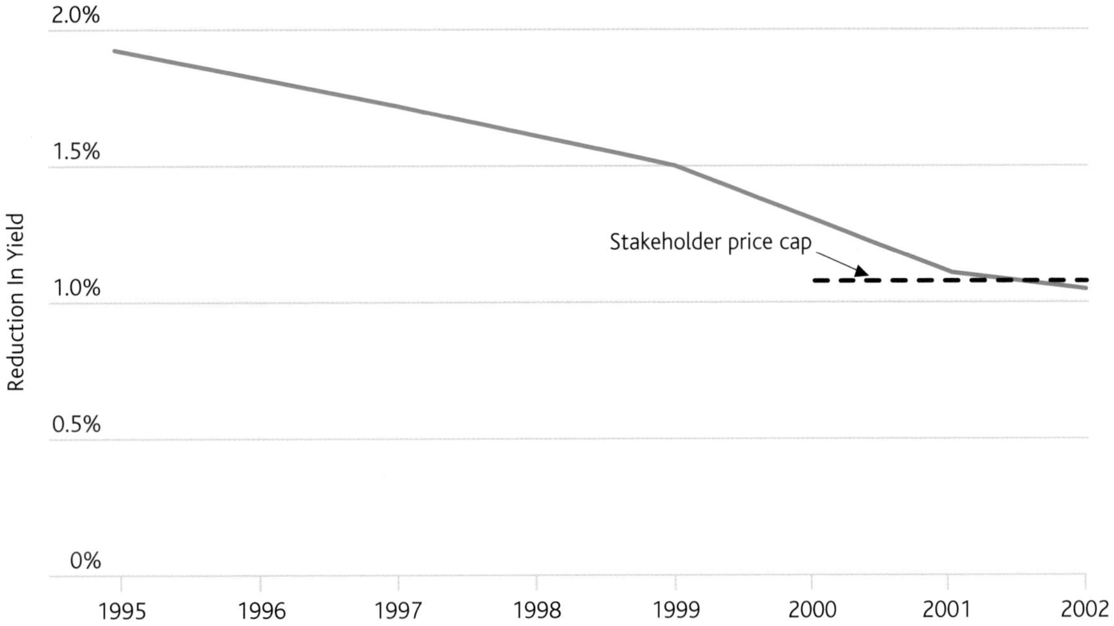

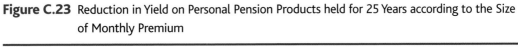

Reduction In Yield

2.0%

1.5%

Stakeholder price cap

1.0%

0.5%

0%

1995   1996   1997   1998   1999   2000   2001   2002

Source: FSA disclosure surveys

Figure C.23 Reduction in Yield on Personal Pension Products held for 25 Years according to the Size of Monthly Premium

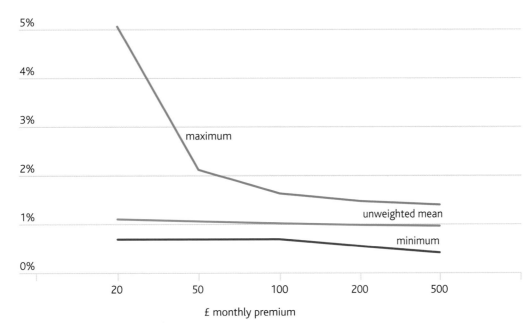

5%

4%

3%

maximum

2%

unweighted mean

1%

minimum

0%

20   50   100   200   500

£ monthly premium

Source: FSA comparative table June 2004

Occupational pensions: The available data on occupational pensions is more limited (due to the absence of required regulatory disclosure) but it is clear that members of occupational schemes benefit from economies resulting both from scale and from more cost-efficient product design. The need for individual interviews is eliminated, communication requirements are fewer, and the schemes act as bulk buyers from the financial services industry. A GAD survey of administrative costs in 1995 suggested total costs falling from about 0.5% for small occupational schemes (less than 1000 members) to below 0.2% for the largest schemes [Figure C.24]. A similar profile is suggested by a survey conducted by Watson Wyatt in 2003, and is confirmed by Pensions Commission discussions with individual schemes.

Group Personal Pensions: Comprehensive data on GPPs is more difficult to obtain, but logic and industry discussions suggest explicit costs lying between those for occupational schemes and for individual personal pensions. GPP arrangements achieve lower costs than individual personal pensions, both because the employer is acting as a bulk negotiator with the provider, and because the provider's costs per successful sale are reduced by the higher success rate which results when there is an employer contribution. But costs are higher than in the occupational scheme environment, since the actual contract is still with the individual employee, which requires individualised communication.

From industry discussions we believe that large GPP schemes may have costs in the 0.5-0.8% RIY range, but it is clear that costs are much higher for small schemes. The model produced by Aegon, focusing on the small company GPP market, as input to the HM Treasury review of the Stakeholder price cap, suggests that an RIY of 1.5% is required to make sales to an employee in a 25 employee company profitable, even when the employer makes a contribution.

Explicit cost assumptions for modeling: For the purpose of our Macro and Group Modelling we assume that:

■ Members of occupational schemes face explicit costs of 0.3%.

■ Members of personal pension schemes (averaging across individual personal pensions, and GPPs of all sizes) face explicit costs of 0.8%. But it is clear that these costs will be significantly higher for employees of small firms (even if in GPP schemes) and for people purchasing personal pensions on an individual basis, particularly at low premium levels. Our group modelling results presented in Chapter 4 [and explained in more details in Appendix B] will therefore tend to underestimate the number of lower income undersavers in small firms.

Figure C.24 Administrative Costs as a Percentage of Fund Value for Occupational Pension Schemes

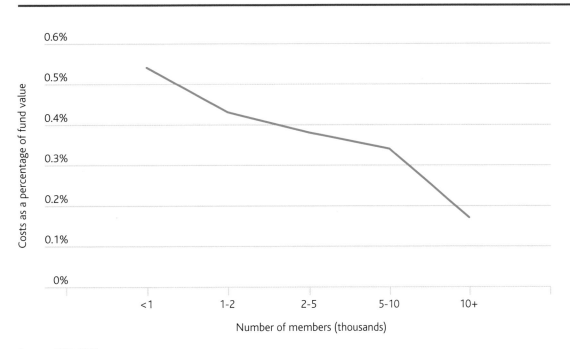

Source: GAD, 1998

3. Overall assumptions for modelling

Integrating all of the assumptions made above, and assuming a typical asset allocation of 60% equities, 20% corporate bonds, and 20% government bonds, gives the figures set out in Table C.2.

■ We estimate the overall real return on the balanced portfolio after implicit costs but before explicit to be 4.08% real. We round this to 4.0% for our illustrations of how "post-everything" rates of return vary for different people facing different explicit costs, employer contributions, tax rates, and means-testing. [See the next Section of this Appendix and Chapter 6].

■ Subtracting explicit costs of 0.3% for occupational schemes and 0.8% for personal, gives us returns after explicit costs of 3.78% (occupational) and 3.28% (personal) which we round to 3.8% and 3.3% and use in our Group Modelling exercise, which aims to estimate the number of under-savers [See Appendix B and Chapter 4].

Table C.2 Summary of Real Rates of Return Assumptions (percentages)

	Gross returns	Implicit costs	Return after implicit costs	Weight in portfolio	
Equities	6.0	0.65	5.35	x 60	= 3.21
Corporate bonds	2.7	0.25	2.45	x 20	= 0.49
Government bonds	2.0	0.10	1.90	x 20	= 0.38
Total real return after implicit costs					**= 4.08**
Explicit costs assumed on average to be:			Occupational schemes	0.3	
			Personal pensions	0.8	
Therefore returns after explicit costs are:			Occupational schemes	3.78	
			Personal pensions	3.28	
			Average for all schemes	3.5	
Returns used in different modelling exercises are therefore:					
			Macro modelling (after costs and across all schemes)	3.0 – 4.0	
			Group modelling assumptions (after all costs)		
			Occupational schemes	3.8	
			Personal pensions	3.3	
Rate of return illustrations (after implicit costs but before explicit costs which are then deducted)				4.0	

Source: Pensions Commission analysis

■ The overall average post-cost real return is therefore about 3.5%, and we have used a range of 3.0-4.0% in our Macro Model. [See Appendix B and Chapter 4].

These rates of return apply to the accumulation stage of a pension product. For the decumulation stage we assume a return of 1.3% real (after all costs), which is the rate implicit in recent annuity prices given official life expectancy forecasts. This is reasonably consistent with the underlying wholesale return of 2.0% real on government bonds, minus selling and administration costs, risk capital costs and insurance company profits. Rates of return on assets held for people already in retirement can be significantly higher for people in Defined Benefit (DB) schemes, since the fund does not need to buy annuities and can stay invested in higher return assets. But with the shift to Defined Contribution (DC), and with mature DB schemes (i.e. those with a predominance of retired members) increasingly switching to bond-rich asset allocations, our annuity equivalent assumption will be increasingly applicable. Clearly, however, this may raise policy issues about whether annuitisation at retirement (and the underlying legal requirements) remains appropriate as life expectancy during retirement increases.

4. Effective rates of return of pension for different categories of saver

This section explores the model which we have created to investigate the effective rates of return on private pension saving which are faced by different categories of individual. Key results from this model were presented in Chapter 6 of the main report.

The return which an individual receives on private pension saving depends on the rate of return available after implicit costs (which will tend to be the same for all investors provided asset allocation decisions are the same) but also on:

■ The rate of tax relief on pension contributions including the possible impact of Working Tax Credit and Child Tax Credit.

■ Whether or not there is an employer contribution.

■ The level of explicit selling and administrative costs which could vary from as low as 0.1% per year for someone in a large occupational scheme, to 1.5% per year for someone in a personal pension contract.

■ Whether or not pension income will be subject to means-testing and the tax treatment of pension income.

Our model assumes that all investors receive the same return of 4% real after implicit costs but before explicit costs during the accumulation phase, and 1.3% real (after all costs) in the annuity phase. For any given life expectancy in retirement this gives a blended rate across the combination of the accumulation and decumulation period: this is equal to 3.18% when someone saves from age 35 to 64 and has a life expectancy of 18.7 years at 65, which is the current estimate for men. Our model then investigates how, with these common gross return assumptions, net return varies as the other factors are changed.

Model structure

The model is based on a man who reaches age 65 during the financial year 2004/05 and retires at this point (i.e. is subject to the tax and means-testing rules that apply today and which will apply during his retirement). It is assumed that he has worked every year since he was 20, and we either assume a constant percentage earnings increase each year, or that wages remain constant in real terms. We assume he has a full Basic State Pension (BSP), was contracted in to SERPS since 1978 and will receive any means-tested benefits in retirement to which he is entitled.[6]

In modelling the accumulation of a pension fund, we have assumed that once saving begins, he saves a constant proportion of his net earnings in a money purchase scheme. In calculating income tax we have assumed that the current tax thresholds and rates have applied in the past and will be uprated in the future to maintain their value in 2004 price terms. The only exception to that is the uprating of the pensioner personal tax allowance which is uprated in line with earnings, in line with current government policy. The savings threshold in the Pension Credit remains fixed in price terms and the Guarantee Credit increases in line with average earnings, which assumes current uprating arrangements are continued in the long-term, this means that over time higher incomes become eligible for some Pension Credit. We also assume that he pays Council Tax at the rate of the national average, and if he is a renter then his rent is at the national average.

In converting the pension fund into retirement income we have annuitised the pot using the highest annuity rate available according to the Annuity Bureau for an index-linked single life annuity for a healthy man aged 65 (the real rate of return implicit within this is about 1.3%). According to GAD the expectation of life for a man aged 65 in 2004 is almost 19 years, so we assume in the model that the man dies during between his 84 and 85 birthdays. Under current tax rules individuals can take up to 25% of the pension fund as a tax free lump sum, but capital is taken into account for entitlement to means tested benefits. Therefore to mimic this we have only calculated income tax on 75% of the total annuity stream, but calculated means tested benefit entitlement based on the whole annuity plus contributory benefits minus income tax.

[6]Note: A more complex version of the model which we will develop during the next year of our work will model the situation of people who will retire at future dates. Such people will tend to have slightly higher replacement rates from BSP and S2P combined at lower incomes but lower replacement rates at middle and high incomes [see Figure F.16]. An increasing proportion of them would be subject to means-tested Pension Credit withdrawal on an increasing proportion of their income if current indexation arrangements continue indefinitely. The net effect of this would be that an increasing proportion of people would over time be facing the negative impact on net returns which is illustrated in Figure C.23.

To analyse the separate impact of the different factors affecting the return individuals achieve on their private pension saving, we model and then compare the accumulation of different pension funds bringing in different factors. The baseline pension fund is the one based only on individual contributions before tax relief, and ignoring the effect of administration charges; this gives the pure return that an individual would get in a 'frictionless' taxless market with no employer contributions. The other pension funds were then based on variations to this. The final stage was to calculate benefit entitlement for the person who had made voluntary saving, and for the same individual who had not made any voluntary saving.

The different retirement incomes that are created in the model are:

1   Pension based only on personal contributions.

2   Pension based on personal contributions plus tax relief.

3   Pension based on personal contributions, tax relief and employers contributions.

4   Pension based on personal contributions, tax relief, employers contributions and after administrative charges.

5   Pension income produced by option four plus state pensions and means tested benefits and after tax.

6   Net private pension income: This is the pension produced by option five minus what the individual would have received without making any private savings.

In order to estimate the effective rate of return on saving, we then calculate the internal rate of return which makes the net present value of the stream of contributions and pension income equal to zero. In all cases the contributions flow is the contribution that the individual makes out of net income, and the stream of pension income is one of the options as explained above. Therefore it is possible to see how the inclusion of different factors affects the return that the individual achieves.

Key results: stylised constant real earnings cases

A simplified way to look at the results of the model is to take a stylised individual who does not receive any earnings increases in real terms over their whole working life. This means that we can abstract from complexities resulting from different earnings profiles. These are stylised cases, they are not representative of the population, nor of the actual returns that real people may achieve, but they illustrate key factors driving the different returns which real world individuals will face.

Table C.3 shows the net return for such stylised individuals depending on whether they receive employer contributions or not, their rate of tax relief, their means-tested status, and the administration costs they face. In each case the return on own contributions, over both the period of saving and pension receipt, is 3.2%, but the effect of the other factors changes the net return the individual receives.

Looking at these stylised individuals, the most typical is probably the individual who pays basic rate tax in working life, and some tax in retirement, and makes a 7.5% individual pension contribution which is matched by a 7.5% contribution from the employer [Figure C.25]. Basic rate tax relief adds 1% to this individual's rate of return and the employer contribution adds 2.6%. Although he receives an employer contribution, we have assumed that he faces an AMC of 1%, which would be typical for someone in a personal pension scheme, which reduces the overall return over his lifetime by 0.7%. As his pension income is sufficient to keep him above means-testing in retirement, the net impact of taxes and means-tested benefits reduces the return by only 0.8%. The overall effect of the different factors means that he receives a net return of 5.2%.

Figure C.26 shows how the different element interact for an individual who is a higher rate tax payer in working life, a basic rate taxpayer in retirement who makes an individual contribution which is matched by the employer as in Figure C.25. For this person the effect of higher rate tax relief adds 2% to the rate of return, and the employer contribution adds a further 2.3%. The pension fund has a 0.3% AMC which reduces the rate of return by 0.2%, the impact of foregone means-tested benefits and taxes reduces his return by 0.8%. Overall the return he achieves, in this stylised model is 6.5%.

Table C.3 Effective Rates of Return for Stylised Individuals with and without an Employer Contribution: Assuming a 3.2% Return Before all Taxes and Explicit Costs

	No employer contributions	Employer contributions
Higher rate tax payer in both working life and retirement. Not means-tested, 0.3% AMC.	3.9%	6.4%
Higher rate tax payer in working life, basic rate in retirement. Not means-tested, 0.3% AMC.	4.1%	6.5%
Basic rate tax payer in working life and retirement. Not means-tested 1% AMC.	2.6%	5.2%
Basic rate tax payer on Working Tax Credit in working life, and on means-tested benefit in retirement. 1.5% AMC.	4.1%	5.2%
Basic rate tax payer in working life and on means-tested benefits in retirement, 1.5% AMC.	0.7%	3.2%

Figure C.25 Effective Real Rate of Return for Stylised Individual who pays Basic Rate Tax in Working Life and in Retirement

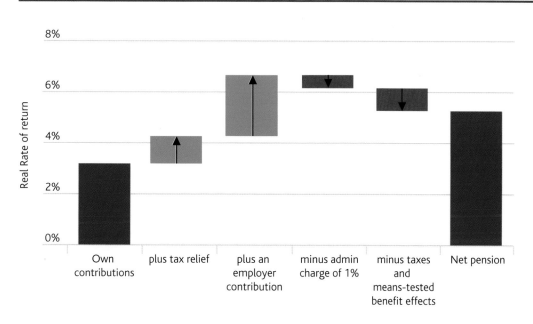

Source: Pensions Commission analysis

Note: The rate of return on individual saving across both accumulation and decumulation is 3.18%. We assume that he starts saving at 35 and makes a 7.5% contribution with a 7.5% employer contribution. To simplify the analysis we have assumed no earnings growth in real terms. He pays an annual management charge of 1%.

Figure C.26 Effective Real Rate of Return for Stylised Individual Who Pays Higher Rate Tax in Working Life and Basic Rate Tax in Retirement

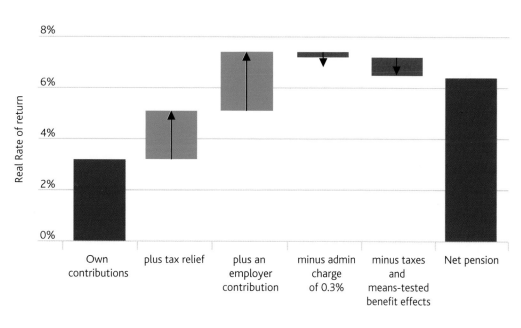

Source: Pensions Commission analysis

Note: The rate of return on individual saving across both accumulation and decumulation is 3.18%. We assume that he starts saving at 35 and makes a 7.5% contribution with a 7.5% employer contribution. To simplify the analysis we have assumed no earnings growth in real terms. He pays a annual management charge of 0.3%.

By contrast, Figure C.27 shows the position of an individual who is on low earnings throughout his life, only paying basic rate tax during working life and falling on the means-tested benefits in retirement, but was not entitled to Tax Credits in working life. He did not receive an employer contribution, but paid 15% of his net salary in pension contributions. Because he was making smaller contributions, and buying the pension individually he faced an AMC of 1.5%. As he pays basic rate tax, the effect of tax relief only adds 1% to the effective rate of return, which is more than eliminated by the effect of charges (-1.1%). This person has only a small pension, so the means-tested benefits foregone as a result of saving are a large proportion of his actual pension income. The negative impact of means-testing is therefore bigger (-2.3%) and the net effective rate of return on private pension saving is 0.7%.

Figure C.28 however illustrates that if the person who was on Pension Credit during retirement [illustrated by Figure C.27] had received Working Tax Credit throughout his working life, and if his earnings fell within the range at which the 37% withdrawal taper applies, his return could look significantly better. This is because pension contributions are taken off gross income in order to calculate entitlement to Tax Credits. This gives this person an effective rate of tax relief of 59% since pension contributions both decrease basic rate tax liability (22%) and increase Tax Credits received (37%). The 3.2% pre-everything return now becomes 4.1% after all effects.

If Tax Credits are received at some point during working life, but not for the whole working life, this will boost the net return but not by as much as Figure C.28 illustrates. Someone who is on means-tested benefits in retirement, but did not receive Working Tax Credit, but who at some stage in his working life received Child Tax Credit on the taper, would received a return somewhere between that illustrated in Figure C.27 and Figure C.28. This reflects the fact the Child Tax Credit would only apply for a proportion of total working life. Finally it should be noted that some people with higher incomes in retirement (and therefore not on means-tested benefits) may receive Child Tax Credit on the taper at some point during their working life. Such people could therefore receive a better return than illustrated in Figure C.25.

Figure C.27 Effective Real Rate of Return for Stylised Individual Who Pays Basic Rate Tax in Working Life and Receives Means-tested Benefits in Retirement: Not on Working Tax Credit during Working Life

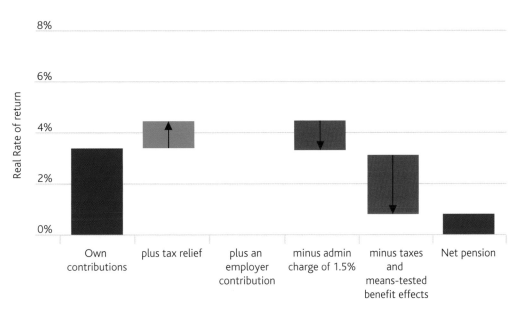

Source: Pensions Commission analysis

Note: The rate of return on individual saving across both accumulation and decumulation is 3.18%. We assume that he starts saving at 35 and makes an individual contribution of 15%. To simplify the analysis we have assumed no earnings growth in real terms. He pays an annual management charge of 1.5%.

Figure C.28 Effective Real Rate of Return for Stylised Indivdidual who pays Basic Rate Tax and is on Working Tax Credit in Working Life and is on Means-tested Benefits in Retirement

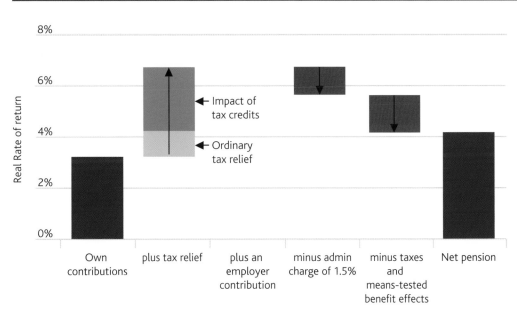

Source: Pensions Commission analysis

Note: The rate of return on individual saving across both accumulation and decumulation is 3.18%. We assume that he starts saving at 35 and makes an individual contribution of 15%. To simplify the analysis we have assumed no earnings growth in real terms. He pays an annual management charge of 1.5%.

Key results: return variations by income, housing tenure and age

An alternative way to look at the impact of the different elements of the system is to look at the overall effect of the different factors at different earnings level. Figure C.29 shows how this works for the base case scenario, which is that someone saves 15% of their net income from the age of 35, faces a 1% AMC and does not rent in retirement.

The effective rate of return increases as income increases, but then declines at very high income levels, for a number of different reasons:

1 Tax relief increases as people become higher rate tax payers. There is a gradual increase in the return as more years of working life are spent as a higher rate taxpayer.

2 At the lower end of the earnings distribution SERPS/S2P entitlement is insufficient to remove entitlement to the Guarantee Credit; therefore by undertaking private pension saving people forego a larger amount of state benefit.

3 As earnings increase, the foregone means-tested benefit is a smaller proportion of total retirement income, therefore the negative impact of means-testing withdrawal is less, and the net return increases.

4 At very high incomes people are paying higher rate tax on some of their pensions, this therefore reduces the return slightly.

This approach then allows us to look at how the return on private pension saving varies as we change elements of the scenario. Table C.4 shows how the return on own contributions increases the longer that people save for retirement. This is a consequence of the fact that there are more years in the accumulation period, during which the return is higher than in the decumulation period. Figure C.30 shows how the net return changes according to the age someone starts saving and their earnings.

Table C.4 Rate of Return on Own Contributions according to the Age Someone Started Saving

Age started saving	25	35	45	55
Return on own contributions	3.3%	3.1%	2.9%	2.5%

Source: Pensions Commission analysis

Note: Assuming his earnings increase by 1.5% per year, 4% real return during the accumulation and 1.3% during the annuity phase. Once he starts saving he saves 15% of earnings and pays 1% AMC.

Figure C.29 Effective Rates of Return at Different Earnings Levels

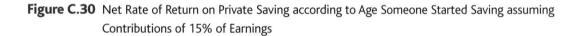

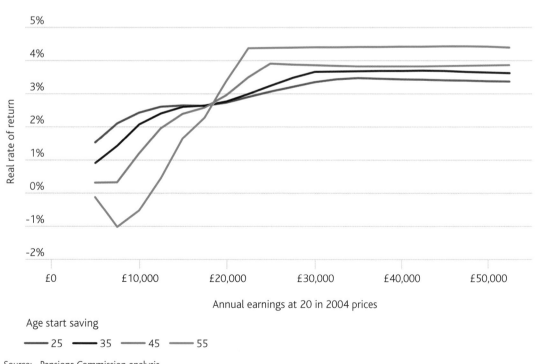

Annual earnings at 20 in 2004 prices

—— Own contributions ——— Plus tax relief —— Minus charges —— Net return after taxes and means-testing effects

Source: Pensions Comission analysis

Note: Assuming his earnings increase by 1.5% per year, 4% real return during accumulation and 1.3% during the annuity phase. He starts saving at 35, saves 15% of earnings and pays 1% AMC. He is not a renter in retirement. Tax credit effects have been ignored.

Figure C.30 Net Rate of Return on Private Saving according to Age Someone Started Saving assuming Contributions of 15% of Earnings

Annual earnings at 20 in 2004 prices

Age start saving

—— 25 —— 35 —— 45 —— 55

Source: Pensions Commission analysis

Note: Assuming his earnings increase by 1.5% per year, 4% real rate of return during accumulation and 1.3% during the annuity phase. Once he starts saving he saves 15% of earnings and pays 1.5% AMC. He is not a renter in retirement. Tax credit effects have been ignored.

The net rate of return for men on lower earnings who start saving earlier is higher; this is because their private pension income increases, so the foregone income from the state is a smaller proportion of their private pension income, boosting the net return. But for those on higher earnings who start saving earlier, this reduces their net return as they have a higher income in retirement and therefore pay proportionately more tax than they would have done had they saved later. For people who start to save later the reverse pattern is true; those who are on lower earnings have worse rates of return because they forgo a large proportion of the private pension income in means-tested benefits. Whereas those who are on higher earnings get a higher net rate of return as proportionately less is taxed.

Another important element is the role of an employer contribution. Figure C.31 shows how for someone aged 35, whose total pension contribution, is 15%, the net return increases as the employer contributes more of that 15%. Even a small employer contribution significantly boosts the return an individual receives on their own pension saving.

Another aspect of the system that will affect the return an individual achieves on pension saving is whether they are a renter in retirement which could create an entitlement to Housing Benefit. Figure C.32 shows how being a renter reduces the net return an individual achieves. For those who start saving at a later age the impact is even greater. Someone who earns £10,000 per year, starts saving at 55 and who is a renter in retirement earns a negative real rate of return. He is still better off in retirement as a result of saving, but the net increase in income in retirement is small compared to the contributions, as the foregone Housing Benefit is a significant proportion of their retirement income.

This modelling shows that there is wide divergence in the actual returns that individuals get on their savings, even holding investment returns and charges constant. This is because of the interactions between different components of the tax, benefit and pension systems. People who start saving early, have an employer contribution, receive higher rate tax relief and do not rent in retirement get significantly higher returns than individuals with the opposite characteristics.

However low and possibly negative real rates of return (or even negative nominal returns) may not mean that people should not save for their retirement. Even when individuals have a negative rate of return their absolute income in retirement is higher than it would have been had they not saved. This increase in income in retirement may be desirable for individuals compared to the increase in consumption that they could have achieved in working life had they not saved. Moreover it is worth noting that the individuals who are likely to get very poor rates of return are also likely to be those who receive adequate replacement rate from the state. Thus in our group modelling [see Appendix G and Chapter 4] we find some people who have adequate retirement income even if they make no private savings.

The most concerning impact of low returns therefore relates not to the lowest income earnings, but to 'lower-middle' income earners, who do need to make private saving to achieve adequate replacement rates, but who may face relatively poor incentives to save.

Figure C.31 The Impact of an Employer Contribution on the Net Return of an Individual who starts Pension Saving aged 35 and where Total Contributions are 15% of Earnings

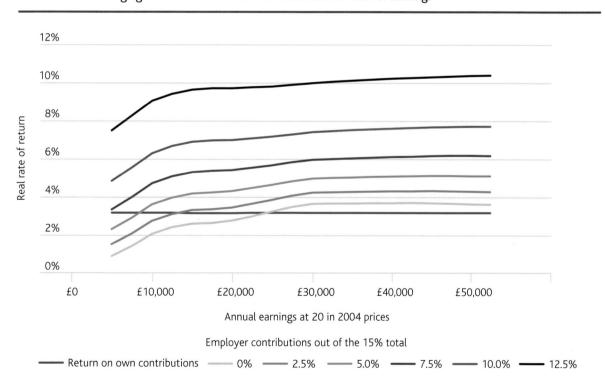

Source: Pensions Commission analysis

Note: Assuming his earnings increase by 1.5% per year, 4% real rate of return during accumulation and 1.3% during the annuity phase. He starts saving at 35 and his total pension contribution is 15% of earnings. He is not a renter in retirement. Tax credit effects have been ingored.

Figure C.32 The Impact of being a Renter in Retirement for Someone who Started Saving at Age 35 or 55

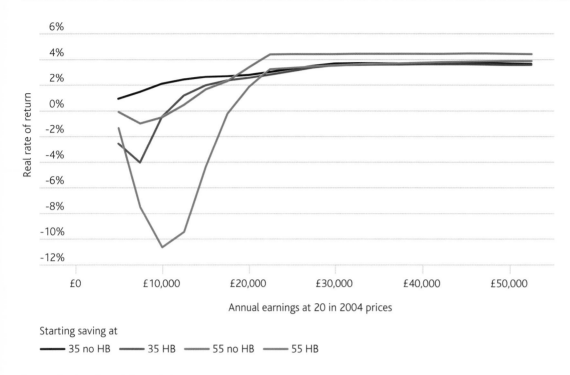

Starting saving at
—— 35 no HB   —— 35 HB   —— 55 no HB   —— 55 HB

Source: Pensions Commission analysis

Note: Assuming his earnings increase by 1.5% per year, 4% real rate of return during accumulation and 1.3% during the annuity phase.
Once he starts saving he saves 15% of earnings and pays 1% AMC. Tax credit effects have been ignored.

International comparisons

This Appendix covers eight topics in turn:

1   The structure of mandatory pension systems in developed countries, covering both Pay As You Go (PAYG) systems and compulsory savings systems.

2   The generosity of these systems, once the systems are fully mature at different levels of income.

3   Pension levels and pension adequacy for today's pensioners.

4   Total resource transfers as a percentage of GDP, fiscal cost and fiscal sustainability.

5   Pension system reforms in developed countries.

6   The scale and asset allocation of funded pension savings, voluntary as well as compulsory.

7   Compulsory savings in developing as well as developed countries:

    –   Impact on aggregate savings rates.

    –   Importance of administrative charges.

8   Seven country case studies: New Zealand, the Netherlands, Switzerland, Australia, USA, Sweden and Germany.

1. The structure of mandatory pension systems

In order to compare the generosity of public pension systems, we need first to be clear what is included. All developed countries have a PAYG pension paid for out of insurance contributions or taxes. Most of these systems provide at least a minimum pension irrespective of earnings. Most also include an earnings-related element, with both contributions and benefits rising with earnings. In most cases these earnings-related elements are only compulsory for employees not for the self-employed. Some countries' systems in addition have compulsory or quasi compulsory savings: where these exist they also usually apply only to employees not to the self-employed.

The pattern of provision by OECD country is shown on Table D.1.

■ For most countries the PAYG system is the entire compulsory system, with no compulsory savings element in addition. In these countries there may in addition be voluntary private savings, but these are not part of the compulsory public system.

■ Switzerland has a long established system of compulsory private savings. Australia has developed a system of compulsory private savings during the 1990s. Sweden's system is primarily PAYG, but now has a small tier of compulsory private savings as well.

■ The Netherlands has an extensive system of private funded pensions. While these are not strictly compulsory in law, they are so integrally bound in with a system of national collective bargaining that they are considered (e.g. by the OECD) to be effectively part of the public compulsory system.

■ The UK has a compulsory second tier of pension provision. Employees must either participate in the state PAYG earnings-related pension scheme (SERPS/S2P) or "contract-out" into a funded pension scheme, with the minimum contributions designed to ensure that the funded schemes will deliver a pension equivalent to the SERPS/S2P system [see Appendix F for more details of the UK system].

2. Generosity of compulsory pension systems

This section compares the pension income which pensioners would receive from different mandatory systems (including any compulsory funded savings element) if they were fully paid-up members of the systems which now exist.

The OECD has recently published the results of a comprehensive analytical framework that enables quantitative comparison to be made of mandatory pensions.[1]

[1]Note: These results are preliminary and it is expected that a new set of revised indicators will be published in the last quarter of 2004.

Table D.1 Structure of Mandatory Pension Systems in OECD Countries

Provision Type	First tier: mandatory, redistribution			Second tier: mandatory, insurance		
	Public Targeted	Public Base	Public Minimum	Public DB	Private DB	Private DC
Australia	■					■
Austria	■			■		
Belgium	■		■	■		
Canada	■	■		■		
Czech Republic		■	■	■		
Finland	■				■	
France	■		■	■	■	
Germany				■		
Hungary	■		■	■		■
Iceland	■				■	
Ireland		■				
Italy						■ notional
Japan		■		■		
Korea				■	■	
Luxembourg	■		■	■		
Mexico	■					■
The Netherlands		■			■ [1]	
New Zealand		■				
Norway	■	■		■		
Poland	■					■ notional and funded
Slovak Republic			■	■		
Spain				■		
Sweden	■				■	■ notional and funded
Switzerland	■		■	■	■ [1]	
United Kingdom	■	■	■	■	■ [2]	■ [2]
United States	■			■		

Source: Monitoring the Future Social Implications of Today's Pension Policies with additional notes from the Pensions Commission.

Note: "First tier: mandatory redistribution": covers those elements of the system which aim to provide a minimum level of income for all retirees and which effectively entail redistribution (provided by social security contributions or taxes which are earnings-related but which fund partly flat rate benefits)

"Second tier: mandatory, insurance" covers those elements of the system which give earnings-related benefits, paid for by earnings-related contributions.

Purely voluntary savings are not included in this framework.

"Public-targeted": refers to a system which is focused on low income pensioners. The benefits can be either pension income tested, broader income tested or means-tested.

"Public-base": refers to a system in which the value of the pension is flat rate or only depends on years of service and not individual earnings.

"Public-Minimum": refers to a system which a minimum pension value exists in earnings-related schemes for workers earning below a given level and have not met the contribution requirements.

[1] The Netherlands and Switzerland's mandatory private saving schemes are effectively close to DB given the surplus funding rules and asset allocation choices made.

[2] The UK "contracting-out" arrangements allow individuals to chose a private pension as an alternative to the mandatory public DB system.

The OECD's framework calculates the pension entitlement from currently legislated mandatory pension systems for full-time lifetime workers at various levels of earnings. The key features are:

- All mandatory systems are included. For The Netherlands the occupational funded pension is included because, through collective bargaining agreements, it has coverage of over 90% of employees. For the UK the pension includes the Basic State Pension (BSP) and the State Second Pension system (S2P). Although it is expected that many workers will opt out of the S2P into an approved private or occupational pension, the level of the rebate paid to those who opt out is designed on reasonable rates of return assumptions to ensure that these private pension systems should deliver a benefit equal to that provided by the State. This equivalence is used to simplify the modelling: all employees are assumed to receive their entitlement to the S2P. It is therefore for the UK a minimum estimate of future pension provision.

- The framework provides forward-looking indicators because it calculates replacement rates for workers entering employment in 2002 and accumulating pension entitlement during their working lives under the currently legislated pension systems.

- The economic assumptions used such as GDP growth, earnings growth and changes in the general price level are held constant for all countries. This means differences are solely the result of differences in the pension systems rather than a mix of pensions and different forecasts for the economic environment in each country.

- The first indicator is the pension value earned at different earnings levels expressed as ratios of average earnings. These pension values are expressed in units of national average earnings.

- Using a synthetic earnings distribution the OECD also calculates the average pension value and this indicates the average generosity of the pension system.

Countries can be grouped according to whether the pensions rise
with earnings.

**1. Almost purely earnings-related: The Netherlands, Italy, Spain and
Sweden [Figure D.1]**. In these countries the mandatory pension scheme is
almost all earnings-related. The earnings link covers a relatively wide
segment of the income distribution and where there are earnings ceilings
they are around twice average earnings. The relative generosity of these
pension systems is placing increasing burdens as populations age where the
schemes are financed from government revenues. Sweden and Italy have
introduced notional accounts to make the link between pensions and
contributions more transparent. They have both linked the annuity factor,
that converts the notional accumulated balance into a pension with
expected longevity at the point of retirement. The rationale for all four
pension systems is to establish a strong link between contributions and
benefits to achieve solidarity across all earnings groups.

**2. Strong but less generous earnings-related pensions: France,
Germany, US, Switzerland and Australia [Figure D.2]**. These countries all
have earnings-related pensions but are not as generous as the countries in
the first group. Moderation in generosity is achieved either through relatively
low earnings ceilings or a less generous link between earnings and pension
entitlement. The earnings link in Switzerland is up to 120% of average
earnings and this gives a flat rate pension above this level. France's scheme
achieves high replacement rates of 90% at half average earnings with a still
generous 85% at average earnings but the replacement rate falls off after
this and is only 59% at 2.5 times average earnings. Germany's system
produces rising replacement rates up to 1.5 times average earnings after
which the pension is flat and the replacement rate declines for higher
earnings. In the US the earnings-related pension link has a relatively high
ceiling at 2.5 times average earnings but the comparative generosity erodes
the higher the level of earnings. Flat rate basic pensions give most of the
curves a kink at low earnings levels.

3. Weak link or flat rate pension systems: UK, NZ & Ireland [Figure D.3].
The UK, Ireland and New Zealand have either a flat rate public pension or
as in the UK a very weak earnings element in the public pension system.
The main rationale of these three pension systems' is avoidance of
destitution in old age and to leave further provision to the private funded
pension schemes that are mainly voluntary.

Figure D.1 Gross Pension Value for Almost Purely Earnings-related Countries

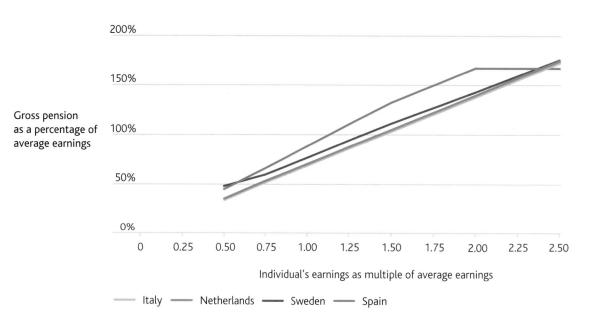

Source: Monitoring Pension Policies, Annex: Country Chapters, 2003

Note: The Netherland's figures reflect the input of the quasi-mandatory private savings systems as well as the PAYG pension.
The values for Italy and the Netherlands are almost identical and the two lines converge

Figure D.2 Gross Pension Value for Strongly Earnings-related Countries

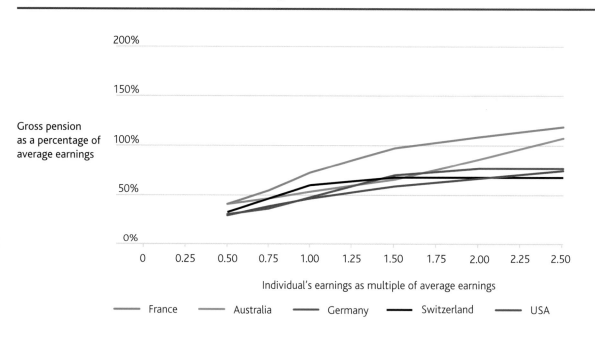

Source: Monitoring Pension Policies, Annex: Country Chapters, 2003

Note: The Australian figures reflect the input of the mandatory private savings system as well as the PAYG pension.

Figure D.3 Gross Pension Value for Basic Flat-rate/Modest Earnings-related Countries

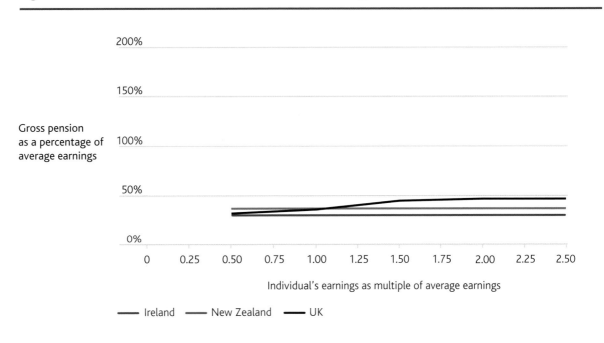

Source: Monitoring Pension Policies, Annex: Country Chapters, 2003

Figure D.4 Percentage of Population with Income Below 60% of Median Employment Income: 2001

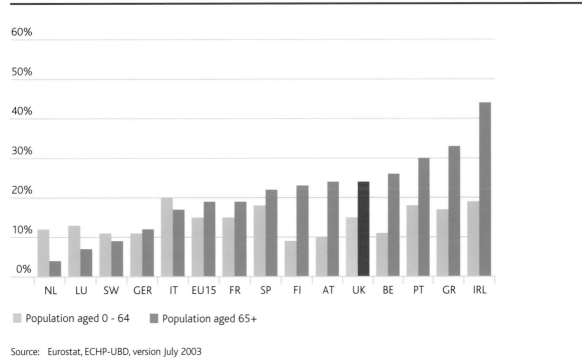

Source: Eurostat, ECHP-UBD, version July 2003

Note: Data for Sweden only cover people aged less than 85.

3. Pension levels and pension adequacy for today's pensioners

The previous section compared the pension a theoretical individual would receive from a full working lifetime in the mandatory or quasi mandatory system (including any compulsory savings). This section presents a different comparison: pensioner incomes today. This differs from the analysis above in two respects:

■ First, it looks at total incomes in retirement, including pensions from voluntary schemes as well as compulsory, and including non-pension savings, benefits and earnings.

■ Second, the pensions received **today** from the public compulsory systems can be significantly different from those which would be received by lifetime members of the systems which now exist. The position of today's pensioners is the outcome of accumulated pension rights under previous pension policies interacting with people's labour market histories, patterns of household formation as well as the impact of indexing regimes. The maturity of a pension system will also affect the incomes of the retired population. Mature pension systems, where the newly retired are as likely to have accumulated full pension rights as the older retirees, will be in a different position relative to immature systems. For example in Spain and Ireland many of the existing pensioners will not have gained the same second pension rights as the cohorts retiring today.

The Member States of the EU adopted a body of indicators designed to compare the income position of people over retirement age, using standard definitions and common data. The first indicator is the proportion of people aged 65 and over who live in households with an income below 60% of median income of all households [Figures D.4 and D.5]. Some key findings are:

■ The UK has a relatively high proportion of people aged 65 and over in low income households: 24% compared with 19% the average for the EU15 Member States.[2]

■ In the UK as elsewhere the risk of belonging to a low income household for people aged 65 and over (24%) is higher than it is for the rest of the population (15%).

■ There are however some countries where pensioners are at lower risk than the rest of the population of living in low income households: Italy, Luxembourg, The Netherlands and Sweden; with Germany showing the same risk for both groups. Some of the differences may not be significant but these countries may have more problems in sustaining generous pension provision in the response to rapid ageing in their populations.

[2]Note: The figures quoted in this annex are provided by Eurostat and differ from the DWP's *Households Below Average Income* in two ways. First the data sources are different: DWP uses the Family Resources Survey and Eurostat use the ECHP but this will make little difference. Second and more important is the equivalence scale used. Eurostat uses the OECD scales and this increases the number of people aged 65 and over living in low income households relative to the DWP's figure of 21%.

■ Women aged 65 and over have a higher risk of being in a low income household (28%) than men aged 65 and over (19%). There is a minority of EU15 countries where women are at no greater risk of poverty than men. In the Netherlands, Luxembourg and Belgium the differences are small or non-existent. In all other countries women are always at greater risk but the differences are greatest in Ireland, Austria, Finland, and the UK where the percentage point difference is greater than the EU15 average.

■ In the UK the proportion of people aged 65 and over in households with incomes below 50% of median income is 13% and 34% are in households with an income below 70% of median household income. This bunching around the low income threshold of 60% of median income means small changes in policies affecting the population aged 65 and over can shift relatively large numbers above or below this "poverty line".

Figure D.5 Percentage of Men and Women Aged 65+ with Income Below 60% of Median Employment Income: 2001

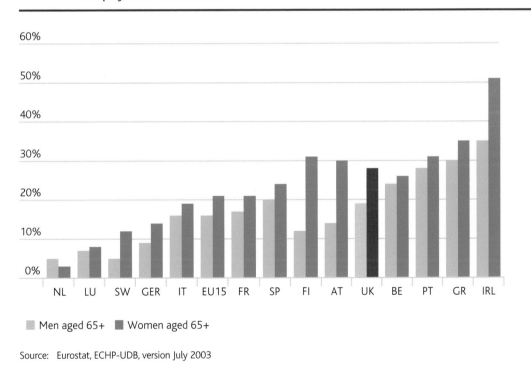

■ Men aged 65+   ■ Women aged 65+

Source: Eurostat, ECHP-UDB, version July 2003

Note: Data for Sweden only cover people aged less than 85

■ Most other countries with relatively high proportions of people aged 65 and over living in low income households are also countries with relatively immature pension systems: Ireland, Greece and Portugal. In addition Ireland has enjoyed very rapid economic growth and this will tend to raise the incomes of workers faster than the retired.

■ The UK is alone in having a relatively mature pension system and a high proportion of the elderly in low income households.

The second indicator used by the EU, average relative household income, confirms the UK's low ranking. Figure D.6 shows the average household income of the population aged 65 and over relative to the average for the population aged less than 65. Countries such as the Netherlands, Luxembourg, Italy and Germany have incomes that are very close to the rest of the population. France has a retirement age of 60 and the ratio shown leaves out the youngest cohort of the retired who will always have higher incomes than older cohorts. The relative incomes of the population aged 60 and over in France are closer to the rest of the population's income than the incomes of the population aged 65 and over.

The UK with a ratio of 0.76 is significantly below the EU15 average of 0.86.

Figure D.7 shows the percentage shares of pensioner income in the EU15 countries. Most of the countries where the incomes of the population aged 65 and over are high relative to the rest of the population are also countries where pensions rather than other social benefits and earnings form a very high share of household income. The exception is Italy. Here a higher proportion of the elderly live with working age relatives whose earned income boosts the average incomes of households with people aged over 65.

Figure D.6 Median Income of People Aged 65+ as a Percentage of Median Income of People
Aged Less Than 65: 2001

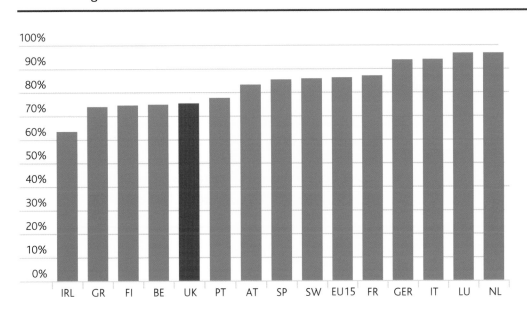

Source: Eurostat, ECHP-UDB, version July 2003

Note: Data for Sweden only cover people aged less than 85

Figure D.7 Composition of Equivalised Income of People Aged 65+ by Main Source: Ranked by Pension Income

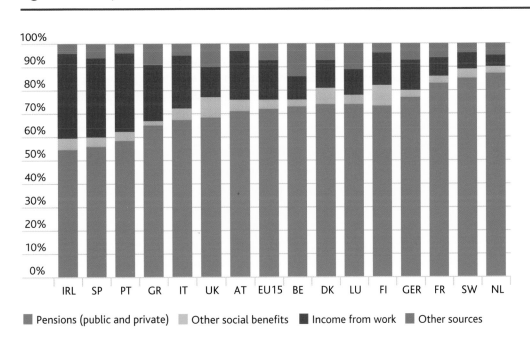

Source: Eurostat, EHCP-UDB, version November 2003

4. Total resource transfers as a percentage of GDP, fiscal cost and fiscal sustainability.

All pension systems, public or private, compulsory or voluntary, involve the transfer of resources from the current working generation to current pensioners. It is therefore useful to compare the size of these transfers as a percentage of GDP, distinguishing two measures:

■ The total percentage of GDP transferred by the whole system, public or private, funded or PAYG, mandatory or voluntary.

■ The percentage transferred by the PAYG element of the compulsory system. This is equivalent to the fiscal burden on taxation or contributions.

Both of these measures are influenced not only by the generosity of the system and the level of individual pensioner incomes, but by demographics i.e. by the proportion of pensioners in the population. A relatively generous system could be combined with a low percentage of GDP transferred if the demographics were favourable.

Great care is needed in drawing comparisons from the data because of the different ways resources are transferred to the retired in different countries. Many countries offer a considerable range of free services to the retired e.g. free transport, free care services and help with medical costs such as exemptions from prescription charges, as well as different ways of meeting the costs of long-term care.

The series that has been made as comparable possible is one from the OECD but it is still highly imperfect. Figures for the UK from the OECD differ from those used in the report [for example in Figure 1.12] because all pension transfers are included not just those to the population aged over 65. In addition disability benefits paid to below retirement age are often included (though not necessarily on a fully comparable basis) because of the way that individuals' countries categorise expenditure. The public share for the UK for instance includes all disability and survivor benefits paid regardless of age and the private share includes private pensions paid to people who are younger than 65.

The data classifies pensions of public employees as part of public pension transfers. It also includes all social assistance and other means-tested benefits such as help with housing costs.

Figure D.8 illustrates these OECD estimates of the total percentage of GDP transferred to pensioners today in different countries, and the element within that which is explained by the public PAYG system.

The results initially seem at odds with the measures of adequacy presented in Section 3. There are two reasons. First, the dependency ratios differ across the countries; for example, the ratio is 20% in the Netherlands and 24% in the UK. Rankings by percentage of GDP transferred would therefore differ from rankings of generosity per pensioner even if the figures were on a fully comparable basis. Second, the figures are not strictly comparable.

It is therefore difficult to assess how the overall UK's overall pension system compares with those of other countries as a mechanism for transferring resources to pensioners. But the figures tend to support our judgemental conclusions made in Chapter 3, that the UK system overall (public and private combined) probably transfers a percentage of GDP somewhat similar to that transferred by other systems which have a larger public pension element and where the demography is similar. What the figures also suggest, however, is that the percentage of total transfer deriving from all government payments is larger than much commentary on the UK pension system often suggests.

Figure D.8 Total Pension Expenditure as a Percentage of GDP: Very Imperfect Estimates

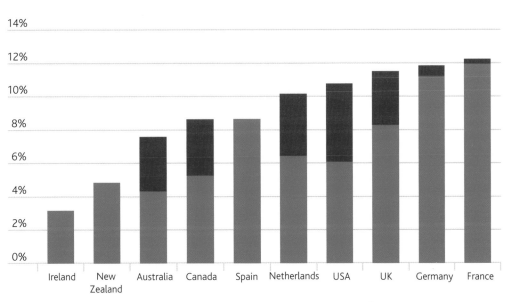

■ Public ■ Private (data was not available for Ireland, New Zealand and Spain)

Source: OECD, 2004, Social Expenditure Database, 1980-2001

Note: The figures from the OECD for the UK differ from those used in the report because all pension transfers are included not just to the population aged over 65, and because disability benefits paid at all ages are included.

Despite the imperfections of the data, moreover, the reasons for some of the relative rankings are clear.

■ Spain has a lower level of transfer, despite reasonable generosity, because it has a less mature demography, and thus at present a smaller proportion of pensioners to support. But it faces one of the biggest demographic challenges over the next 50 years.

■ Ireland has a very low level of transfer because of an immature demography and a low level of provision per pensioner.

■ The US public transfer is lower than the UK because of a less mature demography, rather than lower generosity.

■ New Zealand, despite a reasonable mature demography, transfers a small percentage of GDP to its elderly because of its flat rate state system, with no earnings-related element.

How the PAYG burden will develop in the future will be determined by:

■ The different demographic evolution of each country. Some countries face significantly more dramatic rises in the dependency ratio than the UK.

■ The planned evolution of the system, planned changes to generosity, retirement ages etc.

Table D.2 presents the combined effects of these two factors, allowing for pension system reforms legislated before 2000 but not any merely under discussion. The UK's figures are lower than used elsewhere in the report because they relate to 2000 before changes such as the introduction of Pension Credit and before the latest demographic projections. The total for the UK does not include pensions paid to former public sector employees. The figures reflect the government's interpretation of the definitions used in this exercise by the European Commission.

The projections show that in terms of public pension provision the UK and Ireland are least likely to face problems of fiscal sustainability as populations age in the first half of this century. The UK's projections were based on the assumption that the public pension would continue to be indexed against prices and would therefore fall relative to earnings. Work is currently in hand to produce a new set of pension projections that will incorporate changes to pension systems in all the Member States but they are not expected before the end of 2004.

Table D.2 Public Pension Expenditure as a Percentage of GDP

	2000	2010	2020	2030	2040	2050	Peak Change
AT	14.5	14.9	16.0	18.1	18.3	17.0	4.2
BE	10.0	9.9	11.4	13.3	13.7	13.3	3.7
DK[2]	10.5	12.5	13.8	14.5	14.0	13.3	4.1
EU15	10.4	10.4	11.5	13.0	13.6	13.3	3.2
FI	11.3	11.6	12.9	14.9	16.0	15.9	4.7
FR	12.1	13.1	15.0	16.0	15.8		4.0
GE[3]	11.8	11.2	12.6	15.5	16.6	16.9	5.0
GR	12.6	12.6	15.4	19.6	23.8	24.8	12.2
IRL[4]	4.6	5.0	6.7	7.6	8.3	9.0	4.4
IT	13.8	13.9	14.8	15.7	15.7	14.1	2.1
LU	7.4	7.5	8.2	9.2	9.5	9.3	2.2
NL[5]	7.9	9.1	11.1	13.1	14.1	13.6	6.2
PT	9.8	11.8	13.1	13.6	13.8	13.2	4.1
SP	9.4	8.9	9.9	12.6	16.0	17.3	7.9
SW	9.0	9.6	10.7	11.4	11.4	10.7	2.6
UK[6]	5.5	5.1	4.9	5.2	5.0	4.4	-1.1

Source: Economic Policy Committee (2001), "Budgetary challenges posed by ageing populations: the impact public spending on pensions, health and long-term care for the elderly and possible indicators of the long-term sustainability of public finances", Economic Policy Committee/ECFIN/655/01-EN final.

Note: 1. A number of countries introduced important reforms after 2000, or generated new national demographic projections which the EPC could not assess in detail. Caution must therefore be exercised when interpreting those figures and comparing them with the results for other countries.

2. For Denmark, the results include the statutory labour market supplementary pension schemes (ATP, SAP and SP).

3. Updated German national results based on the common EPC assumptions would show the following evolution of pension expenditure:

2000	2010	2020	2030	2040	2050	Peak Change
10.8	11.1	12.1	13.8	14.4	14.9	4.1

4. For Ireland, the results are expressed as a percentage of GNP.

5. In the Netherlands, the second pillar is well developed. This has a direct positive impact on the public pension scheme by reducing the burden of ageing populations on the first pillar. However, there is also an important indirect implication: taxes on future pension benefits (which are drawn from the private funds) are expected to be quite high and may partially counterbalance the rise in public pension benefits.

6. Figures are on a different basis to those used in the main report and other appendices.

5. Pension reforms in developed countries

This section summarises some of the more important pension reforms, mainly in the EU, that have been agreed in an attempt to make public pension costs sustainable in fiscal terms. The changes are grouped under three headings:

■ Pension age

■ Automatic adjustments for life expectancy

■ Increasing private funded provision to offset reductions in public pension provision.

Pension age: Raising the pension age is one response to the resource implications of growing numbers of pensioners. Table D.3 shows for a selection of OECD countries the legislated plans for pension age. In both EU and non-EU countries a majority of countries have used pressures on equal opportunities to equalise pension ages for men and women. In all countries where this has happened, the age has been raised for women. Those countries in the EU where the age for women is lower these Member States face strong legal pressures to equalise. A minority of countries have deliberately raised the age of retirement for men as well as women: Norway, Denmark, Iceland and the USA.

Automatic adjustments: Faced with fierce opposition at a political level whenever pension reform is introduced some countries have introduced an element of automatic adjustment. Within the EU, Sweden [see Box 6 at the end of this Appendix] and Italy have incorporated life expectancy at the point of retirement into the calculation of pension entitlement.

Germany [see Box 7 at the end of this Appendix] has two automatic elements: one relates to ceilings to contribution rates and the other to demography. There is a ceiling to contribution rates: 20% up to 2020 and 30% after 2030. If 15 year projections of expenditure show the need for rates to be higher to balance the fund the government is obliged to come to parliament with plans to reduce generosity. Recently the government has introduced the idea of linking pension levels automatically to changes in the dependency ratio whether or not they arise from changes in life expectancy.

Increasing private pensions: Several countries are making the growth of private pensions a key strategy for coping with the fiscal burden of ageing populations. Spain, Portugal, Germany and Greece have introduced legislation and regulatory frameworks designed to encourage the growth of private pensions. Tax incentives were introduced in the German 2001 reforms to encourage more private pension savings.

In Italy the development of private pension provision, occupational or individual, is a strategic priority for the government. Supplementary pension schemes will have to play a major role in supplementing adequate income levels for pensioners in the new Notional Account Defined Contribution pension scheme.

Most of these countries are also expecting the growth to be facilitated through the collective bargaining process. Here the success of the Dutch model [see Box 2 at the end of this Appendix] is seen as the ideal where collective bargaining has made occupational pensions virtually mandatory.

Even countries with high levels of private pension provision such as the Netherlands and the UK are assuming the role of the private sector will grow further.

Silver Funds: Several countries are explicitly building up a silver fund like Ireland where surpluses in the public budget are put aside into a fund earmarked for future higher pensions; another example is Belgium. Belgium with a public debt to GDP ratio of over 100% is banking on there being a substantial reduction in public debt and therefore future interest payments. This reduction will make room for the Government to continue paying pensions to an enlarged pensioner population.

France, Spain and Portugal have also set up a public pension reserve; payments will be made either from surpluses from the social insurance fund or the wider public sector surpluses that are hoped for.

Table D.3 Legislated Pension Ages

Australia	Austria	Belgium	Czech	Denmark	Finland	France	Germany	Greece
65	65	65	62	67	65	60	65	65
	60		57 – 61					

Hungary	Iceland	Ireland	Italy	Japan	Lux.	NL	NZ	Norway
62	67	66	65	65	65	65	65	67

Poland	Portugal	Slovakia	Spain	Sweden	Swtz	Turkey	UK	US
65	65	60	65	65	65	55	65	67
60		53 – 57			64	50		

Source: Monitoring the Future Social Implications of Today's Pension Policies, 2003.

Note: For pension ages, second line gives this for women where this is different. Pension ages vary with the number of children in the Czech and Slovak Republics.

6. The scale and asset allocation of funded pension savings in developed countries

The structure of the public pension system described in Section 1 has consequences for the scale of pension funds relative to GDP. Table D.4 shows pension funds for a number of OECD countries as a percentage of GDP.

Where there is a generous earnings-related PAYG system, such as Germany, Italy and Spain, pension funds are limited: since people receive significant income replacement from the state PAYG system, only a small voluntary funded element of the system exists.

Large pension fund assets have therefore developed in two categories of country:

■ In the countries with compulsory or quasi-compulsory savings schemes i.e. Switzerland, the Netherlands, Australia.

■ In the UK, where there has been only moderate compulsion, (either SERPS/S2P or the contracted-out alternative) but where voluntary private pension saving (primarily driven by occupational schemes) developed in the 1950s-1970s to compensate for the limited generosity of the state system. Large pension funds have for similar reasons developed in the USA and Canada.

Within the countries with significant funded pension provision, however, there are important differences in asset allocation approaches and thus sometimes in the risks born by individuals. Table D.5 shows the allocation of funds in the late 1990s.

■ In the Swiss scheme, funds have been primarily invested in bonds and the pension achieved as a result of the compulsory savings has been somewhat predictable. In the Dutch schemes, equities play a larger but still minor role. This, together with approaches to funding levels and surpluses, ensures that benefits to members are close to Defined Benefit (DB) in nature.

■ In the recent past, no other country has invested as high a share of pension funds in equities as the UK. In the past, the UK's large investments in equities have been balanced by the role of DB pension fund sponsors as effectively "return guarantors" and of insurance companies (through the with-profits product) as "return smoothers". Both of these roles are now in retreat. Individuals in Defined Contribution (DC) schemes which invest in equities will in future be fully exposed to equity market allocations: many are now shifting to lower risk, lower return bond strategies.

■ Australia's compulsory savings system has developed as an undiluted DC system and the investments in equities at around 40% have been higher than in the Netherlands and Switzerland but far lower than in the UK or in the USA.

Table D.4 Size of Total Investments of Autonomous Pension Funds as a Percentage of GDP

	2000	2001
Australia	67.0	67.4
Canada	48.3	48.2
Germany	3.3	3.3
Italy	4.5	4.4
Netherlands	113.7	105.1
Poland	1.4	2.6
Spain	8.4	8.2
Switzerland	105.2	113.5
UK	78.7	66.4
USA	69.3	63

Source: OECD, Global Pension Statistics Project

Note: The data for 2001 is provisional
The figures for the UK only include self-administered pension funds and not pension policies held via insurance companies.

Table D.5 Pension Fund Portfolios: Ranked by Percentage of Portfolio in Equities

	Equities	Fixed interest		Equities	Fixed interest
United Kingdom	78	14	Malaysia	16	55
United States	62	27	Switzerland	14	69
Ireland	58	30	France	14	38
Australia	41	15	Hungary	14	19
Belgium	40	46	Austria	13	71
Brazil	38	38	Greece	10	53
Peru	35	60	Finland	9	61
Canada	28	48	Portugal	9	27
Chile	28	68	Germany	8	74
Sweden	28	62	Italy	8	63
Argentina	27	70	Spain	5	76
Denmark	27	63	Singapore	0	70
Netherlands	26	63	Mexico	0	96
Average	**24**	**56**	Uruguay	0	100
Luxembourg	21	61			

Source: Srinivas, Whitehouse and Yermo (2000), De Ryck (1998), Asher (1998)

7. Compulsory savings across the world

Mandatory savings for pensions exist in many countries. The Netherlands scheme [see Box 2 at the end of this Appendix] dates back to 1957 and the UK's National Insurance based earnings-related scheme, now S2P, was brought in 1978 and expanded and modified in the following two decades. Chile's funded DC pension scheme was started in 1981 and has served as a model for mandatory savings pension schemes introduced extensively in South America. The World Bank's advocacy of a three pillar pension scheme with a private funded DC scheme as the second pillar has meant that many Central and East European countries introduced these schemes in the 1990s. The World Bank has argued that their model spreads the risks by having a mix of public and private and DB and DC; but a key has been their belief that a compulsory funded pension scheme will raise national savings.

A key issue is therefore whether any increase in savings rates has been achieved from the introduction of compulsory savings. It is very difficult to work out in the countries with long established compulsion and experience of Latin America is of limited relevance. But Australian evidence suggests their mandatory scheme has raised the level of national savings; the best estimate suggests that for every Au$1 of compulsory contributions there has only been a 38 cent offset from reductions in other forms of savings (Connolly and Kohler, February 2004).

The impact on net savings is only one factor that determines if mandatory savings schemes are worth introducing: administrative charges are also important. Well-run PAYG systems can cost less than 0.1% of implicit value of implicit funds. Forced savings systems typically cost much more.

International comparison of administrative charges for pensions highlights the different factors that determine these costs and demonstrates the impact of different ways of controlling these charges. In a discussion paper for the World Bank, E. Whitehouse compares 13 countries charges. The group includes a number of Latin American Countries[3] where mandatory funded pension schemes have been introduced over the last 25 years, as well as OECD countries.[4]

Most of the 13 countries have some system for controlling charges. Australia and the UK (apart from Stakeholder Pensions) have no restrictions and rely on competitive forces to keep charges down. El Salvador, Kazakhstan and UK (Stakeholder Pensions) have fixed ceilings on charges and Sweden and Poland have partial (Poland) or variable (Sweden) ceilings. Mexico has cross subsidies for low income workers and the remaining Latin American countries have limits on the type of charges designed to ensure cross subsidies for low paid workers. Bolivia uses competitive tendering.

[3] Note: Mexico, Argentina, Peru, Chile, El Salvador, Uruguay, Colombia, and Bolivia

[4] Note: UK, Sweden, Poland and Australia

Figure D.9 shows the variation in estimated administrative charges. Charges are highest in Mexico, Argentina and the UK's (non-Stakeholder) personal pensions and lowest in Bolivia, Australia (Industry Funds only) Kazakhstan and Colombia. An important determinant is whether the relevant pension organisation has to win customers in the retail market as this involves high marketing costs. In contrast these costs disappear in Bolivia where workers are allocated to the two pension funds chosen by competitive tender.

Other factors affecting costs include the use of a clearing house to collect contributions and administer accounts, for example Sweden. Transparency is also important. Chile, El Salvador and Peru require charges to be imposed on top of the mandatory contribution. Members are then more aware of the impact of these charges on their accumulating funds. If the UK were to go down the road of extending compulsion further then care would be needed in the design of such a scheme to minimize these costs whilst also retaining the advantages of a funded pension scheme.

Figure D.9 Charge Ratio in Compulsory Savings Schemes: 2000, Total Percentage Reduction in Accumulated Pension Fund

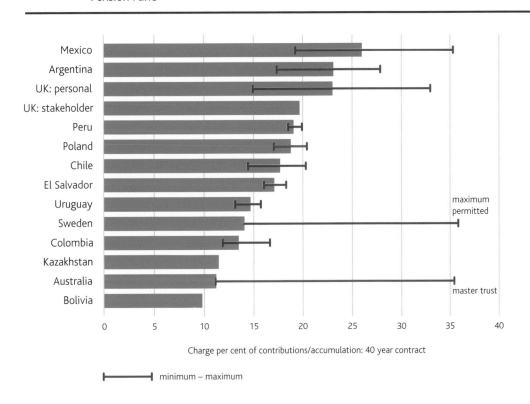

Charge per cent of contributions/accumulation: 40 year contract

⊢────────⊣ minimum – maximum

Source: Whitehouse, June 2000

Note: The charge ratio shows the total reduction in the value of the pension accumulation resulting from annual charges over the entire contract length for example a AMC of 1% per year for a contract length of 25 years, and assuming gross returns of 6% per year, produces a charge ratio of 15%.

8. Drawing some lessons from the country case studies

This section sets out information on pension reform in seven countries. The individual case studies are in Boxes 1-7: New Zealand, the Netherlands, Switzerland, Australia, USA, Sweden and Germany.

New Zealand is a special case as they have decided to limit the Government's involvement to a flat rate citizens' pension and they have a policy of tax neutrality towards private pensions. Pensions policy is seen as solely about the prevention of destitution with individuals left to decide for themselves how if at all they want to make additional private funded provision. Relative to earnings the New Zealand basic pension is more generous than the UK's and their projections of public expenditure suggest that the New Zealand Government is expecting public expenditure to adapt proportionately to the ageing of the New Zealand population.

The Netherlands, Switzerland and Australia are examples of countries that have a basic flat rate pension that is affluence tested because the second earnings related pension is compulsory or in the case of The Netherlands virtually mandatory. The Netherlands scheme is now virtually mature and with relatively high contribution rates it also delivers high incomes in retirement and there are relatively few people aged 65 and over living below 60% of median income. The Netherlands has the strongest commitment to replace earnings before retirement and as a result delivers a pension with a high replacement rate across a wide range of earnings. Switzerland with a cut off for the compulsory earnings-related funded pension at 120% of average earnings delivers more modest replacement rates above this level and higher earners are expected to make their own voluntary provision. Australia's mandatory scheme has raised the level of national savings; the best estimate suggests that for every Au$1 of compulsory contributions there has only been a 38 cent offset from reductions in other forms of savings (Connolly and Kohler, February 2004).

The USA. There is a flat rate means-tested and a compulsory PAYG public earnings-related second pension. This second pension is more generous than the UK's S2P. It delivers a higher net replacement rate for someone on average earnings and it provides an earnings-related element further up the wage distribution: the ceiling is 2.5 times average earnings although the target replacement rate is lower for higher earnings. The combined system is more generous than the combination of the UK's BSP and earnings-related S2P. But as recognition of possible future problems of affordability the official retirement age is being raised to 67 by 2027.

Sweden. The reformed pension system in Sweden is often held up as a model of a reformed mixed provision system. The first layer is a flat rate means-tested pension for those with little or no alternative pension or income. The next two layers, "Notional Account Defined Contribution" and a mandatory funded occupational pension ensure a mixed provision for nearly all pensioners in Sweden. The notional account pension has a direct link to longevity forecasts at the time of retirement and provides can be withdrawn for others because the next two layers are mandatory.

Germany. Until recently this was an example of a state insurance based earnings-related scheme. Generosity and an ageing population have driven reform based on (i) reduced generosity and not automatic adjustment within the state PAYG system, and (ii) a hope of greater reliance on funded private schemes.

Box 1: New Zealand

New Zealand has a single basic flat rate citizen's pension, The New Zealand Superannuation, and voluntary private pensions but the tax treatment is neutral for these schemes. The basic pension is for all people who reach 65 provided they have lived in New Zealand for at least 10 years and five of those have to be since reaching 50. In 2002 it was worth £4,638 for a single person not sharing (there is a small reduction for those who share) and about £7,050 for a married couple.

In addition over one in five receive the Disability Allowance that helps with the costs of ongoing, additional costs of a disability e.g. ongoing visits to the doctor or hospital, medicines and extra clothing or travel. Over 70% have a Community Services card that reduces the cost of doctors' appointments and prescriptions.

Voluntary occupational schemes

These schemes are available but few belong and those that do exist are switching to DC from DB schemes. There are no tax incentives.

Private personal pensions

These are available to all but there are no tax incentives and in this respect New Zealand is the only OECD country to operate a tax neutral policy towards private pensions.

Public pension expenditure as a percentage of GDP was 4.5% in 2000 and is projected to increase by a third to 6.0% by 2020.

Box 2: The Netherlands

First Pillar Algemene Ouderdomswet (AOW)

This is a PAYG flat rate pension based on residence or on the basis of working and paying social security contributions in The Netherlands.

- Everybody who either lives in the Netherlands or who lives abroad but is subject to Dutch taxation on the basis of employment in The Netherlands, is covered by the Dutch AOW State Pension scheme.

- The AOW pension level is the so called "social minimum". The social minimum amounts to 70% of the statutory minimum wage for a single person living alone and 100% of the statutory minimum wage for a couple living together. Both partners of the couple receive an individual AOW State Pension of 50% of the statutory minimum wage, adding up to 100%.

- The minimum wage is raised in line with average wages. This indexing of the AOW State Pension to the minimum wage is statutory. However, there is also statutory provision to suspend this wage indexing for any period. This happened in the first half of the 1990s because of unfavourable economic conditions. It is up to the government to decide when such conditions exist.

- For every uninsured year, for instance due to residence and/or work outside the Netherlands, the pension benefit is reduced by 2%.

- However, people who are not entitled to the full AOW State Pension can receive social assistance provided they do not have other sources of income that would bring them above the social minimum.

- In principle, no resident is exempt from paying contributions. However, in practice, people do not pay contributions as long as they have no income, yet they are considered to be insured and are accruing pension rights. Some people residing in the Netherlands are exempt from paying the contribution, for example, people employed by international institutions with a pension schemes at least comparable to the AOW. These people are not entitled to AOW State Pension.

Second pillar

This is a voluntary funded second pension with more than 90% of employees participating. The contributions paid are deductible against income tax liability and the pension funds are exempt from tax. Participation is as high as this because this pension pillar is seen as part of workers remuneration and is negotiated by the trades unions as part of the Netherlands highly centralised pay bargaining system. This second pillar is not statutorily compulsory but the coverage is so high that virtually all workers are covered.

The second pillar pension is mainly a DB scheme with most benefits defined by final salary. There are 64 industry wide schemes and 95% are DB. Companies in the Netherlands can opt out of these industry schemes if they offer schemes of equivalent value. There are 866 of these single employer schemes and a further 30,000 schemes offered by small employers are operated by insurance companies.

The value of the pension for final salary schemes is equal to the number of years worked times 1.75 of the final wage. These occupational schemes are integrated (in The Netherlands this is referred to as "Franchising") with the AOW first pillar. Total pension is the second pension minus the first pillar pension for a single person. This means that across all levels of earnings a Dutch worker with a full work history will receive a net pension that is 70% of net earnings. A minority (about a quarter) of second pension schemes are average salary with the average indexed to the growth of earnings. The value of the pension for these schemes is calculated using a factor of 2.25%.

The second pillar pension entitlement keeps up with wage growth during working life because the majority are final or near final salary schemes. After retirement the second pillar is up-rated by wage growth but this is customary rather than statutory.

Contributions and taxes

Pensioners pay 11% of pension income for health insurance and survivors' pensions.

People over 65 receive preferential treatment by the tax system. The basic allowance is some 12% higher than for those of working age. Low income pensioners also receive extra allowances.

Box 3: Switzerland

The Swiss system is often held up as the gold standard for other countries seeking to reform their pension policies in response to the ageing of their populations. It has three tiers but considerable integration between these tiers. There is a first, public unfunded tier, a second level that is private funded and compulsory; finally a set of savings schemes, encouraged by tax breaks, increase the provision individuals make for their retirement.

First tier

This has very wide coverage; almost 90% of the economically active are covered. The benefits are modestly earnings-related with a minimum and maximum of 20% and 40% of average earnings. Pensions for married couples are equal to 150% of single pensions and widows receive 80% of the single pension. The minimum pension on its own puts households below the official poverty line and therefore attracts income related social assistance as well.

Pension benefits as well as the cumulated lifetime earnings (used to calculate the pension benefit on retirement) are Swiss indexed. This means an average of the rate of growth of prices and earnings.

There is no upper earnings limit to the contributions paid and this together with the low level of the maximum benefit makes this tier highly redistributive. The contribution rate for old age benefits is 8.4% of covered earnings with a further 1.4% for the associated disability benefit. The total of 9.8% is split evenly between employers and employees. The government also provides funds from general taxation. Government co-financing covers, by design, 20% of the cost of old age and survivor pensions and 50% of disability pensions.

The first tier pension is also linked to a disability scheme that has grown very rapidly as it has come to be used as an early retirement pension for long term unemployed workers.

Swiss second tier

The second tier is private, funded and compulsory. All eligible workers over 17 have to belong to the disability scheme and compulsion for the retirement benefit starts at 24. Eligibility is defined in terms of co-ordinated earnings. These are defined as earnings between one and three times the maximum pension from the public pillar, i.e. between 40% and 120% of average earnings. This is the minimum definition of "coordinated " earnings. Individual schemes can impose wider limits either by having no lower limit or setting higher upper earnings limits.

The second pillar covers over three million workers and 90% of eligible workers are covered. The self-employed, unemployed and disabled workers as well as those on short term contracts are not obliged to belong.

Schemes' boards of trustees are free to choose between DC and DB. Eighty percent of pension funds with members, covering 70% of affiliates, operate DC plans. Eighteen per cent of pension funds offer DB plans for 29% of affiliates. Most DC plans operate in practice as hybrid plans crediting investment income at 4% or higher rate and placing any excess income in special reserves, but aiming to achieve targeted replacement rates.

The law regulates minimum conditions including age-related credits for contributions as well as minimum credits for investment income. The law also specifies a minimum annuity conversion factor. Pension plans are required to maintain notional individual retirement (ageing) accounts and must guarantee an annual nominal rate of return of 4%.

The minimum conditions aim to achieve a 30% to 35% replacement rate that together with the public pension would result in an overall replacement rate of 60% to 70% for workers with average earnings.

Benefits for survivors and disability benefits have to be adjusted for inflation every three years. Retirement pensions are adjusted at the discretion of fund trustees.

Insured workers have no choice of fund but have to join the employers scheme. There are no minimum contribution rates but employers must at least match employee contributions: in practice employers account for 63% of contributions. Workers who leave an employer can choose to leave their contributions with the old employer or take them into the new employer's scheme.

The regulations do not allow senior management from the employer to be on the board of trustees. This together with the prohibition on choice has resulted in very cautious investment policies and correspondingly low returns compared with other pension funds around the world. The proportion of equities has grown but is currently only 30%. The returns are low primarily because of the low proportion of equities but also because the equity investments produced low returns.

Box 4: Australia

Australia combines a flat rate affluence tested basic pension with a compulsory private funded scheme.

Flat rate public pension: The Age Pension

All men aged 65 and all women aged 62 (this is being raised progressively to 65 by 2013) are entitled to this state PAYG pension if they have lived in Australia for 10 years. For a single person in 2003 it is worth £4,518 for a single person and £7,907 for a married couple. These two values are 25% and 42% of average earnings.

This flat rate pension is affluence tested against income and assets except the value of a house for homeowners. After pension receipts equivalent to about 70% of average earnings it is withdrawn at 40%. There is also an asset test but only 10% of pensioners subject to withdrawal are affected by the asset test. Owner-occupied houses are not part of the asset test. Two thirds of all pensioners receive the full value of the Age Pension.

Compulsory private funded pension: Superannuation Guarantee

After a growth in occupational pensions as a result of National Collective bargaining the Government introduced a compulsory tax incentivised funded pension in 1992, The Superannuation Guarantee. Employers' compulsory contributions are currently 9%. Benefits can be withdrawn from 55 (being raised to 60 by 2025) either as a lump sum or as an annuity or drawn down in stages.

The tax treatment of benefits and contributions means that the net replacement rates are higher than gross.

Box 5: United States

The foundation of the pension system in the United States is a contributory earnings-related, PAYG public pension system: the Old Age, Survivors and Disability Insurance. In addition there is a means-tested flat rate state pension for those on low incomes. Private, employer based, pensions also play an important role together with private savings including tax favoured savings schemes.

Contributory earnings related PAYG state pension

The pension is based on up-rated average earnings during working life with the five lowest years excluded and earnings before 21 excluded. Forty years earns full eligibility and currently the retirement age is 65 but this will rise to 67 by 2027. Early retirement from 62 is available but at a reduced benefit and receipt of benefit can also be postponed with a corresponding enhancement. The reduction and enhancement rate is 6.5% for each year postponed or retired early.

The formula for calculating the pension is progressive and has a ceiling of 2.5 average earnings, $84,900 pa. The first $592 of monthly uprated earnings attracts a replacement rate of 90%; between $592 and $3,567 a month is replaced at 32%. These thresholds are 37% and 220% of average earnings respectively. A replacement rate of 15% applies between the latter threshold and the earnings ceiling. A 50% dependants' addition is available to married couples where secondary earners have built up a smaller entitlement.

The vast majority of people over 65 receive some Old Age Survivors and Disability Insurance pension and for 16% it is the sole source of income. Once in payment pensions are indexed against prices.

Means-tested scheme

This is a flat rate PAYG scheme available to people on low incomes. For single people in 2003 the maximum was $6,372; couples receive an additional 50% making the maximum $9,558. Eligibility is withdrawn where assets in 2003 are greater than $2,000 for an individual and $3,000 for couples. Income above $20 per month attracts a withdrawal of the benefit at a rate of 100%. In 12 States this Federal system applies; in another the State offers a supplement to the Federal system but in 28 states they administer their own system.

Private voluntary occupational schemes and tax incentivised savings

Nearly half the American work force participate in employer provided supplementary pensions. These and individual savings benefits are exempt from employment taxes but not from federal tax.

American tax provisions, both Federal and many State, give special concessions to people who are over 65. This explains the difference between gross and net replacement rates.

Sources of retirement income

The non-employment income of people over 65 currently is 50% from state provision and a quarter from occupational pensions with the balance from private savings.

Box 6: Sweden

The newly reformed pension system is being gradually phased in to replace a DB PAYG public pension system that was showing signs of accumulating deficits. People born before 1938 are entirely exempt and people born between 1938 and 1954 have a rising share of their pension calculated under the new system. People born after 1953 are covered only by the new system introduced in 1999.

The four Swedish pillars

The Swedish pension system has a first basic pension that is designed for people with a lifetime of low earnings. This **minimum guarantee benefit** is financed by general revenues from the central government budget. The benefit is graduated to make it possible to have a small guarantee component, while receiving the main part of a benefit from the two earnings-related systems. This benefit also covers the lifetime poor and will mainly do so in the future. The guarantee together with a means-tested housing allowance is higher than the minimum income standard. The benefit is also based on years of residence in Sweden with a special clause for elderly immigrants. The guarantee benefit can be received from the age of 65, not earlier. For a single person in 2003 its full value was £6,461 per year. It is indexed against general prices and is withdrawn as a retired person receives the public earnings-related pension. The first withdrawal rate is 100% and thereafter it is 48%. Social assistance is available for those who have not resided in Sweden.

The new Swedish second pillar is a **Notional Account Defined Contribution** system. Employees and employers pay a contribution of 16% of earnings. Contributions are also paid by the government to cover pension entitlements credited for income replacement social insurances, e.g. for unemployment, sickness and disability and for parental leave. The self-employed are also included in the system. Each employer has a personal account that is credited with these contributions. The contributions in this notional account are cumulated over the working life using the average growth in wages. The revenue is used to pay current pension liabilities.

At retirement, the capital sum is converted into an annual pension using an annuity factor that reflects the age of retirement (Sweden has a flexible retirement age starting at 61) as well as the life expectancy at the point of retirement. Subsequent revisions to life expectancy do not affect the pensions of the already retired. The conversion factor also includes a wage growth assumption of 1.6%. After retirement, pensions are indexed in line with earnings less the assumed trend rate of growth of 1.6%.

For this pension, there is a floor and ceiling to the earnings on which contributions are payable. The floor is a little over 47% and the ceiling nearly 130% of average earnings.

The third part of the Swedish system is a **fully funded compulsory system**. A further contribution of 2.5% of average earnings is credited into funded individual accounts. Individuals choose, from a large number of mutual funds, how their money is to be invested during the saving period and can choose a fixed or variable annuity upon retirement. The annuity can be claimed at any time from age 61, in part or in full.

The fourth layer of the Swedish pension system is a **semi-mandatory occupational pension**. It is semi mandatory because the four occupational pension systems are the result of national pay bargaining and result in 90% of the employed workforce being covered. The different schemes offer DB and DC pensions and on average offer about 10% of final earnings.

Box 7: Germany

The German pension system is dominated by the single tier, earnings-related public pension. In addition, about a quarter of private sector employees are covered by occupational schemes. These occupational schemes account for no more than 5% of pensioners' income. Civil servants but not other public sector workers are covered by a separate scheme.

The public pension system

The German pension uses a points system. One point is awarded for a full year of contributions at the average earnings of contributors under the ceiling of the scheme. Contributions are levied on earnings between €315 and €51,500 in 2002. Average covered earnings are about 90% of average production earnings. At retirement, the sum of these points is multiplied by a "pension value". The points of low income workers can be increased by up to 1.5 times up to a maximum equal to 75% of average earnings of contributors.

The pension is payable from 65 for people with five years of contributions and at 63 for those with 35 years.

The "pension value" factor is up-rated in line with net wages. This affects both the pre-retirement revaluation of earnings in the benefit formula but also affects post-retirement benefits.

The effective ceiling to pensionable earnings and the revaluation of pension points of low earners makes the system progressive up to 1.75 of average earnings where the pension hits a ceiling.

Social assistance

There is social assistance available at 13% of average earnings for a single person. Pension entitlement at 30% of average earnings is enough to preclude entitlement to social assistance.

Civil servants

Civil servants with more than five years service are covered by a special scheme that calculates the pension as 1.875% of final salary times the number of years' service. There is a maximum replacement rate of 75% after 40 years. Pensions in payment are up-rated in line with the growth of civil servants pay.

Occupational pensions

Fifty seven per cent of employees are covered by one of the four occupational schemes. There are four different types of scheme:

■ Book reserve financed scheme is the dominant type, accounting for about half of the schemes. There is no formal funding but a pension reserve is shown as a liability on the form's balance sheet. Forty six per cent of people covered by occupational schemes are in book reserve schemes.

■ The next most popular are "pension funds" covering 19% of those with occupational pensions. These are captive insurers set up as mutual benefit associations.

■ Twenty five per cent of occupational pension membership is covered by an individual or group policy taken out by the employer.

■ The fourth type is where occupational pensions are provided through "support funds".

Pensionable age is aligned with the public pension. More than half pay only a flat rate pension regardless of years service once onerous vesting conditions are met – 10 years membership. But the pension often varies with grade with higher grades getting higher replacement rates. More than a third pay a flat rate depending on scheme tenure. Only 10% of schemes are fully earnings-related. Two thirds pay an annuity income stream but the other third only pay out a lump sum.

An explanation of past and future trends in the old-age dependency ratio

Longevity has been increasing steadily over the last 50 years and is projected to increase significantly further over the next 50 years. As people live longer, the ratio of older people to younger people tends to increase. However, over the last 20 years the ratio of people aged 65 and over to those aged 18-64 has been almost stable.

This Appendix sets out to explain this conundrum and to draw out the implications for the demographic challenge that the country faces over the coming half century.

We therefore explain past and future trends in the old-age dependency ratio. For the purposes of this analysis, in this Appendix the ratio is defined as the number of people aged 65 and over divided by the number of people aged 18-64. This is slightly different from the analysis in Chapter 1 where the ratio was defined as the number of people aged 65 and over divided by the number of people aged 20-64, but this will make little difference to the overall results.

The Appendix has six sections:

1. Overview of trends in the old-age dependency ratio.

2. Factors affecting the old-age dependency ratio and definition of key terms: Total Period Fertility Rate, Completed Family Size, General Fertility Rate, period life expectancy and cohort life expectancy.

3. The impact of fertility rates on the old-age dependency ratio: past and future.

4. The impact of increased life expectancy on the old-age dependency ratio.

5. The impact of the baby boom: delaying the impact of the underlying life expectancy effect.

6. Conclusions: possible implications for retirement age policies of the causes of dependency ratio increases.

1. Trends in the old-age dependency ratio

Figure E.1 sets out the past trend in the old-age dependency ratio and shows how this ratio is expected to evolve over the next 50 years, on the basis of GAD's "Principal Projection".

It shows a significant increase between 1953 and 2053 but shows that the rate of increase has not been smooth. In particular, the last 20 years has seen very little increase in the ratio while the next 30 years will see a very rapid increase.

2. Definition of factors affecting the old-age dependency ratio

The old-age dependency ratio is determined by the historical pattern of:

a) Fertility rates

b) Mortality rates

c) Net migration

For the purpose of this analysis we will ignore the effects of migration which, while potentially substantial in the future, are of little relevance to explaining past and future trends in the old-age dependency ratio.

Fertility Rates: Fertility rates provide a measure of the number of children being born per female in the population. There are several different ways of calculating a fertility rate:

a) The Total Period Fertility Rate (TPFR) is calculated by adding up all the age-specific fertility rates for women in a given year. To calculate the TPFR, one needs to know the number of births for women of each age (16, 17, 18, etc up to 44) and the total number of women of each age. An age-specific fertility rate is calculated by dividing births to women of a given age by the number of women of that age. The TPFR is calculated by adding up all these age-specific rates. Effectively, the TPFR calculates the mean number of children a woman would have if she behaved over her lifetime exactly as women were doing at each age in the year being examined.

b) Completed Family Size (CFS) is probably the best way of measuring the fertility rate but it can only be obtained reliably for cohorts of women who have already reached the end of their childbearing years. The CFS measures the mean number of children that women in a given birth year cohort will have over their lifetimes. For example, women born in 1955 had 2.02 children on average. It is a better measure of the fertility rate than the TPFR particularly when the timing of childbirth is changing. For example, if there is a general move towards later childbearing there is a tendency for the TPFR to

produce an artificially low measure of the fertility rate for as long as
the average age of childbearing is increasing. This is because the TPFR
is a "snapshot" measure that will pick up the temporary fall in the
fertility rate brought about by a delay in childbearing but will not be
able to make any allowance for the increase in births at older ages
that would follow some years later. When the pattern of age-specific
fertility rates is stable, the CFS and TPFR measures will produce the
same result. To calculate the CFS for cohorts of women still in their
childbearing years, we would need to make assumptions about future
trends in fertility rates. As a result, it is harder to produce an estimate
of the CFS and the TPFR measure tends to be favoured. In our analysis
we use the TPFR but always with an eye on the potential biases that
are inherent in its calculation.

c) The General Fertility Rate (GFR) is calculated as the number of births
in a year divided by the number of women of childbearing age
(usually, but not always, 16-44). We use this definition in some parts
of our analysis where we are looking at very long run trends and where
detailed information to construct the TPFR is not available. The main
drawback of this measure is that changes in the age composition of
the female population can lead to changes in the GFR even when the
TPFR is stable.

Figure E.1 Evolution of the Old-age Dependency Ratio: 1953-2053, GB

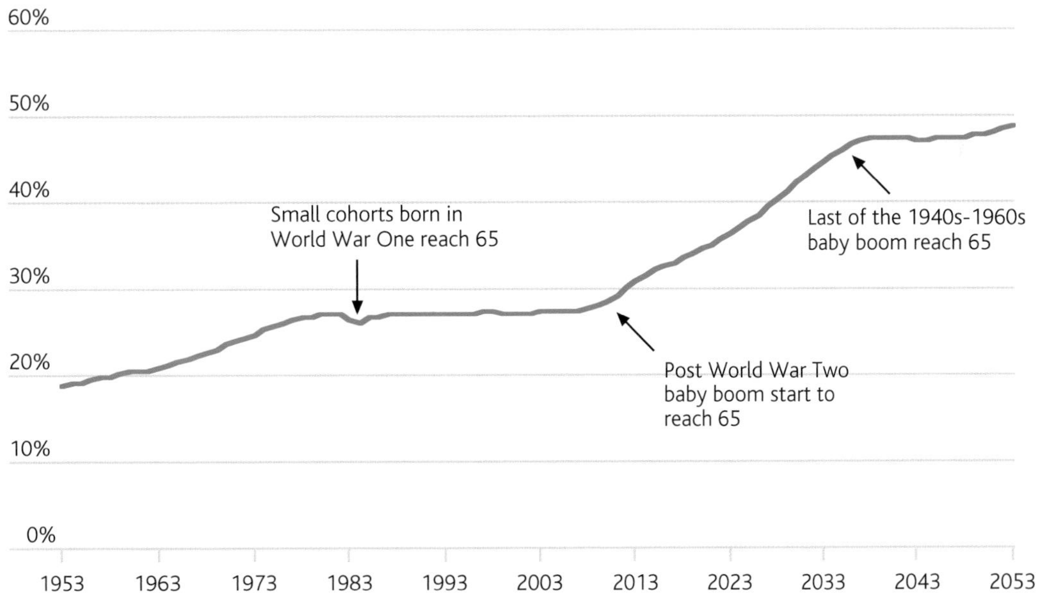

Source: GAD 2002-based population projection, GB
          Population Estimates Unit, ONS

Mortality rates and life expectancy: Mortality rates are calculated as the probability of a person of a given age and sex dying in a particular year. For example, the mortality rate for a 65 year old man (living in England and Wales) in 2002 was 1.7%.

Using age-specific mortality rates it is possible to produce an estimate of the mean expected duration of life, also referred to as longevity. Expectation of life effectively calculates the mean age at which someone will die. It is usually calculated as expectation of life at birth but can be calculated as expectation of further life from any age. In our analysis, we pay particular attention to changes in the expectation of life at age 65.

To calculate the mean expected duration of life, we need to have a figure for the mortality rate at each single year of age. There are two methods by which expectations of life can then be calculated:

a) The period approach

b) The cohort approach

The period approach is similar in concept to the Total Period Fertility Rate discussed above in the section on measuring fertility. The period approach uses the pattern of age-specific mortality rates observed in a given year to calculate the mean expectation of life if those mortaility rates remained unchanged in the future. Effectively, this approach calculates the longevity of somebody whose personal probability of dying at the age of one is the same as a one year old today, whose probability of dying aged 10 is the same as a 10 year old today, etc, etc, including a probability of dying at, say, age 80 equal to that of an 80 year old today. However, in a world where mortality rates are improving (i.e. decreasing), the period approach will tend to underestimate the mean expectation of life for people alive today or who will be born in the future.

As a result, the cohort approach to calculating longevity is more useful and is to be preferred. This approach uses estimates of future age-specific mortality rates to calculate the life expectancy of current and future generations. Thus, a person who is 55 in 2004 will have an estimated mean expectation of life calculated using the projected mortality rate of a 56 year old in 2005, a 57 year old in 2006, a 58 year old in 2007, etc. Although this approach requires projections of future changes in age-specific mortality rates, such information is readily available and it is straightforward to conduct sensitivity analyses to establish a range within which longevity is likely to lie.

Figure E.2 shows projected life expectancy at age 65 for men using the period and cohort bases. As can be seen, the period figures significantly underestimate the true life expectancy which is given by the cohort figures.

Given the importance of people understanding the increases in life expectancy they are likely to enjoy and need to provide for, it is unfortunate that the most commonly cited figures in Government publications and press reports are based on the period calculation. **We recommend that official publications as much as possible use the cohort approach when describing current and future trends in longevity**.

In the section on fertility measures, we explained that we were using a period measure of fertility rather than a cohort measure. However, for mortality, our preference has been reversed. To some extent the choice is expedient and reflects the nature of the data available. However, improvements in mortality have been large and systematic and the cohort approach is the only possible way of avoiding a misleadingly low estimate of future life expectancy. On the other hand, Total Period Fertility Rates have been stable for a number of years and although the timing of births is changing this is unlikely to lead to major errors in the conclusions we are drawing from fertility trends.

Figure E.2 Life Expectancy of Men at 65: Comparison of Cohort and Period Measures

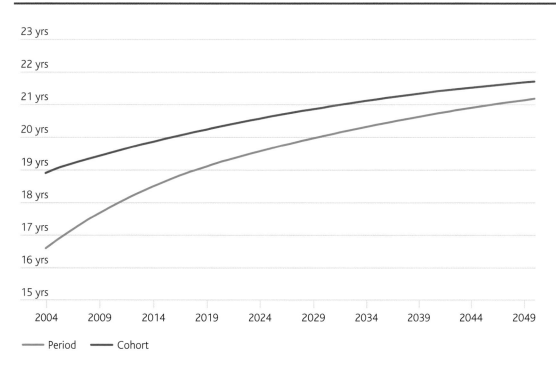

Source: GAD 2002-based population projections, UK

127

3. Changes in fertility rates and the old-age dependency ratio

The next section will show that past and future improvements in longevity will account for much of the coming increase in the old-age dependency ratio. However, over the last century, much of the increase in the ratio has been caused by a substantial and sustained fall in the fertility rate.

Figure E.3 shows the long-run trend in the General Fertility Rate. The figure shows two series: (a) the GFR for all live births; (b) this rate weighted for the probability that a live birth reaches 18 and moves into the "working age" population. The latter series is of most use for considering the effects of falling fertility rates on the old-age dependency ratio.

Figure E.3 shows that the adjusted GFR fell from around 3.2 in the 1880s to around 1.7 in the 1930s. During the period 1945-1970 there was a significant "baby boom" but, since 1970, the adjusted GFR has settled at around 1.7-1.8.

To understand the impact of these trends we will first focus on the impact of falling fertility up to the 1930s. The "baby boom" although by definition a "fertility rate" phenomenon will be analysed separately because it plays a crucial, but transient, role in the development of the UK old-age dependency ratio.

The sustained long-run fall in the fertility rate is important for two reasons:

a) A lower fertility rate (all other things being equal) will result in a slower rate of population growth or even a falling population;[1]

b) A sustained lower fertility rate leads to an increase in the level of the old-age dependency ratio.

Of these, b) is the focus of our attention in this Appendix. If any given fertility level is maintained indefinitely (and mortality rates remain constant), it is possible to calculate an "equilibrium" old-age dependency ratio towards which the age structure of the population will gravitate. Simply put, the lower the fertility rate, the higher the equilibrium old-age dependency ratio.[2] This fact is best understood by thinking about what happens when fertility rates start to fall. A smaller generation follows a larger and, therefore, the ratio of older people to people of working age must be higher.

[1] Note: A fertility rate of around 2.07 is required to maintain the population at a stable level (given a stable pattern of mortality rates and no net migration). This "replacement level" of fertility is a little higher than two because: (a) a slightly higher proportion of births are male rather than female (51.3% of births were male in 2002; (b) some women die before the end of their childbearing years.
If the fertility rate is above the replacement level, the size of the population will tend to increase (all other things being equal) while if the fertility rate is below the replacement level, the size of the population will decline.

[2] Note: It is worth noting that a given TPFR tells us nothing about the timing of childbirth. For any given TPFR, the age distribution of births does affect the size of the population but it has only a trivial effect on the long-run old-age dependency ratio.

Figure E.3 The Long-run Evolution of the General Fertility Rate

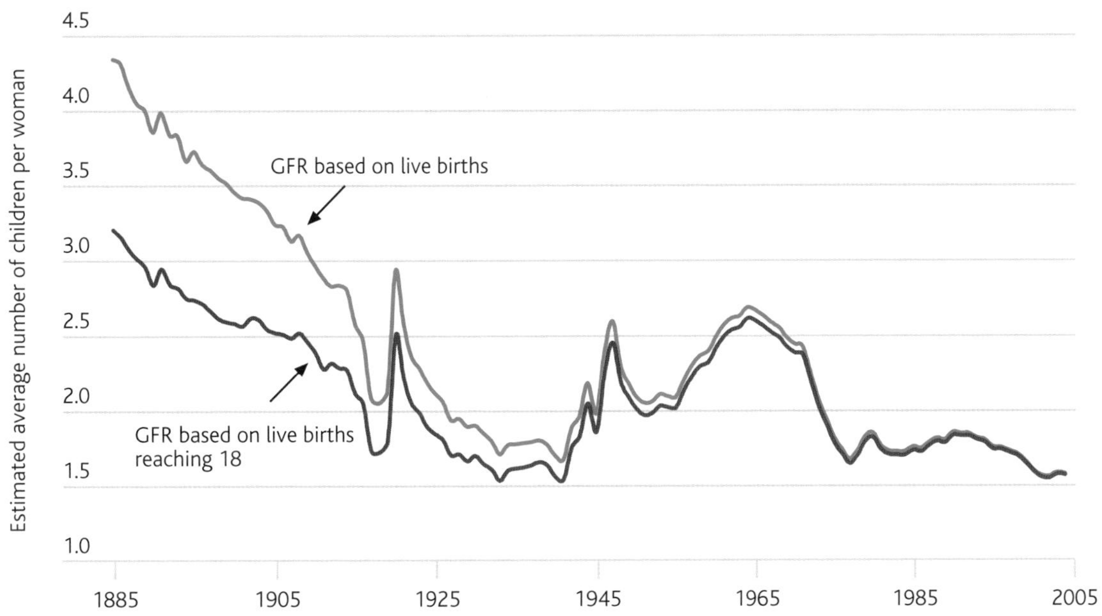

Source: Pensions Commission analysis based on a synthetic model of the England and Wales population

We can use this insight to understand the effect of the substantial fall in the UK fertility rate on the old-age dependency ratio. Figure E.4 sets out a stylised model of the impact of the decline in the fertility rate.

The fertility trend in Figure E.4 is a simplified version of the actual fertility trend in Figure E.3 and removes the "baby boom" so that we can concentrate solely on the impact of the long run fall in fertility rates.

Figure E.4 shows clearly that for a given life expectancy, the decline in the fertility rate that occurred between 1885 and 1930 has acted to more than double the old-age dependency ratio from around 18% to around 37%. The Figure shows that the impact of a decline in fertility takes many years to work through and that even though fertility rates stabilised in 1930, growth in the old-age dependency ratio carried on up to the present day. Figure E.4 also suggests that the effects of the long-run fall in fertility will have little effect on future trends in the dependency ratio.

Possible future changes in fertility: The Government Actuary's Department's current principal projection is for TPFR to increase gently from its current level to 1.74 and then to stabilise. This is the assumption we use for our dependency ratio forecasts and reflects the view of most demographers that a return to the levels of fertility well above 2.0 are unlikely in rich developed countries.

It is worth considering whether the experience of the post-war baby boom contradicts this. Figure E.5 compares the trend in the CFS with that of the TPFR.

The CFS is the best measure of long-term underlying trends and, in the 1945-65 period, the CFS did go up, but far less dramatically than TPFR, reaching a peak of 2.4 for the cohort born in 1934 versus the TPFR peak of 2.9 in 1963. The difference arises because the baby boom involved not only an increase in TPFR but also a reduction in the average age of childbirth, which drove the TPFR temporarily above its long-term trend level.

Thus while fertility rates once fallen can recover, and did so in the mid-20th century, the recovery was less dramatic than the GFR and TPFR figures would suggest. And since the second wave of CFS reduction began, (for women born after 1934), the trend has been, as best as GAD can estimate, continually down. This reflects the experience of other rich developed countries, none of which has seen a reversal of the late 20th century movement of fertility rates to below replacement levels. GAD's principal projection of 1.74 is therefore a reasonable assumption looking forward.

Figure E.4 Impact of Falling Fertility on the Old-age Dependency Ratio: Hypothetical Figures for the UK Given no Increase in Life Expectancy and with One-off Fall in Fertility Rates Rather than Oscillations

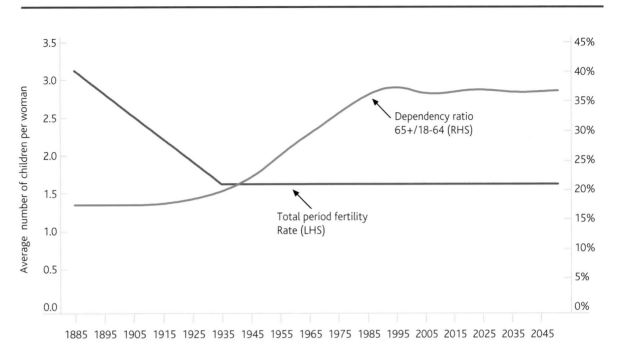

Source: Pensions Commissions analysis

Figure E.5 Comparison of Total Period Fertility Rate and Completed Family Size Measures of Fertility

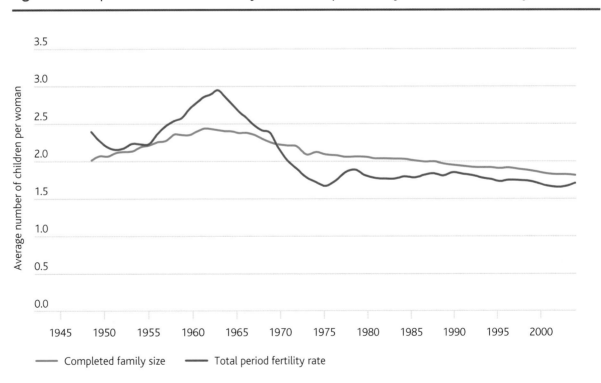

CFS is plotted at the year of birth of the cohort plus the mean age of birth, for example, the peak CFS is the 1934 cohort which is plotted at 1961.4 (1934 plus mean age of 27.4).

Source: ONS

4. Changes in life expectancy and the old-age dependency ratio

Over the last 50 years, there have been significant falls in mortality rates bringing about significant increases in longevity. All the indications are that the future will see further significant increases. Figure E.6 shows the probability of living to various ages for different cohorts of men.

Figure E.6 shows that there have been enormous increases in the likelihood of a 65 year old male reaching the age of 85. For men born in 1900, only 17% of those who had reached the age of 65 would live to the age of 85 (and only 47% of men born in 1900 would have reached the age of 65 in the first place).

Of men born in 1939 and reaching 65 this year, 48% could expect to live a further 20 years to reach the age of 85 (and 75% of the 1939 birth cohort would have reached the age of 65).

Figure E.6 also shows that the probability of a live birth reaching 18 improved significantly for cohorts born in the first half of the 20th century but is now largely stable. The probability of an 18 year old reaching 45 has always been high and, again, has been largely stable for cohorts born in the second half of the 20th century.

The probability of a 45 year old male reaching 65 increased significantly for cohorts born after 1925 (i.e. reaching 45 after 1970) but further improvements in these middle age survival rates will be more modest, simply because the survival rate is already over 90%.

These increases in longevity have usually (but not always) acted to increase the old-age dependency ratio. When considering the link between longevity and the old-age dependency ratio, reductions in mortality rates can be split into three types:

a) Decreases in childhood mortality rates actually act to decrease the old-age dependency ratio. This is because lower childhood mortality is similar in effect to an increase in the fertility rate. The previous section showed that increases in the fertility rate tend to reduce the old-age dependency ratio.

b) Decreases in the mortality rates of people of working age will tend to increase the old-age dependency ratio in the long run. In the short run, the initial boost to the size of the working age population may act to decrease the ratio but in the long run the ratio will rise. The extent of this increase will depend on which parts of the age distribution are affected by an improvement in mortality rates. In general, the older the age group affected, the greater will be the increase in the old-age dependency ratio.

Figure E.6 Trends in Male Survival Rates on a Cohort Basis

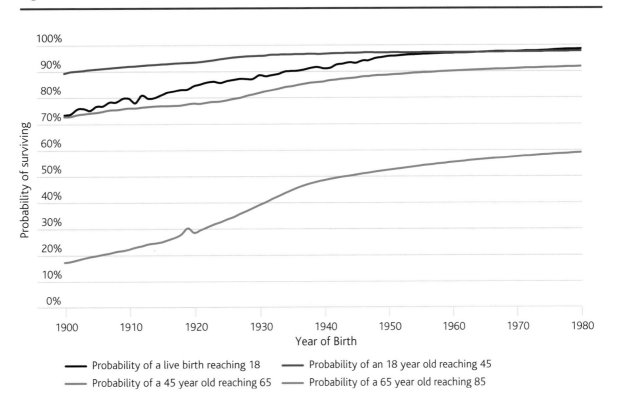

Source: GAD historical data for England and Wales and 2002-based principal projection

c) A decrease in the mortality rates of over 65s will increase the old-age dependency ratio in both the short and long runs.

An analysis of actual changes in mortality rates between 1940 and 2000 suggests that in the long run:

a) Improvements in childhood mortality **decreased** the long-run old-age dependency ratio by around 2.5 percentage points;

b) Improvements in working age mortality increased the long-run old-age dependency rate by around 4 percentage points;

c) Improvements in mortality rates among the over 65s increased the long-run old-age dependency rate by around 13.5 percentage points.

We have constructed a stylised model of the England and Wales population to enable us to examine the implications of improvements in longevity for the old-age dependency ratio. Figure E.7 compares the current projection for the old-age dependency ratio with scenarios where no improvements to longevity had taken place.

The top line in Figure E.7 shows the current projection for the evolution of the old-age dependency ratio. The other lines show how this ratio would have changed if mortality rates had remained fixed at their 1941, 1961, 1981 or 2001 levels.

Figure E.7 shows that by 2051, the old-age dependency ratio is around 95% higher than it would have been if mortality rates had not improved after 1941. The Figure also shows that even without further mortality improvements after 2001, the old-age dependency ratio would continue to increase. Part of the reason for this increase is that the full effect of past mortality improvements have yet to feed through into the old-age dependency ratio. Another reason is because of the impact of the 1945-70 baby boom which we will now examine.

5. The impact of the baby boom on the old-age dependency ratio

So far we have seen that the long run decline in the UK fertility rate and the sustained improvements in longevity have both acted to increase the old-age dependency ratio. Despite this, the last 20 years have seen almost no increase in the ratio and yet the next 30 years will see a very rapid and significant rise.

The reason for this paradox is the role of the baby boom. Figure E.5 showed how the fertility rate grew sharply after the Second World War and again, and even more significantly, during the late 1950s and early 1960s. Since 1970, the fertility rate has been fairly stable at 1.7 to 1.8.

Figure E.7 Impact of Increasing Longevity on the Old-age Dependency Ratio: Hypothetical Figures Given Actual Fertility Trends and Different Mortality Scenarios

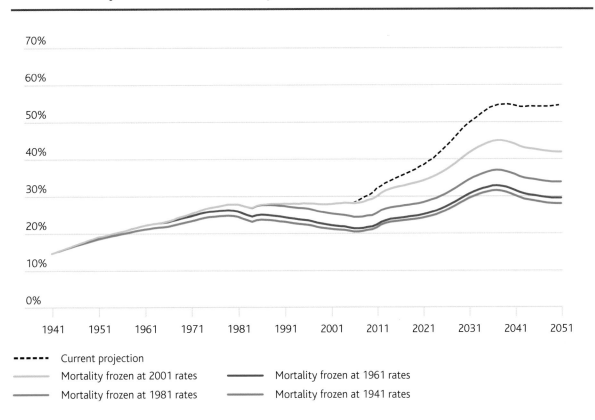

- - - - - - Current projection
——— Mortality frozen at 2001 rates   ——— Mortality frozen at 1961 rates
——— Mortality frozen at 1981 rates   ——— Mortality frozen at 1941 rates

Source: Pensions Commission analysis based on a synthetic model of the England and Wales population

Note: The old-age dependency ratio for the current projection is higher than that in Figure E.1 as it is based on a synthetic model of the England and Wales population and does not account for inward migration.

This sharp increase in the fertility rate led, 18 or so years later, to an increase in the size of the working age population. The peak year for births was 1963 and people born in this year did not start entering the labour force until the early 1980s. At the moment, all of the people born during the baby boom years have now entered the working age population but none of them has yet reached pension age.

This temporary phenomenon has had a significant downward impact on the old-age dependency ratio. In effect, the increase in the size of the working age population brought about by the ageing of the baby boom generation has acted to offset the increases that would have been expected due to the long run fall in fertility and the significant increases in adult longevity.

Figure E.8 reports results from our synthetic model of the England and Wales population and shows the impact of the baby boom on the evolution of the old-age dependency ratio. The solid line shows how the old-age dependency ratio is projected to evolve while the dotted line shows what would have happened if there had not been a baby boom.

Figure E.8 shows that the baby boom had no impact on the old-age dependency ratio until the mid 1960s (when the first baby boomers entered the working age population) and that the effects of the baby boom will have disappeared by around 2035 (when most baby boomers are well into old age).

But in the intervening years, the baby boom has the temporary effect of reducing the old-age dependency ratio. During this period, the baby boom shields society from the long-run implications of fertility and mortality reductions. The downward impact of the baby boom on the old-age dependency ratio will reach its peak in the next five years or so. After that, the baby boom generation starts to reach retirement age (2011 for men born in 1946) and the old-age dependency rate starts to increase rapidly.

Figure E.9 shows how the baby boom affects the size of the populations of children, working age adults and 65+ age group. It shows that, in the long run, the baby boom acts to increase the sizes of all age groups by the same proportion. However, the baby boom first affects the under 18 population, then the working age population and then pensioners. From 1961 until today, the baby boom has an unambiguously downward effect on the old-age dependency ratio.

Figure E.8 Impact of the 1940s-1960s Baby Boom on the Old-age Dependency Ratio

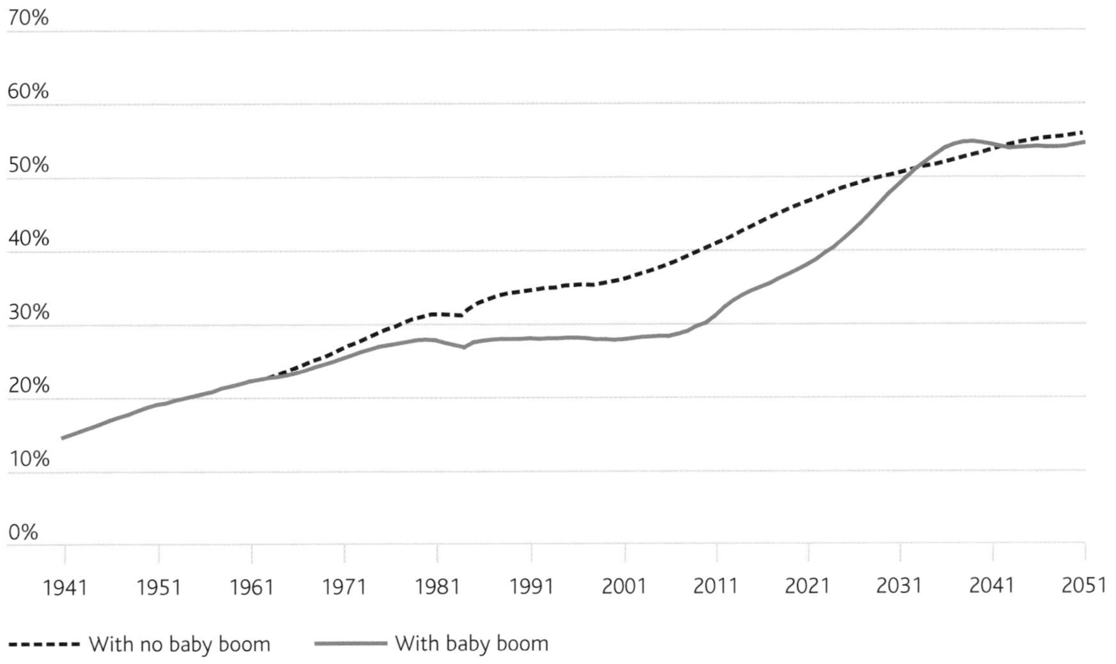

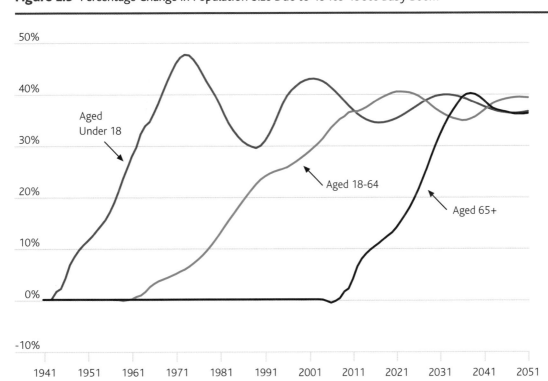

Source: Pensions Commission analysis based on a synthetic model of the England and Wales population

Figure E.9 Percentage Change in Population Size Due to 1940s-1960s Baby Boom

Source: Pensions Commission analysis based on a synthetic model of the England and Wales population

6. Conclusions

This Appendix explains past and future trends in the UK old-age dependency ratio. The analysis has shown that long-run declines in the fertility rate coupled with long-run improvements in longevity have both acted to significantly increase the old-age dependency ratio.

However, the analysis has also shown that for the last 20 years, we have been sheltered from the long run implications of these trends by the temporary impact of the baby boom on the old-age dependency ratio. The surge in births that took place between 1945 and 1970 has acted to keep the old-age dependency ratio stable even as significant improvements in longevity have continued.

The impact of the baby boom on the old-age dependency ratio is shortly to go sharply into reverse as the large cohorts of people born during the boom start to reach 65. The next 30 years will see an increase in the old-age dependency ratio that is much more rapid than would be implied by longevity improvements alone. One implication of this is that the old-age dependency ratio is not only increasing because people are living longer but also because of decisions taken by the baby boomers' parents over 35 years ago.

As a result the old-age dependency ratio cannot be stabilised over the next 50 years simply by raising retirement ages to keep the proportion of life spent working stable (which would suffice if life expectancy increases were the only factor at work). Instead more-than-proportional increases in the retirement age would now be required to stabilise the old-age dependency ratio.

The appropriate response to this can be debated:

a) Some might argue that it is unreasonable for people living now to accept more-than-proportional increases in retirement age just because they happen to be part of a large generation.

bi) But others might argue that: (i) it is only because of the baby boom that we have been able to delay proportional rises in the retirement age for the last 50 years; (ii) there is no reason why we should not now catch-up, and; (iii) that the baby boom generation during its working life has enjoyed a historically low total dependency ratio (pensioners and children) as a result of being a bigger generation than both the preceding and the following one.

Description of the UK state pension system

This Appendix explains key features of the UK state pension system. It deals in turn it with:

1 The Basic State Pension (BSP).

2 The Pension Credit.

3 The impact of present plans for the uprating of BSP and Pension Credit.

4 Other benefits.

5 State Earnings Related Pension Scheme/State Second Pension (SERPS/S2P): now and as the S2P system will evolve.

6 Contracting-out: and the implications of future plans for the level of compulsion within the system.

7 Total income replacement rates at different income levels at different dates given current plans.

8 Forecasts of total government expenditure on state pensions and benefits to retired people.

1. The Basic State Pension

The Basic State Pension (BSP) is currently £79.60 per week for a single person and £127.25 for married couples. A married couples pension is payable when the wife has an insufficient contribution record to receive more than 60% of the full amount in her own right.[1] The state pension is currently payable at 65 for men, 60 for women, but will equalise at 65 between 2010 and 2020.

---

[1]Note: From 2010 it will be possible for husbands to receive this pension based on their wives' contribution record if that is more favourable.

Receipt of the BSP is based on someone's National Insurance (NI) contribution history, not on citizenship or residency. Contributions of 11% are paid by employees on earnings between the Primary Earnings Threshold and the Upper Earnings Limit (UEL) and 1% over the UEL.[2] However if someone has earnings between the Lower Earnings Limit (LEL) and the Primary Earnings Threshold they are treated as if they have made contributions. The self-employed make compulsory weekly contributions of £2.05 plus contributions of 8% on profits between £4,745 and £31,720 per year and 1% above £31,720 per year.

At present a man will receive a full BSP after making contributions, or being treated as if he had made contributions, for 44 of the 49 years between 16 and 65. If someone does not have a full contribution record then they receive a partial award. However if they have made contributions that would give them a pension of less than 25% of the full amount then they receive nothing [Figure F.1]. As the State Pension Age (SPA) for women is 60, a woman's working life is considered to be 44 years, and a woman needs to make contributions for 39 years in order to receive a full pension. Once SPA is equalised at 65, both men and women will need 44 years of contributions to receive a full pension.

To help mitigate the effects of a broken work record on pension entitlement, a range of credits are available which credit contributions to an individual even when they did not have earnings in a specific week. The main reasons for receiving a credit are being unemployed, claiming certain NI benefits, or being a man aged 60-64.

In addition to credits, Home Responsibilities Protection (HRP) is available for those who are not in work because of caring for children or the long-term sick or disabled. HRP is available to someone who does not have earnings but is in receipt of Child Benefit for at least one child aged 16 or under. HRP does not treat the recipient as if they had made NI contributions; instead it reduces the number of years for which someone has to make contributions in order to receive a full pension. As Figure F.1 shows, a woman who has made contributions for 20 years is entitled to 50% of the full rate, but the effect of 10 years of HRP is to increase that to two-thirds of the full rate. However, HRP is an inflexible benefit. In a given year you can either accrue a year of contributions or be awarded a year of HRP. Therefore individuals who have earnings in part of the year do not receive the benefit of their contributions.

[2]Note: This Appendix refers to a number of different thresholds and limits in the National Insurance system. The Lower Earnings Limit (LEL) (£4,108 per year or £79 per week in 2004/05) is the point at which individuals accrue entitlement to National Insurance benefits, but employees and employers do not make contributions until earnings reach the Primary Earnings Threshold (£4,745 per year or £91 per week in 2004/05). The Lower Earnings Threshold (LET) (£11,600 per year or £211 per week in 2004/05) and the Upper Earnings Threshold (UET) (£26,600 per year or £511 per week in 2004/05) affect the accrual of S2P. The Upper Earnings Limit (UEL) (£31,720 or £610 per week in 2004/05) is the point at which National Insurance contributions for entitlement to benefits cease to be paid.

Figure F.1 Accrual of Basic State Pension

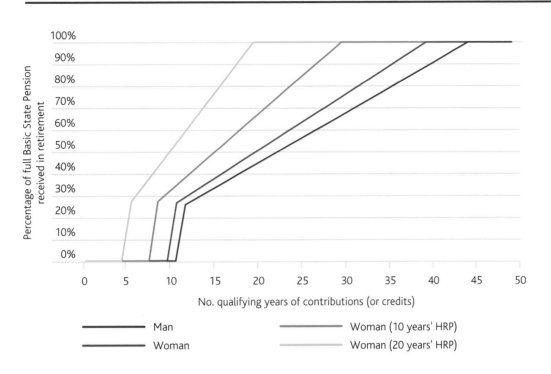

Source: Pensions Commission calculations based on state pension rules.

Figure F.2 shows that the majority of men aged 65-69 receive full BSP. Women aged 65-69 on average have smaller state pensions, and significantly when we look at pension entitlement based only on personal contribution history, which is the Category A pension. In the future women should increasingly receive higher levels of BSP in their own right, as the impact of HRP matures (it has only been available since 1978) and as the historic impact of married women making reduced rate NI contributions even when in work (the choice to make reduced contributions was only available up to 1977) works out of the system.

Over the last 20 years the BSP has increased by less than average earnings, [Figure F.3]. The law requires that the BSP is increased in line with prices, however in recent years there have also been occasional increases greater than the level of inflation. Present indicative plans, reflected in the expenditure forecasts presented in the final section of this Appendix, assume continued indexation with prices as measured by the RPI, but with a guarantee of a 2.5% increase each year. Therefore assuming that this policy continues in the future the value of the BSP as a proportion of average male earnings will fall.

If someone wishes to defer their entitlement to their pension (both BSP and SERPS/S2P), they are able to do so. There is no requirement for an individual to be in work to defer their claim. In return for delaying a claim, the amount of pension is increased, at present, by approximately 7.5% per year of delay. The maximum reward for deferment is 37% which is achieved by deferring for five years. If someone defers their pension for five years, their BSP per week becomes £107 per week instead of £79.60. The DWP estimates that 20,000 people in Great Britain currently defer their claim to their state pension each year and on average they defer for around two years.

The Government has proposed to increase the level of uplift for deferral to 10.4% per year and to remove the five year maximum. It is also proposing to allow a lump sum payment, as an alternative to the increased weekly pension. This would be equivalent to the pension not received, plus interest, for anyone who delays a claim for more than one year. If someone has a total state pension entitlement of £100 per week and delays their claim for five years they could receive an increased state pension of £152 per week or a lump sum of £30,000 assuming a 6% rate of return (this lump sum would be taxable). These proposals to increase the generosity of the reward for deferring a claim are part of the Pensions Bill which has not yet completed its passage through Parliament. They are intended to take effect from April 2005.

Figure F.2 Percentage of Basic State Pension Received by 65-69 Year Olds: September 2003

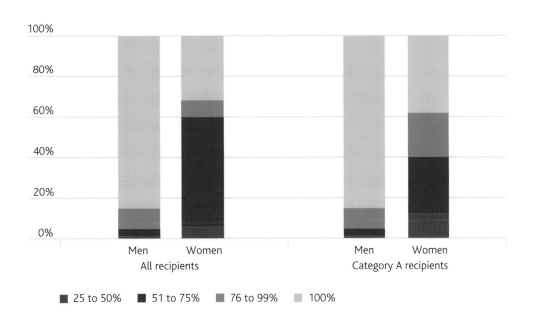

25 to 50% ■ 51 to 75% ■ 76 to 99% ■ 100%

Source: Retirement Pension and Widows Benefit Administrative Data, 30 September 2003, DWP

Notes: Category A entitlement is based only on the individual's contributions.
The figures for all women recipients shows much higher percentage of receipts than for category A because many women will receive 51-75% of the BSP as wives of fully paid-up men, and some will receive 100% as widows.

Figure F.3 Full Basic State Pension as a Percentage of Average Male Earnings

Source: DWP

Note: Assuming that real earnings growth is 1.5% per year

2. Pension Credit

The contribution based but non-means-tested BSP is not, however, the minimum income which society guarantees to pensioners in Britain. Rather this is determined by means-tested benefits, of which the Pension Credit is the most important.

Pension Credit is a means-tested benefit available to people aged 60 and over. This means that it tops up the income of people with low and moderate incomes. It has two elements: the "Guarantee Credit" and a "Savings Credit" which is only available to people aged 65 and over. These two components add up to a benefit which tops people's income up to a level of income and then is tapered away at 40p for every extra pound of pre-benefit income above a particular level. The impact of the Pension Credit is therefore to make many people better off, but to reduce the incentive to save for some of them.

Structure of the Pension Credit

The impact of the Guarantee Credit is shown in Figure F.4. It simply tops people's income up to a particular level (£105.45 per week for a single person in 2004/05) with a pound for pound withdrawal rate for any pre-benefit income. For example someone with £90 pre-benefit income (including BSP, SERPS/S2P and private pension income), ends up with £105.45 post-benefit income, as does someone with £100 in pre-benefit income. Since people aged 60-64 can receive the Guarantee Credit but not the Savings Credit, this is the situation they face. This was also roughly the situation faced by all people over 60 before Pension Credit was introduced in 2003, under what was then called the Minimum Income Guarantee (MIG). The Savings Credit is an additional means-tested benefit relating to income above the level of the BSP. Its value is calculated in such a way as to mean that the effective withdrawal rate of the Pension Credit (Guarantee Credit and Savings Credit) is 40% if pre-benefit income is above the BSP (while withdrawing 100% if income is below the level of the BSP).

The addition of the Savings Credit initially affects only people with pre-benefit income in a fairly narrow range either side of the Guarantee Credit, as shown in Figure F.5. For example someone with £90 pre-benefit income now receives a further boost to her income resulting in a total post-benefit income of £111.69 per week. However, for every extra pound of pre-benefit income, she would now face a reduction of 40p in the total Pension Credit received. Thus the person who has £100 in pre-benefit income now receives £117.69. Compared with the situation where only the MIG existed, therefore, this person does have a greater incentive to save, since they keep 60% of their private income, whereas previously they kept none. But someone who has pre-benefit income above the level of the Guarantee Credit (i.e. £105.45 per week) has a reduced incentive to save.

Figure F.4 Guarantee Component of the Pension Credit

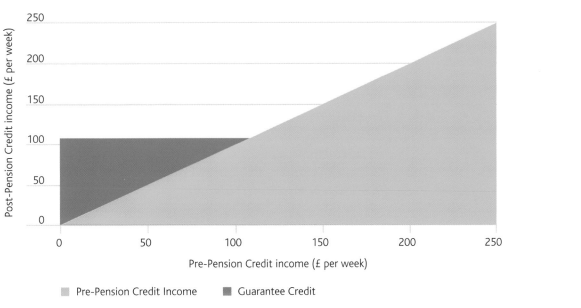

Source: DWP

Figure F.5 Guarantee and Savings Credit Components of the Pension Credit

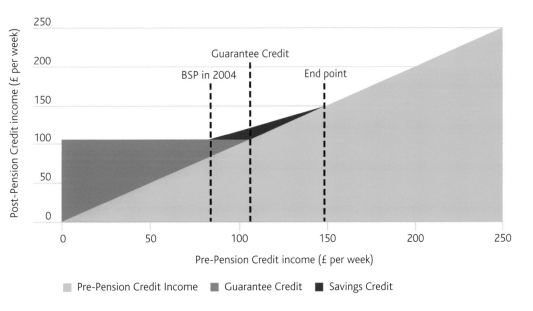

Source: DWP

The impact of the introduction of the Pension Credit has, therefore, been to reduce the proportion of people on very high marginal withdrawal rates, but to increase the proportion on moderate rates. Looking at the impact of the Guarantee Credit and the Savings Credit together (but ignoring Housing Benefit (HB) and Council Tax Benefit (CTB)) there are fewer people on 100% withdrawal rates, but many more on 40%. Once the impact of HB and CTB is also included the effect of the introduction of the Savings Credit has been to reduce the number of people in the 75-100% withdrawal band, but to increase the number in the 51-74% band. Figure F.6 shows the total marginal deduction rates that pensioners face and therefore also includes the effect of HB and CTB withdrawal.

Take-up of the Pension Credit

Although the Pension Credit guarantees pensioners an income of at least £105.45 per week, it does rely on pensioners actually correctly claiming their entitlement. However, the DWP estimates that during the financial year 2001/02 between one-quarter and one-third of benefit units were on incomes below the guaranteed level due to failure to claim their entitlement. But when we look at the take-up according to expenditure, it is clear that those who are not taking up their entitlement are entitled to lower levels of benefit than the average, as take-up according to expenditure is between 73 and 83%.

3. The impact of present up-rating plans

The current uprating arrangement is that the BSP is indexed to prices. Figure F.3 showed how this would affect the future value of the BSP as a proportion of average male earnings, if this policy was continued indefinitely. However the income of poorest pensioners would not fall if the Pension Credit continues to be as generous, relative to average earnings, as today.

The number of people who will in future gain the benefit of income uplift from Pension Credit, but who will also as a result face the potential disincentive effect of the 40% withdrawal rate will depend on the level of the Guarantee Credit and the starting point of the Savings Credit. The current approach is that the Guarantee Credit should increase in line with average earnings, (to ensure that the poorest pensioners maintain their income relative to the rest of society), but that the starting point of the Savings Credit (currently equal to the BSP) is indexed to prices.[3] If continued over the long-term this would mean that over time the gap between the Guarantee Credit and the start of the Savings Credit widens. Figure F.7 shows this by displaying the possible shape of the Pension Credit at different points in time. All figures are in constant earnings terms.

[3]Note: It also depends to a smaller degree on longevity post SPA, since many people who are not recipients of Pension Credit at the point of retirement become so during retirement, and thus the longer people live in retirement the bigger this effect.

Figure F.6 Distribution of Marginal Deduction Rates for Pensioners Before and After the Introduction of the Pension Credit

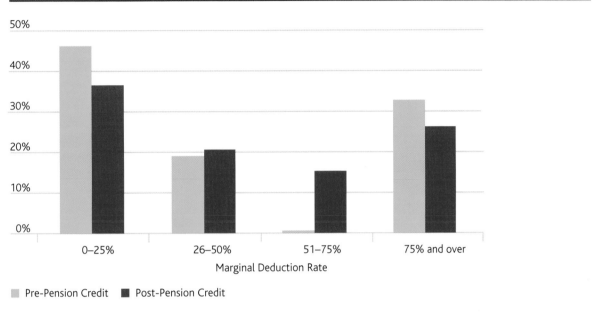

Marginal Deduction Rate

■ Pre-Pension Credit   ■ Post-Pension Credit

Source: DWP Policy Simulation Model 2004-05

Figure F.7 Evolution of the Pension Credit

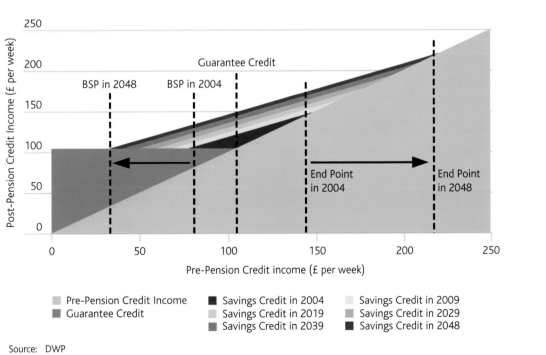

Source: DWP

Note: Income is given in 2004 earnings terms

Over time the starting point of the Savings Credit falls in earnings terms, whilst the level of the Guarantee Credit is constant. As a result, the Savings Credit extends over a wider range, which means more people will be entitled to it and many people will be entitled to more. Clearly this represents a boost to these people's income and will mean more and more people's net income keeps pace with average earnings. However, it also means more people gain a reduced increase to their net income from their private saving.

The impact of this indexation, pursued over the long-term, would result in Pension Credit covering a wide income range. Almost 65% of all pensioner households in 2050 would be entitled to Pension Credit, and would thus be having pension income withdrawn at the margin.

However if we had different uprating regimes, the evolution of the Pension Credit would be quite different.

■ If the starting point for the Savings Credit and the maximum level of the Guarantee Credit are both increased on the same basis, then the range of income over which the Savings Credit is applicable remains constant, and there would not be large changes in the number of people claiming the Pension Credit.

■ If the starting point for the Savings Credit were increased faster than the Guarantee Credit, then the range of income over which the Savings Credit applies would become smaller. As a result there would be fewer people eligible for the Pension Credit.

4. Other benefits

In addition to Pension Credit, there are other benefits available to some categories of pensioner. The main ones are:

■ **Housing Benefit** is a means-tested benefit paid to people living in rented accommodation. Pensioners who receive the Guarantee Credit automatically receive full HB which will cover all their rent.[4] HB is withdrawn at the rate of 65p for each additional pound of pre-benefit income. But in order to prevent pensioners from having their Pension Credit payments removed through the HB taper, the point at which HB begins to be tapered away is the level of the Guarantee Credit plus the maximum Savings Credit. In 2004/05 this level is £120.96 for a single person.

[4]Note: Housing Benefit covers what is called the eligible rent. If the actual rent for the property is greater than the local rent officer thinks appropriate for the area and size, then only what the rent officer deems appropriate will be eligible for Housing Benefit.

■ **Council Tax Benefit** is a means-tested benefit that assists people with paying Council Tax. It is structured in the same way as HB, and entitlement to CTB is calculated using the same income as for HB. The taper rate for CTB is a 20p reduction for each pound in excess of the threshold.

As HB and CTB are calculated together the combined taper where someone is entitled to both is 85p for each pound of extra pre-benefit income.

■ **Disability Living Allowance** (DLA) provides a tax free, non-contributory and non-income-related contribution to the disability-related extra costs of people who are severely disabled (mentally and/or physically) before SPA. It has two components:

  – A care component for people who need personal care from another person which is paid at one of three rates depending on the degree of disability and the level of care needed.

  – A mobility component for people with walking difficulties which is paid at one of two rates.

It is not possible for someone aged 65 and over to make a new DLA claim, but people who claim and qualify for the allowance before reaching age 65 can keep it after that age, provided they continue to satisfy the entitlement conditions. (Around 24% of the DLA caseload are aged 65 and over; around 31% are over SPA.)

For people who are aged 65 and over when they claim help with disability-related extra costs, **Attendance Allowance** (AA) provides a tax free, non-contributory and non-income-related contribution towards those costs. It has a two-rate care component only, for which the entitlement conditions and the rates paid are the same as for the higher and the middle rates of the DLA care component.

DLA and AA are not taken into account in calculating entitlement to Pension Credit, HB or CTB. But they give rise to entitlement to disability premiums in HB and CTB and to the disability additional amount in Pension Credit.

In addition the UK state system provides to all pensioners a variety of cash and non-cash benefits. These include:

- The Winter Fuel Payment which is £200 for a household with someone aged 60 or over. This is made during the winter to help elderly households meet the additional costs of cold weather. Households where someone is aged 80 and over are entitled to an additional £100 per year. In 2004 an additional £100 payment is to be made to households where someone is aged 70 and over. Therefore households in which there is someone aged 70 and over will receive £300 in winter 2004 and households were there is someone aged 80 and over will receive £400.

- A free TV licence for those who live in a household where someone is aged 75 and over.

- Free prescriptions and eye tests for those aged 60 and over.

The total cash cost of the Winter Fuel Payment and the free TV licence is expected to be £2.9 billion in 2004/05 and a further £7 billion is expected to be spent on Housing Benefit and Council Tax Benefit for pensioners. Expenditure on AA and DLA for pensioners is expected to be £6.5 billion in 2004/05. These are included in the state expenditure figures shown later. The estimated value of the other non-cash benefits is not included.

5. SERPS/S2P

Since 1978, the UK has had a mandatory second tier earnings-related pension system for employees but not for the self-employed.[5] This system requires all employees either to be members of the State Second Pension (S2P) previously SERPS, or to make equivalent private savings in a contracted-out funded pension. It is therefore worth noting that while the Pensions Commission has been asked to advise on whether the UK should introduce compulsory private pension savings, an element of UK pension savings is already compulsory. All employees (and their employers) are compelled to make contributions either to S2P or to a contracted-out alternative, on all earnings between the Primary Earnings Threshold and the UEL.

S2P, which was introduced in April 2002, is a reformed version of the State Earnings Related Pension Scheme (SERPS) which came into effect in April 1978. The SERPS regime changed a number of times between 1978 and 2002, therefore what a pensioner will receive from the state will depend on the year the pensioner reaches SPA and this will continue to be the case for many years, even if no further changes are made to S2P accrual.

In order to understand how S2P operates, it is helpful first to understand how SERPS accrual operated. SERPS accrued on earnings between the LEL and the UEL. The amount of SERPS that an individual accrued in each year is calculated in two stages:

1. First calculate the value of a given percentage of earnings between the LEL and UEL in each year, revalued to take into account average earnings growth up to the point of retirement. The percentage is between 20% and 25% of earnings depending on when someone reaches SPA.

2. This amount is then divided by a number, which depends on when someone reaches SPA:

   a) If someone reached SPA prior to 1999 then it is divided by 20 years.

   b) If someone was 16 or older when SERPS was introduced, but did not reach SPA before 1999, the number of years is the number of years between 1978 and the year they reach SPA.

   c) If someone was younger than 16 when SERPS was introduced, the number of years is the number of years between 16 and SPA.

---

[5]Note: Between 1961 and 1975 the Graduated Retirement Benefit scheme was in operation. This gave benefits based on the level of National Insurance contributions an individual made but these benefits were initially fixed in cash value. It was also possible for firms to contract-out of Graduated Retirement Benefit if they offered equivalent pension benefits in their own scheme. Because the benefits from Graduated Retirement Benefit were initially fixed, during the 1970s their value was eroded by inflation. In 1978, the benefits became indexed to inflation.

S2P is based on this framework, but introduces different bands of accrual between the LEL and UEL. S2P introduces two important new thresholds into the calculations, the Lower Earnings Threshold (LET) and the Upper Earnings Threshold (UET), as illustrated in Figure F.8.

1. For earnings between the LEL and LET for the purposes of S2P employees are treated as if they are earning at the LET. The accrual rate at this point is 40%.

2. For earnings between the LET and the UET the accrual rate is 10% to compensate for the higher accrual rate on the first band on earnings, so that higher up the earnings distribution the benefits are more equivalent to what would have been accrued under SERPS.

3. For earnings between the UET and the UEL the accrual rate is 20%: that is the same as SERPS.

In addition to treating individuals who have earnings below the level of the LET as if they had earnings at the LET. S2P, unlike SERPS, also gives credits to certain groups who do not have earnings. Credits mean that someone with no earnings above the LEL is treated as if they are earning at the LET. Credits are available for some groups of disabled people and carers, including those who are receiving Child Benefit for a child aged under six.

The effect of the changes made to SERPS accrual and the introduction of S2P means that the level of additional pension an individual receives is dependent on the year of retirement. Figure F.9 shows how the award at the point of retirement varies over time. The high point of SERPS award for someone on average earnings was achieved in 1999, as this was the last cohort who had an accrual rate of 25%.

Figure F.8 S2P Accrual Rates, Compared to SERPS: 2004/05

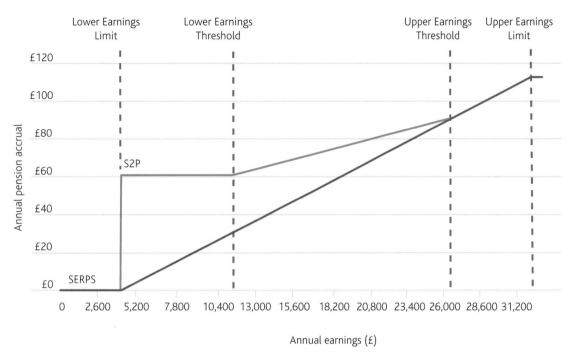

Source: DWP

Figure F.9 State Pension at the Point of Retirement Assuming a Full Contribution Record for a Person who has Been on Average Full-time Earnings Throughout Their Working Life as a Percentage of Average Earnings

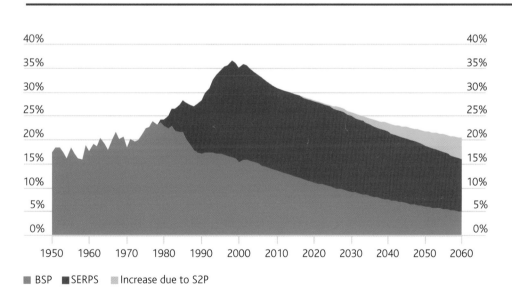

Source: Government Actuary's Quinquennial Review of the National Insurance Fund as at April 2000, GAD

The essence of the present position and changes put in place can be gauged by comparing:

■ The income replacement which would have been achieved by people of different income levels retiring in 2000, whose additional pension entitlement has accrued under SERPS [Figure F.10].

■ And what they will achieve as fully paid-up members of S2P retiring in 2050 [Figure F.11].

These charts show someone with 44 years of working life i.e. starting at 21 and ending at 65. Given current average ages of entry into the workforce and of retirement, it is likely that actual accruals would be lower than this.

As Figures F.10 and F.11 illustrate the overall impact of the change from SERPS to S2P will be that the system will become significantly more flat rate. Thus while for people retiring in 2000 the pension resulting from fully paid up state pension rights (BSP and SERPS combined) would increase with income up to 145% of average earnings, for people retiring in 2050, under the fully mature S2P system, the maximum state pension will be received at 108% of average earnings, but the vast majority of this is achieved at below 20% of average earnings.

Figure F.10 Composition of Income from the State Pension for a Single Male Retiring in 2000 Assuming no Additional Savings: in 2003 Earnings Terms

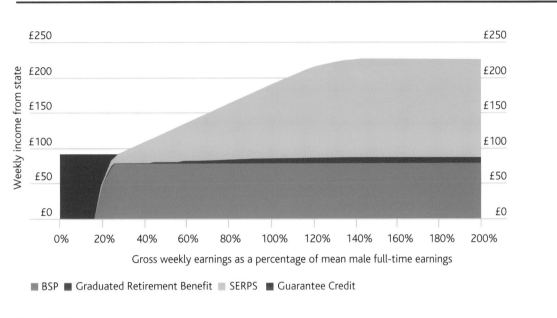

Gross weekly earnings as a percentage of mean male full-time earnings

■ BSP ■ Graduated Retirement Benefit ■ SERPS ■ Guarantee Credit

Source: DWP

Note: Potential entitlement to Housing Benefit or Council Tax Benefit is ignored.
Amounts in 2003 Earnings Terms

Figure F.11 Composition of Income From the State Pension for a Single Male Retiring in 2050 Assuming no Additional Saving: in 2003 Earnings Terms

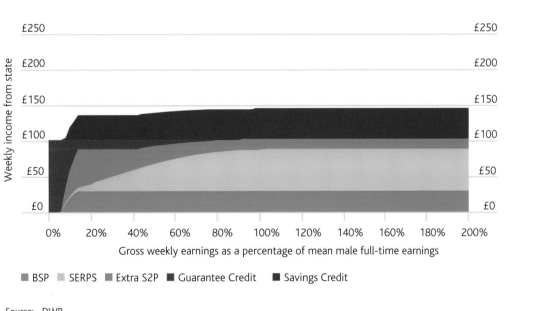

Gross weekly earnings as a percentage of mean male full-time earnings

■ BSP ■ SERPS ■ Extra S2P ■ Guarantee Credit ■ Savings Credit

Source: DWP

Note: Potential entitlement to Household Benefit or Council Tax Benefit is ignored.
Amounts in 2003 Earnings Terms

The main cause of the future flat profile of S2P entitlement is the current plans for the indexation of the LEL and UEL. Current indicative plans (used for state expenditure forecasting) are that these should rise with prices only and therefore fall relative to average earnings. But the LET is linked to earnings, which means that an increasing band of income will be deemed to be earnings at the level of the LET. As a result the accrual system becomes more flat rate in nature [Figure F.12 and Figure F.13].

The other implication of these indexation plans is that not only will the benefits become flat rate at a lower income level, but so too will the employee contributions. If the UEL did indeed rise only with prices not earnings, maximum employee NI contributions would by 2050 be paid at less than average earnings (£14,400 in current earnings terms) whereas today they are paid at £31,720 which is significantly above median earnings. This will be true whether people stay contracted-in to S2P, or if they contract-out into a funded saving alternative.

The implication of this is that current indicative indexation plans, if pursued over the long term, would involve a reduction in the amount of compulsory earnings-related pension provision/saving within the UK system and might therefore actually reduce the level of funded savings, unless we can assume that reduced compulsion is offset by an increase in voluntary savings.

Figure F.12 Accrual of S2P in 2015: in 2003 Earnings Terms

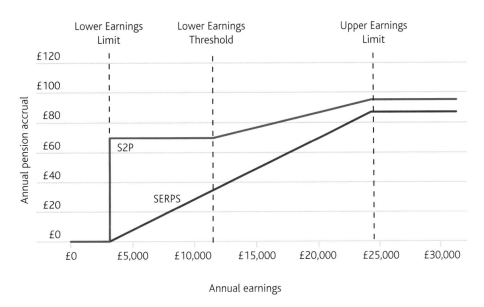

Source: DWP

Figure F.13 Accrual of S2P in 2050: in 2003 Earnings Terms

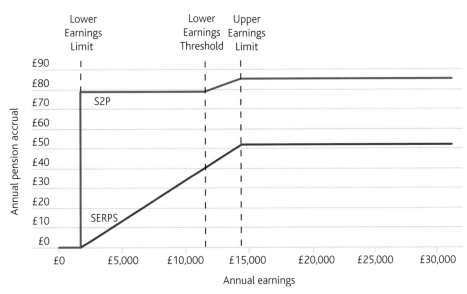

Source: DWP

6. Contracting-out

Employees must either be members of SERPS/S2P or they and their employers must make equivalent contributions to funded pension schemes. If they choose the contracted-out alternative, both employers and employees receive a rebate of NI contributions. The level of these rebates is set by the Government Actuary's Department (GAD) with the aim of ensuring that the contracted-out pension will secure equivalent benefits, given reasonable assumptions about rates of return and the costs of investing.

The operation of contracting-out is complex. Different arrangements are in place depending to whether someone contracts-out into an occupational salary-related (i.e. Defined Benefit (DB)) scheme, an occupational "money purchase" (i.e. Defined Contribution (DC)) scheme or into an Approved Personal Pension. The rules and interactions between different parts of the system have changed many times. We explain below how the system works today.

Contracted-out Salary Related schemes (COSR): An occupational DB pension scheme can contract-out of S2P if the scheme provides benefits that conform to the Reference Scheme Test, which defines a minimum level of pension right accrual. If a scheme is contracted-out both employers and employees pay lower rates of NI contributions. In 2004-05 the total reduction is 5.1% (1.6% employee, 3.5% employer).

The Reference Scheme Test and the 5.1% rebate are not designed to ensure benefits fully equivalent to S2P, but rather to the now replaced SERPS, which was less generous for lower income levels. People who are contracted-out into COSR schemes and who earn below the UET therefore also accrue residual S2P rights equivalent to the difference between S2P and SERPS benefits. For example, someone earning £10,000 per year will build up rights in the occupational pension scheme based on their earnings but in addition will earn rights to S2P on the difference between what they would have got from SERPS (which is the equivalent to their contracted-out pension rights) and what they get from S2P. This is the difference between a pension based on 20% of £10,000 minus the LEL and 40% of the LET minus the LEL, which is an additional £37 per year for one year of earnings.

Contracted-out Money Purchase schemes (COMP): Occupational money purchase schemes can similarly contract-out and secure NI rebates. Contributions at least equivalent to this rebate ("the minimum payment") must be paid into a pension fund. The present rebates have a flat rate element (employee 1.6%, employer 1.0%) and an age-related element, rising with age, to reflect the fact that later contributions earn fewer years of investment return.

Because the "minimum payments" aim to secure a SERPS equivalent pension, this element of the fund ("the protected rights") has to be paid out in a fashion which mirrors the SERPS terms, i.e. used to buy an index-linked annuity, based on a unisex rate, and, if the person is married, a joint life rather than single life annuity. The fact that the use of the "protected rights" has to mirror SERPS in structure, however, provides no certainty that the pension achieved will equal the SERPS benefits in terms of level: the pension achieved can be greater or less than the equivalent SERPS pension depending on investment returns.

And, just as with COSR, since the aim is to mirror SERPS benefits rather than S2P benefits, people contracted-out into a COMP who are earning less than the UET also accrue residual S2P equal to the difference between S2P and SERPS benefits.

Approved Personal Pensions (APP): The option to contract-out through a personal pension was introduced in 1987. If someone is contracted-out into a personal pension, they initially pay the full rate of contributions, but at the end of each year the contracted-out rebate is paid directly to the pension fund by the government. These contracted-out rebates are age-related, increasing with age, to reflect that for older people there are fewer years of investment return. Unlike for COSR and COMP the rebates for an APP are intended (on rate of return and cost of investing assumptions) to secure benefits equivalent to S2P (rather than to SERPS). To reflect the structure of S2P the rebates therefore have a banded structure, with different rates for the different bands of S2P accrual. This means that those who are contracted-out through a personal pension do not build up any element of entitlement to S2P.

Trends in contracting-out: The trend in the number of people choosing the contracted-out versus contracted-in alternatives is shown in Figure F.14. Prior to 1987 contracting-out was only allowed into salary-related schemes. After 1988, however, people could also contract-out into occupational money purchase schemes (COMP) or into APPs, and were encouraged to do so by an incentive payment which was intended to make contracting-out the more attractive option. The recent trend has been, however, for people to contract back in. This will tend, everything else being equal, to reduce funded pension savings and increase future public expenditure on pensions.

The total value of contracted-out rebates is about £11 billion per year. These rebates therefore account for over one-quarter of the value of all funded private saving currently taking place. Figure F.15 shows the trend over time in contracted-out rebates.

Figure F.14 Trend in the Percentage of the Population in a Second Tier Pension

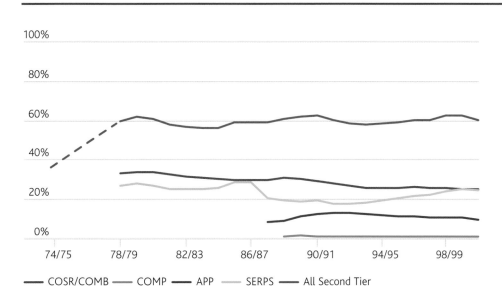

Source: GAD and LLMDB2, DWP

Figure F.15 Trends in Contracted-out Rebates in 2002/03 Prices

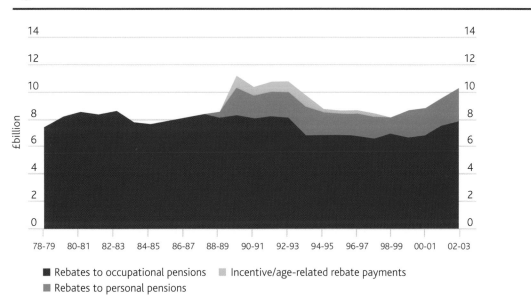

Source: GAD, GB

Note: The data above relates to GB.
Data on COMPs and incentive payments are available for the UK only. GB figures are derived using an assumed GB/NI split. It was necessary to estimate some of the payments to COMPs and some of the figures for the later years may be revised as more data becomes available.

7. Total income replacement rates at different incomes at different times

One way to look at what the state provides in retirement income is to look at the gross replacement rate that state pensions and benefits deliver at different levels of earnings, and how that changes according to when someone reaches SPA. Figure F.16 shows how the replacement rate from the BSP and SERPS/S2P varies depending on earnings and how it would vary with age if current indexation arrangements were continued indefinitely. The decline in replacement rate over time is least for those with lower lifetime earnings, because for them the increased generosity of S2P compared with SERPS offsets the falling value of the BSP relative to earnings. At higher income levels the replacement rate falls because the BSP is indexed to prices, and because, since the UEL is indexed to prices, a decreasing range of income is covered by S2P.

Figure F.17, however, shows the replacement rate that an individual could receive from the state assuming that they made no private pension saving. The increased generosity of the Pension Credit over time means that someone aged 21 on lifetime annual earnings of £9,000 could expect a higher replacement rate than someone on similar lifetime annual earnings aged 60 today. That is also true at £21,250 but only if the person was content with a replacement rate of under 40% and therefore needed no private pension saving. If they did make private pension saving their replacement rate from the state would fall towards that shown in Figure F.16. Public expenditure forecasts assume that people on average earnings will make private pension provision and therefore Pension Credit payments to average earners will be trivial.

Figure F.16 Replacement Rate From the State for a Male Employee, by Earnings Level: Contributory Pensions Only

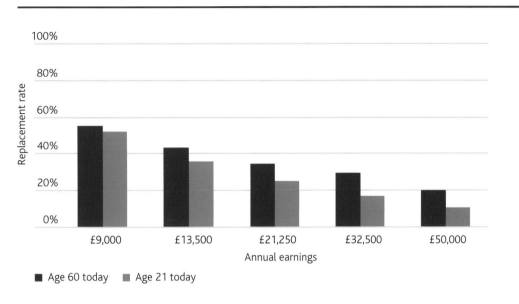

Source: Pension Commission analysis of DWP data

Note: Assuming a 44 year working life

Figure F.17 Replacement Rate From the State Including Means-tested Benefits for a Male Employee Given Age and Earnings Today Assuming No Private Saving

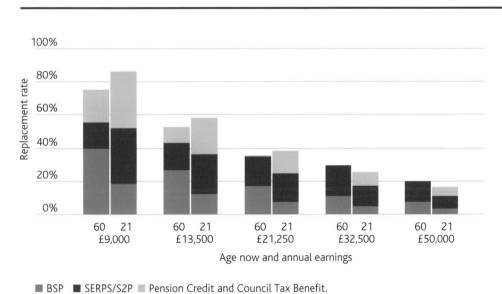

Source: Pension Commission analysis of DWP data

Note: Assuming 44 year working life for SERPS/S2P

8. Forecast public expenditure on state pensions and other retiree benefits

As the number of pensioners will increase over the next 50 years, and since most benefits are indexed to at least prices, the amount being paid in pensions or pensioner benefits is projected to increase in real terms, as shown in Figure F.18.

However, looking at expenditure as a percentage of GDP, the profile is flatter, with declining BSP expenditure (relative to GDP) offset by rising levels of SERPS/S2P and Pension Credit expenditure. Between 2010 and 2020 the growing demographic pressures are offset by the rise in the SPA for women. From 2020 to 2035 demographic pressures are so large that expenditure as a percentage of GDP increases despite falling replacement rates. After 2035 there is a flattening out, but only if the GAD population projections are correct in predicting a slow down in longevity increases at that time.

Finally, it is worth noting that different figures for state expenditure on pensions and benefits are used in different parts of the main report because different measures are appropriate when asking different questions. The panel "Pensions and pensioner incomes as a percentage of GDP: different definitions" of Chapter 1 in the main report explains the different uses of the different definitions, which are set out in Table F.1.

Figure F.18 Forecast Spending on Benefits for Pensioner Households over the next 50 Years, in 2004/05 Price Terms

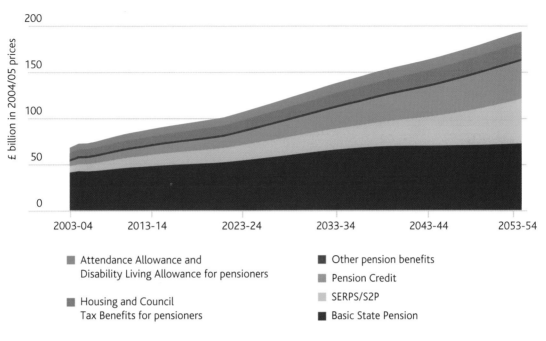

Source: DWP

Figure F.19 Forecast Spending as a Percentage of GDP on Benefits for Pensioners over the next 50 Years

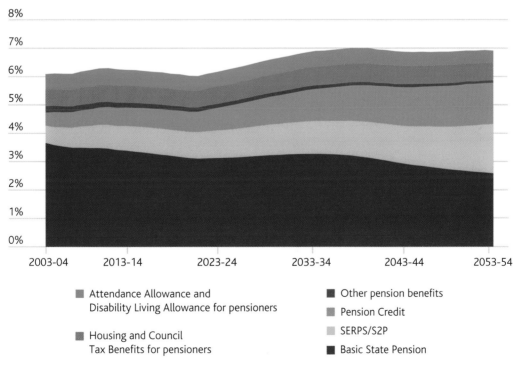

Source: DWP

Table F.1 Pensioner Incomes and Pensions as a Percentage of GDP: 2002

	Incomes received by normal age retirees	Pensions received by early retirees	Lump sums received	Total
State pensions and benefits				
- BSP	3.6			
- SERPS/S2P	0.6			
- Minimum Income Guarantee	0.4			
- Other pension benefits	0.2			
State pension expenditure	4.8	State expenditure on early retirees (e.g. Incapacity Benefit) not included in this analysis		4.8
Housing and council tax benefit	0.6			0.6
Disability benefits	0.6			0.6
State expenditure on pensioners	6.1	n.a		6.1
Unfunded public sector pensions	0.8	0.5	0.2	1.5
Total public expenditure	6.9	0.5	0.2	7.6
Funded occupational and personal pensions	2.0	1.4	0.4	3.8
Non-pension investment income		Non-pension income of early retirees not considered in this analysis		
- Deriving from lump sums	0.2			
- Other	0.8			
Earnings from employment	0.9			
Total Income	10.8	1.8	0.6	n.a
Total occupational and personal pension (including unfunded public) Of which	2.8	1.9	0.6	5.3
Public sector unfunded	0.8	0.5	0.2	1.5
Public sector funded	0.3	0.1	0.1	0.5
Private sector	1.7	1.3	0.4	3.4

The figure of 2.2% used as funded pension income in Figure 1.12 is 2.0% funded occupational and personal pensions plus 0.2% investment income deriving from pension lump sums.

Notes: State pension and benefit expenditure from DWP for financial year 2002/03.
Pension income for normal age retirees and early age retirees based on Pensions Commission estimates from the Family Resources Survey and the Blue Book.
Some rows and colums do not sum precisely due to rounding.

The Pensions Commission's "Group Modelling"

This Appendix provides details of our "Group Modelling," the key results of which were presented in Chapter 4. The purpose of this modelling is to provide an initial indication of which groups of people are making inadequate private pension contributions to supplement what the state will provide.

This analysis can only be considered indicative because of the severe data limitations and the large number of assumptions that need to be made. We describe some of the key uncertainties here: the data problems are described in more detail in Appendix A. Moreover it is important to realise that the results present only a snapshot of current behaviour. This may deteriorate in the future in key ways (e.g. as a result of the DB-DC shift).

We set out below:

■ The details of our approach; and

■ Results, including some of the key intermediate results which are not included in Chapter 4 and sensitivity analysis for different scenarios.

APPROACH

Our approach involves six steps:

1   Divide the working age in-work population into groups.

2   Estimate the level of state pension income a typical person in each group can expect.

3   Make assumptions about the target total income replacement rates which people at different income levels will consider adequate.

4   Work out the adequate level of private pension contributions people in the group need to be making today.

5   Use real data to see how many people in each group are saving above and below this threshold.

6   The weaknesses in this methodology need to be recognised in interpreting the results. They are set out in Section 6 below. Some of these weaknesses can be addressed by more sophisticated modelling over the next year. Some are inherent.

1. Dividing people into groups

We split people into groups using the following dimensions:

■ income band

■ age band

■ sex

■ employed and self-employed

This results in 100 groups in all. An example is employed men aged 25-34, earning between £17,500 and £29,999.

2. Expected state pension income

Given the past and expected structure of the state pension system, and if we assume that current indexation approaches are continued indefinitely, we can work out how much a typical person in each of our groups will get from the state contributory pensions (Basic State Pension (BSP) and SERPS/S2P). However, since we do not know people's lifetime earnings and contribution profiles, we must make a number of assumptions. We have assumed the following:

■ People work continuously for 44 years, retiring at State Pension Age (SPA).

■ Their earnings rise in line with average earnings for the whole of their working life.

■ The decision to contract-out does not affect people's final pension (though obviously it does affect the means of delivery). This effectively assumes that the Government Actuary's Department (GAD) has correctly set the level of contracted-out rebates, i.e. at the level which, when combined with reasonable rate of return assumptions, will result in someone who is contracted-out receiving the equivalent private pension to the SERPS/S2P foregone. This allows us to model all employees as though they have SERPS/S2P and to include only voluntary contributions in our modelling of private pensions. [See the panel in Chapter 3 of the main Report for more details of how contracting-out works.]

We do not include the impact of the means-tested benefit system at this stage, but it is taken into account in step 4.

3. Target replacement rate assumptions

Chapter 4 discusses the philosophical and empirical arguments around what is meant by adequacy of pension income. Based on this analysis, we use benchmark replacement rate targets for modelling as shown in Table G.1. The replacement rate is measured simply as pre-tax pension income (i.e. state pension plus private pension plus means-tested benefits) in the first year of retirement divided by pre-tax earnings in the last year of work. Other sources of income are ignored.

4. Estimating necessary private pension contributions

For a typical person in each of our groups we next work out how much they need to save today as a percentage of their earnings to be on track for the appropriate target replacement rate. This provides us with a threshold rate of adequate contributions for each of our groups.

This requires a number of steps. First, given their earnings at the point of retirement, expected state pension level and our assumptions on the evolution of the means-tested benefit system we can work out the level of private pension they need to achieve the desired replacement rate. Second, we use forecast life expectancy and current implicit rates of return in annuities today to work out an expected annuity rate that will be available to the person at the point of retirement. We can then work out the size of pension pot at retirement that the person will need to generate the requisite private pension income. Finally, based on assumptions that people start contributing to a pension at a particular age and save the same proportion of earnings from then to retirement, we can work out the percentage of salary they need to save each year to achieve their desired replacement rate.

Table G.1 Adequacy Thresholds

Earnings	Target replacement rate (Gross)
< £9,500	80%
£9,500-17,499	70%
£17,500-24,999	67%
£25,000-39,999	60%
£40,000+	50%

We continue to use the assumption that earnings rise in line with average earnings and also assume the following:

■ Contribution profile: people start saving at age 35 and save the same proportion of their salary each year to SPA, when they retire.

■ Real rate of return: 3.3% for personal pensions and 3.8% for occupational pensions. These are after all costs, both explicit and implicit [see Appendix C for details].

■ Annuity rates are fair value based on GAD's principal projection of life expectancy at age 65 and 1.3% real rate of return, which is the rate implicit within existing market pricing.

■ We exclude contracted-out rebates from our analysis of private pensions because we have assumed that individuals are contracted-in in our modelling of state pensions, as discussed above.

■ We assume that the current uprating regime for Pension Credit and state pensions persists indefinitely. [See Appendix F for a description of the state system.] This means the coverage of Pension Credit grows over time, affecting more people to greater extents.

These are our "base case" assumptions. Later, we undertake sensitivity analysis by varying the assumptions on the age at which people start saving, rates of return and target replacement rates.

5. Using real data

The steps above create thresholds of adequate private pension contribution rates for a typical person in each of our 100 groups. Our next step is to use real data to identify those people who are saving adequately (i.e. at a rate greater than or equal to their appropriate threshold) and those who are not (i.e. are not saving at all, or are saving at a rate below the threshold).

This is no easy task because of major data problems, as discussed in Appendix A. This lack of appropriate data meant that we have had to combine information from a number of sources and make some assumptions. Figure G.1 outlines the process used.

A key assumption required was that the GAD estimates of the distribution of contribution levels for Defined Contribution (DC) pensions across the whole population apply within each of our groups. This means, for example, that if GAD found 50% of all people in DC pensions contribute more than 5% of salary (taking account of employer plus employee contributions and adjusted to exclude contracted-out rebates), then we have assumed that 50% of people in each of our groups who are members of DC pensions contribute more than 5% of pay.

The process estimates the number of people in each of our 100 groups who are above and below our contribution thresholds, i.e. determines those who we think are saving adequately (indicated by green shading in the diagram) and those who are not (red and orange shading). Two segments identified in the diagram should be noted:

■ Those who do not need to save. These are people who do not need to save at all in a private pension in order to be on course for an adequate replacement rate. These are mostly fairly low earners who will receive enough income from the state (BSP, SERPS/S2P, Pension Credit, and Council Tax Benefit) to reach the target replacement rate.

■ People in public sector pensions or private sector Defined Benefit (DB) pensions: we have assumed that all such people are saving adequately.

Figure G.1 Use of Real Data

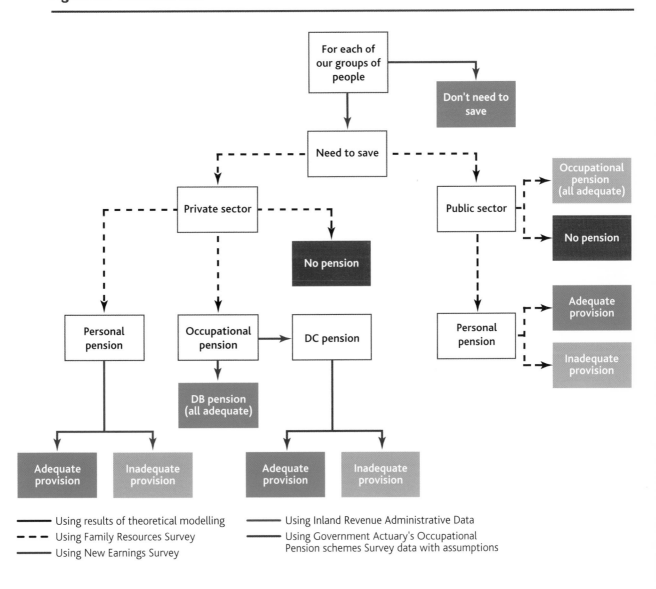

171

6. Weaknesses in the methodology: simplifying assumptions required

To identify accurately whether individuals are on target to meet the benchmarks of income replacement, we would need to know both their rate of current pension saving and their accumulated stocks of past pension savings. In fact, as Appendix A explains, the data available does not allow this: it is highly imperfect in respect to rates of new pension saving, and almost entirely non-existent on accumulated pension stocks.

We have therefore had to make a number of simplifying assumptions. Most of these will tend to result in an underestimate of the number of people making inadequate provision. Our key simplifying assumptions are:

- People save continuously throughout life, starting either at 35 (or 25 in our sensitivity analysis). In fact many people, particularly women, and part-time workers, have interrupted savings patterns.

- All people accrue full BSP rights, and all employees at the relevant income levels accrue 44 years of SERPS/S2P rights. In fact many people, and again particularly women and part-timers, do not.

- We have modelled on an individual basis, ignoring the fact that some people may be able to rely on a spouse's pension. This partly reflects the unavailability of data, but also the principle, proposed in Chapter 8, that we must increasingly focus on an individual rights approach to assessing pension adequacy, given the increasing number of women and men who are entering retirement not as part of an on-going marriage.

- We assume that all current members of private sector DB schemes and public sector pension schemes will be adequately provided for whatever the current contribution rates. This reflects the fact that almost all DB pension promises have an underlying value to the employee of more than 20% of salary (and of close to 20% even on a contributed-in basis), and that future contribution rates will have to rise to fund these obligations. But while this is true for those who stay in their current employment, many current members of DB schemes will leave their employer before retirement and in the majority of cases move to a less generous DC scheme. Our estimates therefore represent a snapshot of under-savers today. The situation will get worse as the DB-DC shift works through.

■ The distribution of DC contributions is the same for all age, sex and income groups. In fact we know that the upper tail of the distribution is heavily influenced by executive pension schemes. We may therefore tend to underestimate the number of DC scheme under-savers of average and lower earnings. One factor that might offset this slightly is that we have used the GAD 2000 source for the distribution of occupational DC contributions, and it is possible that DC contributions have increased slightly since then.[1]

■ For low income house renters we assume that the higher percentage of income replaced by the government (as a result of Housing Benefit) fully offsets the higher replacement rate needed to cover rent expenditure, (i.e. we have assumed no difference in required savings between homeowners and renters). This is an over-generous assumption used for reasons of modelling simplicity. In fact Housing Benefit does not always fully offset the costs of renting. We may therefore underestimate the number of under-savers among low income renters.

■ We have not included taxes or working age benefits/tax credits and have calculated 'gross replacement rates', based on total income before and after retirement.

Our estimates should therefore be treated as indicating the minimum number of people under-saving in pensions. [The issue of whether some of them will be adequately provided for because of housing and other non-pension assets is considered in Chapter 5.] The true figure for pension under-savers is probably already substantially higher and will grow over time with the DB-DC shift. Over the next year the Pensions Commission hopes to develop a more realistic model of under-saving, building on the Pensim2 model being developed within DWP, and drawing on data on the stock of accumulated pension saving being developed (though only for the 50-65 year old group) from the ELSA survey.

[1]Note: The assumption of the same distribution for all ages is also simplistic given that many DC schemes have contributions increasing with age. But this is offset by the fact that we are assuming that savings rates required and actually observed are flat with age, whereas a sophisticated life-cycle consumption model would suggest that they should be lower for younger age groups and higher for older.

RESULTS

These are presented in five parts:

1. Replacement rates from state contributory pensions (with no private saving or means-tested benefits).

2. Replacement rates from private pension saving only (with no state pensions or means-tested benefits).

3. Required private saving rates (taking account of state pensions and means-tested benefits).

4. Are people saving enough?

5. Sensitivity analysis.

1. Replacement rates from state contributory pensions

Figure G.2 shows expected replacement rates from the state for male employees with different earnings levels and ages. Employees will receive both BSP and SERPS/S2P, whereas the self-employed do not contribute to or receive SERPS/S2P so only get the BSP.

Key results are:

■ The less well-off receive a much higher replacement rate from the state than the better-off. This implies that the better-off need to save more privately to achieve any replacement rate target.

■ On the whole, younger people will receive less from the state than older people. This is because the BSP will fall as a proportion of earnings. Whilst this holds at most earnings levels, the exception is the lowest paid, for whom state provision will remain fairly constant. This is because the increased generosity of S2P offsets the declining BSP.

These results do not include the Pension Credit or other means-tested benefits. If these were included and if people were assumed to have zero private savings, then lower and moderate earners would be shown as receiving a higher replacement rate from the state. Among younger people the Pension Credit would have a bigger boosting effect and would extend further up the income distribution.

Figure G.2 Gross Replacement Rates from State Contributory Pensions for a Male Employee

Earning £9,000 per year

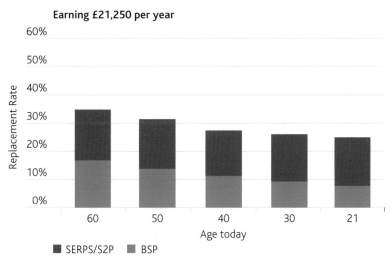

Earning £21,250 per year

Earning £50,000 per year

Source: DWP

Note: This assumes a 44 year working life

2. Replacement rates from private saving alone

In this section we look at the replacement rates people can achieve from a given level of private pension contributions in the absence of state provision [Figure G.3].

Key results are:

■ Women achieve a worse replacement rate from a given level of saving. This is because they have higher life expectancy so receive poorer annuity rates.

■ Younger people also achieve a worse replacement rate than older people for a given level of saving. This is similarly because they will have a higher life expectancy when they reach 65.

■ Delaying retirement by even a few years makes a very significant difference to the replacement rate achieved. This is because people who retire later contribute for longer and then buy an annuity at an older age, and so receive a better rate.

Figure G.3 Gross Replacement Rate from Private Pension Saving Assuming 10% of Pay Saved Each Year From 35 to Retirement

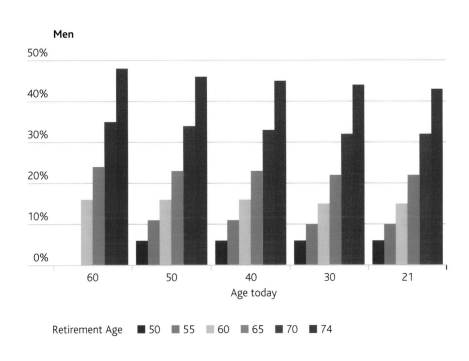

Men

Age today

Retirement Age ■ 50 ■ 55 ■ 60 ■ 65 ■ 70 ■ 74

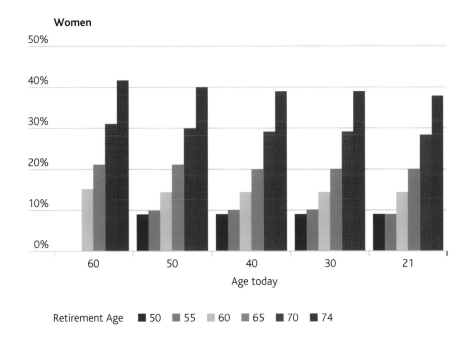

Women

Age today

Retirement Age ■ 50 ■ 55 ■ 60 ■ 65 ■ 70 ■ 74

Source: Pensions Commission analysis.

Note: Assuming 3.3% annual real rate of return during accumulation and the purchase of an index-linked annuity at retirement.

3. Required contributions to private pensions

Combining the above results and an assumption of the future shape of the means-testing system allows us to calculate the levels of contributions people need to make to achieve different target replacement rates.

Some example results are shown based on our base case assumptions [Figure G.4].

Key results are:

■ A typical person needs to save something like 10% of earnings to achieve a two-thirds replacement rate.

■ Women and younger people need to save more to achieve a particular replacement rate because of the reasons discussed above.

■ Many low earners receive enough income from the state that they do not need to save privately at all.

Figure G.4 Private Contribution Rate Needed for Different Replacement Rates for Employees: Given State System Plans

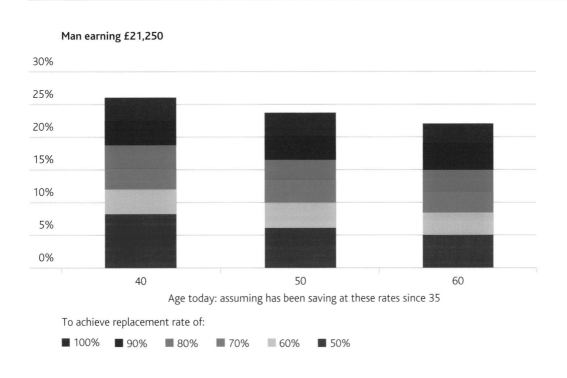

Man earning £21,250

Age today: assuming has been saving at these rates since 35

To achieve replacement rate of:

■ 100% ■ 90% ■ 80% ■ 70% ■ 60% ■ 50%

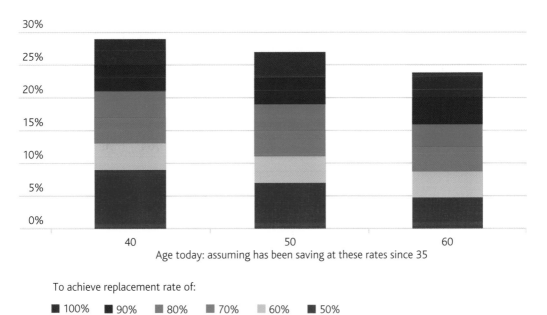

Woman earning £21,250

Age today: assuming has been saving at these rates since 35

To achieve replacement rate of:

■ 100% ■ 90% ■ 80% ■ 70% ■ 60% ■ 50%

Source: Pensions Commission analysis based on DWP data

Note: Assuming 3.3% annual real rate of return during accumulation and the purchase of an index-linked annuity at retirement, 44 year working life for purposes of National Insurance pensions.

4. Are people saving enough?

Chapter 4 of the main Report presents the key findings of our analysis [Table 4.12 and Figure 4.16, in particular]. These findings are reproduced here as Figure G.5 and in Table G.2. We estimate that under our base case, which assumes people start saving at age 35, 9.6 million people are not saving enough for retirement.

However, our modelling approach allows us to present our results in a number of different ways, for example, splitting our under-savers by different characteristics as shown in Figure G.6. For example a majority of those who are not saving enough for retirement are male, and one-third are earning between £9,500 and £17,499.

We identified a number of weaknesses in our modelling approach above. These include a lack of analysis of non-pension assets and partnership. However, we were able to use the FRS to explore these to a limited extent in relation to the base case.

- 71% of people with no pension were homeowners. This suggests they may have some scope to use housing assets to fund retirement, though this issue is explored in detail in Chapter 5 [and also Appendix B].

- 29% of people with no pension have a partner who is contributing to a pension. There are significant differences between men and women: 40% of the women with no pension had a partner who was contributing, compared with only 20% of men.

- Only a quarter of those with no pension both owned a house and had a partner who was contributing to a pension.

Table G.2 Numbers of Under-savers and Non-savers (millions), Assuming Savings Start at 35

Age band	26 - 35	36 - 45	46 - 55	56 - 59/64	All over 35
Income band					
< £9,500	n/a	0.2	0.8	0.5	1.5
£9,500 - £17,499	n/a	1.4	1.2	0.6	3.3
£17,500 - £24,999	n/a	0.9	0.8	0.3	2.1
£25,000 - £39,999	n/a	0.9	0.7	0.3	1.8
£40,000+	n/a	0.5	0.4	0.2	1.0
Total	n/a	3.9	3.8	1.8	9.6

Source: Pensions Commission analysis

Note: Totals may not sum due to rounding.
n/a = not applicable

Figure G.5 Base Case Results: Saving Start at Age 35

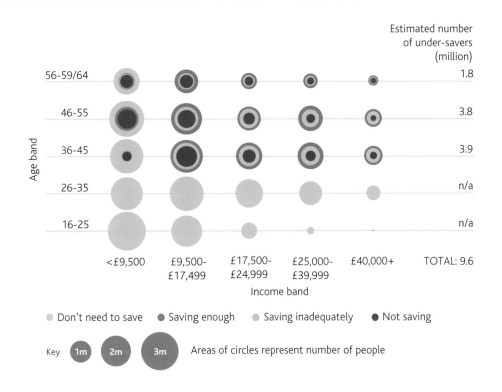

Source: Pensions Commission analysis based on FRS 2002-03, NES, GAD and Inland Revenue data

n/a = not applicable

Figure G.6 Characteristics of Under-Savers in the Base Case

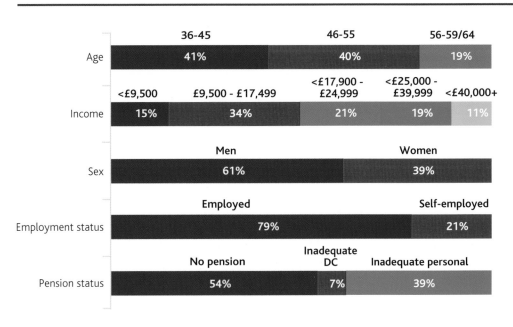

Source: Pensions Commission analysis based on FRS 2002/3, NES, GAD and Inland Revenue data

5. Sensitivity analysis

As well as running our model with our "base case" set of assumptions we have undertaken sensitivity analysis to test the degree to which our results change if we vary our key assumptions. The different scenarios used are explained in Table G.3.

The results of running our model with these different sets of assumptions are shown below. Although these assumptions do affect our results, the overall picture is not changed radically [Figure G.7].

■ Reducing the age at which we assume that people need to save significantly increases both the number of people not saving and under-saving as it brings in an additional age group. This more than offsets the reduction in the number of people under-saving in older age groups caused by the reduction in the necessary savings rate associated with people saving for longer.

■ The lower target replacement rates scenario has a significant impact on the required contribution rate at the lower end of the income distribution. It reduces both the number of people who are not saving but should be (because more people now receive an adequate income from the state), and the number of under-savers.

■ The impact of higher rates of return (increased by 0.5%) reduces the number of under-savers only by 0.1 million, as it only reduces the required contribution rates by around 1 percentage point, and many of the under-savers are under-saving by a large margin or not saving at all.

The following tables break down the high level results by income band and age band for our alternative scenarios. Table G.2 showed the number of under-savers in each group in the base case. Tables G.4 to G.7 show the difference in the number of under-savers in each group under each of our sensitivity scenarios, in comparison with the base case. Figures G.8 to G11 present the numbers of under-savers in the "start at 25", "lower replacement rates", "higher returns" and "combination" scenarios graphically.

Table G.3 Scenarios Used for Sensitivity Analysis

Scenario	Key assumptions		
	Age at which people start saving	Target replacement rates	Rates of return
Base case	35	Base case (see Table G.1)	3.3% (personal) 3.8% (occupational)
Start at 25	25	Base case	3.3% (personal) 3.8% (occupational)
Lower replacement rates	35	Base case minus 5% in each case	3.3% (personal) 3.8% (occupational)
Higher returns	35	Base case	3.8% (personal) 4.3% (occupational)
Combination	25	Base case minus 5% in each case	3.8% (personal) 4.3% (occupational)

Figure G.7 Under-savers in the Base Case and Alternative Scenarios

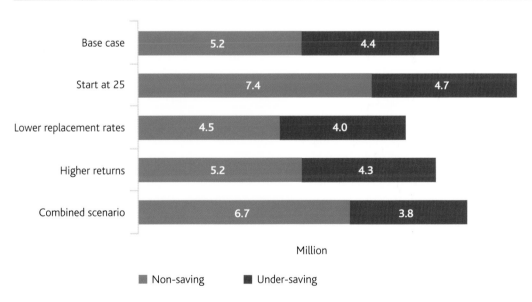

Source: Pensions Commission analysis based on FRS 2002/3, NES, GAD and Inland Revenue data

Table G.4 Numbers of Under-savers and Non-savers (millions), Difference Between Base Case and Start Saving at 25 Scenario

Age band	26 - 35	36 - 45	46 - 55	56 - 59/64	All over 25
Income band					
< £9,500	0.2	0.0	0.0	0.0	0.1
£9,500 - £17,499	1.5	-0.1	-0.2	-0.1	1.1
£17,500 - £24,999	1.1	-0.1	-0.1	-0.1	0.8
£25,000 - £39,999	0.7	-0.1	-0.1	0.0	0.4
£40,000+	0.3	-0.1	-0.1	0.0	0.1
Total	3.7	-0.5	-0.5	-0.2	2.5

Source: Pensions Commission analysis based on FRS 2002/3, NES, GAD and Inland Revenue data

Note: Totals may not add due to rounding.
A positive number indicates an increase in the number of under-savers, a negative number indicates a decrease in the number of under-savers.

Table G.5 Numbers of Under-savers and Non-savers (millions), Difference Between Base Case and Lower Replacement Rate Scenario

Age band	26 - 35	36 - 45	46 - 55	56 - 59/64	All over 35
Income band					
< £9,500	n/a	0.0	-0.6	-0.1	-0.7
£9,500 - £17,499	n/a	-0.1	-0.1	0.0	-0.1
£17,500 - £24,999	n/a	0.0	0.0	0.0	-0.1
£25,000 - £39,999	n/a	0.0	0.0	0.0	-0.1
£40,000+	n/a	0.0	0.0	0.0	-0.1
Total	n/a	-0.1	-0.8	-0.2	-1.1

Source: Pensions Commission analysis based on FRS 2002/3, NES, GAD and Inland Revenue data

Note: Totals may not add due to rounding.
A positive number indicates an increase in the number of under-savers, a negative number indicates a decrease in the number of under-savers.
n/a = not applicable

Table G.6 Numbers of Under-savers and Non-savers (millions), Difference Between Base Case and Higher Returns Scenario

Age band	26 - 35	36 - 45	46 - 55	56 - 59/64	All over 35
Income band					
< £9,500	n/a	0.0	0.0	0.0	0.0
£9,500 - £17,499	n/a	0.0	0.0	0.0	0.0
£17,500 - £24,999	n/a	0.0	0.0	0.0	0.0
£25,000 - £39,999	n/a	0.0	0.0	0.0	0.0
£40,000+	n/a	0.0	0.0	0.0	0.0
Total	n/a	0.0	0.0	0.0	-0.1

Source: Pensions Commission analysis based on FRS 2002/3, NES, GAD and Inland Revenue data

Note: Totals may not add due to rounding.
A positive number indicates an increase in the number of under-savers, a negative number indicates a decrease in the number of under-savers.
n/a = not applicable

Table G.7 Numbers of Under-savers and Non-savers (millions), Difference Between Base Case and Combined Scenario

Age band	26 - 35	36 - 45	46 - 55	56 - 59/64	All over 25
Income band					
< £9,500	0.1	0.0	-0.6	-0.1	-0.6
£9,500 - £17,499	1.3	-0.3	-0.2	-0.1	0.7
£17,500 - £24,999	1.0	-0.2	-0.2	-0.1	0.6
£25,000 - £39,999	0.7	-0.2	-0.2	0.0	0.3
£40,000+	0.3	-0.2	-0.1	0.0	0.0
Total	3.4	-0.8	-1.3	-0.4	0.9

Source: Pensions Commission analysis based on FRS 2002/3, NES, GAD and Inland Revenue data

Note: Totals may not add due to rounding.
A positive number indicates an increase in the number of under-savers, a negative number indicates a decrease in the number of under-savers.

Figure G.8 Alternative Scenario 1 Results: Saving Starts at Age 25

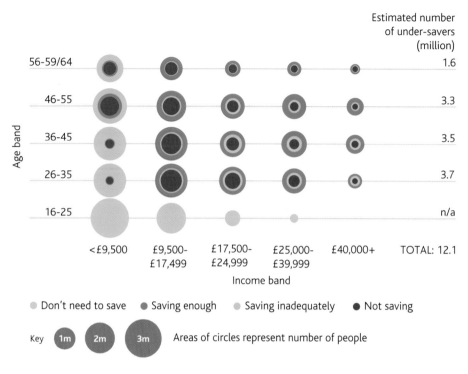

Source: Pensions Commission analysis based on FRS 2002-03, NES, GAD and Inland Revenue data

Note: n/a = not applicable

Figure G.9 Alternative Scenario 2 Results: Lower Replacement Rates

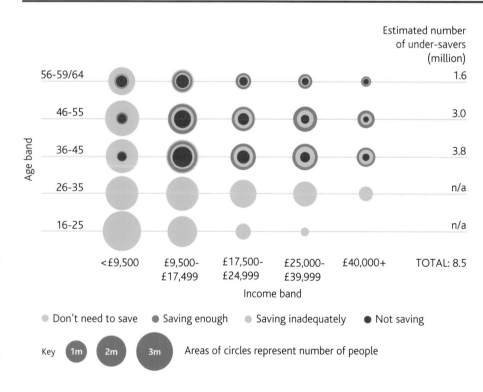

Source: Pensions Commission analysis based on FRS 2002-03, NES, GAD and Inland Revenue data

Note: n/a = not applicable

Figure G.10 Alternative Scenario 3 Results: Higher Returns

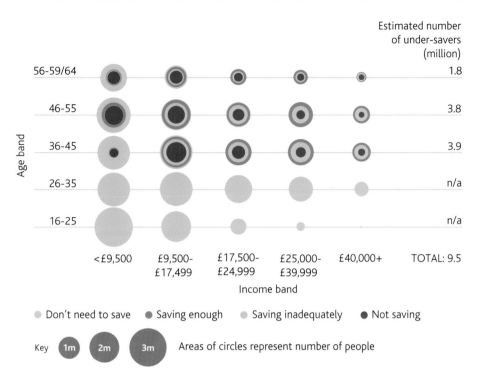

Source: Pensions Commission analysis based on FRS 2002-03, NES, GAD and Inland Revenue data

Note: n/a = not applicable

Figure G.11 Alternative Scenario 4 Results: Combined

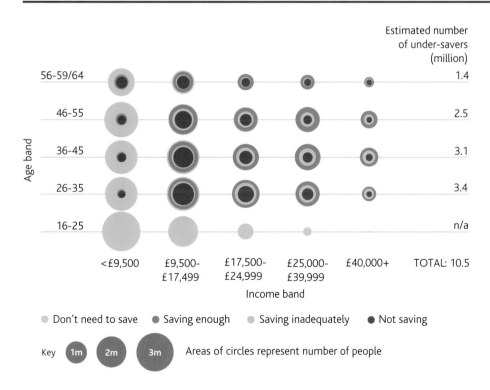

Source: Pensions Commission analysis based on FRS 2002-03, NES, GAD and Inland Revenue data

Note: n/a = not applicable

Glossary

Active membership

Active members are current employees who are contributing (or having contributions made on their behalf) to an organisation's occupational pension scheme. The scheme may be open or closed but cannot be frozen.

Additional Voluntary Contribution (AVC)

These are personal pension contributions made by someone who is also a member of an occupational scheme as a top-up to their occupational entitlement. Additional Voluntary Contributions can be made into the occupational scheme or to a stand-alone product called a **Free-Standing Additional Voluntary Contribution plan**.

Annual Management Charge (AMC)

This is the charge generally applied to personal pension plans where the fee is levied as an annual charge on the value of the fund. This charge covers the sales, administration and fund management costs of the fund.

Approved Personal Pension (APP)

This is a **personal pension** which meets certain regulatory requirements, so that it can receive **minimum contributions** (contracted-out rebates from NI payments) enabling an individual to **contract-out** of **S2P**.

Attendance allowance

A non-**means-tested benefit** payable to pensioners if they have additional needs because of illness or disability. For more details see Appendix F.

Automatic enrolment

A pension scheme where an individual is made a member by default, and has to actively decide to leave the scheme.

Average earnings terms

Figures have been adjusted to remove the effect of increases in average earnings over time. Thus if something shown in average earnings terms increases then it is rising faster than average earnings, whereas if it is constant, it rises at exactly the same pace as average earnings.

Average salary scheme	A **Defined Benefit** scheme that gives individuals a pension based on a percentage of the salary earned in each year of their working life (rather than the final year).
Basic State Pension (BSP)	Non-earnings-related pension based on an individuals' **National Insurance** contribution record. For more details see Appendix F.
Behavioural economics	A class of economic theories using insights from psychology to understand how individuals make economic decisions.
Cohort life expectancy	See life expectancy
Conduct Of Business (COB) regulations	The Financial Services Authority rules on how financial sales persons must sell financial **products**.
Contracting-out	The system by which individuals can choose to opt-out of **S2P** and use a proportion of their **National Insurance** contributions to build up a **funded** pension. For more details see Appendix F.
Contribution holidays	Temporary breaks in contributions by either the employer or employees taken because of a surplus in a **Defined Benefit** pension fund.
Council Tax Benefit (CTB)	A **means-tested** benefit through which the UK government helps qualifying individuals meet their Council Tax payments. Qualification criteria include income, savings and personal circumstances.
Defined Benefit (DB) Pension Scheme	A pension scheme where the pension is related to the members' salary or some other value fixed in advance.
Defined Contribution (DC) Pension Scheme	A scheme where the individual receives a pension based on the contributions made and the investment return that they have produced. These are sometimes referred to as money purchase schemes.
Direct execution	Where individuals buy a financial product directly from the provider without using a financial adviser.
Disability living allowance	A non-**means-tested benefit** which is mainly paid to people under **State Pension Age** if they have additional needs because of illness or disability. For more details see Appendix F.

Earnings threshold	The point at which employers and employees become liable for **National Insurance** contributions. In 2004-05 the threshold is £91 per week or £4,745 per year. Also known as the primary earnings threshold or secondary earnings threshold, since all are the same rate.
Economically inactive	People who are neither employed nor **unemployed**, e.g. those who are not doing paid work but caring for children.
Employer-sponsored scheme	A pension scheme which is organised through the employer, enabling pension contributions to be made through the payroll. Often the employer will also make a contribution. An employer-sponsored scheme can either be **occupational** or **group personal** in nature.
Executive pension scheme	A **Defined Contribution** pension scheme arranged through an insurance company for the benefit of a senior employee.
Final salary scheme	A **Defined Benefit** scheme that gives individuals a pension based on the number of years of pensionable service, the accrual rate and final earnings as defined by the scheme.
Free-Standing Additional Voluntary Contribution (FSAVC)	An **Additional Voluntary Contribution** plan which is separate from the individual's **occupational** pension fund.
Funded	Pension schemes in which pension contributions are paid into a fund which is invested and pensions are paid out of this pot.
Gilts	An abbreviation for 'gilt-edged securities'. These are bonds, loans etc issued by the UK government. They are often similar in structure to corporate bonds, paying a fixed amount to the owner following a given schedule. Gilts are generally considered to be one of the safer forms of investment so generate a correspondingly lower return than some more risky assets such as corporate bonds or equities. Some gilts make payments which are fixed in cash terms, whereas others make payments which go up in line with inflation (**indexed-linked gilts**).
Graduated retirement pension	A **National Insurance** pension scheme which ran from 1961-1975, providing earnings-related benefits based on contributions. For more details see Appendix F.

Group Personal Pension (GPP)	A **personal pension** scheme which is organised through the employer, but still takes the form of individual contracts between the employee and the pension provider.
Guarantee Credit	A **means-tested benefit** which is part of the Pension Credit and provides pensioners with a minimum level of income. In 2004-05 the level of the Guarantee Credit for a single person is £105.45 per week.
Guaranteed Minimum Pension (GMP)	The minimum pension that must be provided by a **contracted-out** salary-related scheme for pensions accrued between 1978 and 1997. The GMP is roughly equivalent to the **SERPS** foregone by **contracting-out**.
Healthy life expectancy	An index that combines measures of mortality and health to indicate expected years of life in good health.
Higher participation scenario	A "stretching but feasible" scenario of how employment rates might develop in the UK developed by the Pensions Commission for use in analysis. For more details see the panel in Chapter 2.
Home Responsibilities Protection (HRP)	This helps protect the **National Insurance** record of people who have caring responsibilities and are eligible for certain benefits. For more details on how this works see Appendix F.
Home reversion schemes	An equity release scheme where the individual sells all or part of their house to a company. On death the provider receives the value of the part of the property sold.
Housing Benefit (HB)	A **means-tested benefit** through which the UK government helps qualifying individuals to meet rental payments. Qualification criteria include income, savings and personal circumstances.
Implicit costs	The costs of trading which reduce the return achieved on an invested fund prior to applying explicitly identified management charges.
Income draw-down or income withdrawal	Where an individual takes the tax-free lump sum but does not convert the remaining pension fund to an annuity but draws income directly from the fund.

Independent Financial Adviser (IFA)	An independent financial adviser is someone who is authorised to provide advice and sell a wide range of financial products. They are distinguished from tied financial advisers, who can only give advice on investment products offered by a specific company.
Index trackers	A type of investment fund which is designed to follow a particular published index of the performance of **securities**, e.g. the UK all-share-index.
Indexing regimes	Policy on the up-rating of thresholds used in the calculation of tax or benefits. Typically these thresholds increase each year in line with inflation or average earnings. Over the long-term, indexing regimes can dramatically change the impact of taxes and benefits.
Index-linked gilts	**Gilts** which pay an income which increases in line with inflation and the capital values of which increase in line with inflation.
Individual Savings Account (ISA)	ISAs are accounts which can be used to hold many types of savings and investment products including cash, life insurance and stocks and shares. They are available to most UK residents and there are strict rules regarding the maximum amount allowed for each component and the overall amount you can invest in any one tax year. The returns earned in an ISA (capital growth and income) are tax free.
Insurance-managed occupational pension schemes	**Occupational pension** schemes where an insurance company is responsible for the administration of the fund and may also provide some guarantees relating to investment performance.
Large firm	For statistical purposes, the Department of Trade and Industry usually defines a large firm as one with 250 or more employees.

Life expectancy	Life expectancy (or the expectation of life) at a given age, x, is the average number of years that a male or female aged x will live thereafter, and is calculated using age and gender-specific mortality rates at ages x, x+1, x+2 etc. Period life expectancy is calculated using age-specific mortality rates for the period under consideration and makes no allowance for changes in age-specific mortality rates after that period. Cohort life expectancy is calculated allowing for subsequent known or projected changes in age and gender-specific mortality rates after that period as he or she gets older. For example, a period life expectancy calculation for a male aged 50 in calendar year 2000 would use male mortality rates for age 50 in 2000, age 51 in 2000, age 52 in 2000 (and so on). The cohort life expectancy would be calculated using male mortality rates for age 50 in 2000, age 51 in 2001, age 52 in 2002 (and so on). The cohort definition is the better measure of true life expectancy.
Life-cycle consumption model	An economic theory which suggests that people aim to smooth consumption from year to year over their lives. Since their income tends to vary, they use saving and dis-saving to meet this aim, for example, building up a pension pot while in work and running it down during retirement.
Lighter touch sales regime	A common financial services industry term referring to the new sales regime for financial advisers which will be simpler and quicker and hence cheaper to comply with than the current **Conduct of Business** rules. See the FSA's CP04/11, published in June 2004, for details.
Limiting longstanding illness	An illness, disability or infirmity that has troubled an individual over a period of time or that is likely to affect them over a period of time and limits their activities in some way. Survey respondents are asked to assess their own health according to these criteria. The responses are used as measures of chronic sickness.
Long-dated bond yield	The return received by owners of **long-dated gilts**.
Long-dated gilts	**Gilts** with many years (e.g. 20) left until maturity.
Longevity	Length of life.

Longitudinal	A research study which follows a group of individuals over a period of time.
Lower Earnings Limit (LEL)	The level of earnings at which an individual is treated as if they have made **National Insurance** contributions. In 2004-05 the limit is £79 per week or £4,108 per year.
Lower Earnings Threshold (LET), also referred to as the underpin	For the purposes of calculation of **S2P** anyone earning less than the Lower Earnings Threshold (£11,600 in 2004-05) and above the **LEL** is treated as if they had earnings at the Lower Earnings Threshold.
Matching contributions	An arrangement common in **employer-sponsored Defined Contribution** pension schemes by which a contribution made by an individual is added to by their employer. A pound of individual contributions might be added to by 50p or £1 up to a limit.
Mean	The average value of a group, calculated as the total of all the values in a group and dividing by the number of values.
Means-tested benefits	State benefits where the amount paid depends on the level of income, capital and other personal circumstances.
Median	The median of a distribution divides it into two halves. Therefore half the group are above the median value and half below.
Medium-size firms	For statistical purposes, the Department of Trade and Industry usually defines a medium firm as one with 50-249 employees.
Minimum contributions	Contributions paid into a **contracted-out personal pension** scheme from the **National Insurance** scheme in place of building up rights to **S2P**.
Minimum Income Guarantee (MIG)	The forerunner of the **Guarantee Credit**.
National Insurance (NI)	The national system of benefits paid in specific situations, such as retirement, based on compulsory earnings-related contributions by employers and employees. Self-employed people make contributions on a different basis.

New Deal 50 plus	A programme of help provided by DWP for people aged 50 and over who want to work.
Nominal gilts	**Gilts** which pay an income which is constant in cash terms (i.e. is not **index-linked**)
Normal age pensioners or normal age retirees	Used by the Pensions Commission to refer to people who are aged at or above the **State Pension Age** and who are retired.
Notionally funded	A form of **unfunded** pension scheme in the public sector, where pension contributions are theoretically paid from the relevant department to HM Treasury to purchase **gilts** but where the future cost still has to be met out of future tax revenue.
Occupational pension	A pension which is provided via the employer, but the pension scheme takes the form of a trust arrangement and is legally separate from the employer.
Old-age dependency ratio	Used by the Pensions Commission to measure the number of people above 65 to the number of people aged 18 or 20 to 64 in the population.
Pay As You Go (PAYG)	A pension system where the pension is paid out of current revenue and no funds are accumulated to pay future pensions. The **National Insurance** system is a Pay As You Go system.
Pensim2	A model being developed by DWP that simulates the future life course of a current population sample to estimate their future pension income. It will enable aggregate and distributional analysis of alternative policy, demographic and economic scenarios.
Pension accrual	The build up of pension rights. In a **Defined Benefit** scheme this may be based on the number of years of contributions.
Pension Credit	The main **means-tested benefit** for pensioners, which combines the Guarantee Credit and the Savings Credit. For more details see Appendix F.
Pensioner Benefit Unit (PBU)	A single (non-cohabiting) person aged over **State Pension Age** (SPA) or a couple (married or cohabiting) where the man, defined as the head, is over SPA.
Period life expectancy	See life expectancy.

Persistence	Where someone continues to make contributions to a pension scheme over time.
Personal pension	A pension which is provided through a contract between an individual and the pension provider. The pension produced will be based on the level of contributions, investment returns and annuity rates. A personal pension can either be employer provided (a **Group Personal Pension**) or purchased individually.
Price-indexed	Increasing each year in line with inflation.
Primary earnings threshold	See Earnings threshold.
Private equity	Ownership claims on companies which are not listed on a public exchange.
Protection products	Financial products which provide insurance against specific events, such as unemployment or illness.
Quartile	The quartiles of a distribution divide it into four parts.
Quintiles	The quintiles of a distribution divide it into five parts.
Quoted equities or bonds	Are listed on a public exchange. They therefore tend to be more easily traded than **unquoted equities** (i.e. **private equity**) or bonds.
Real terms	Figures have been adjusted to remove the effect of increases in prices over time (i.e. inflation), usually measured by the **Retail Price Index**. Thus if something shown in real terms increases then it is rising faster than prices, whereas if it is constant, it rises at exactly the same pace as prices.
Reduction In Yield (RIY)	This measures the effect of all charges (whether **Annual Management Charges** or **implicit costs**) on the return an individual achieves on investment. If the rate of return before charges was 6% but the individual receives a rate of return of only 4% after charges, then the Reduction In Yield is 2%.
Replacement rate	This measures income in retirement as a proportion of income before retirement.

Retail Prices Index (RPI)	This is an average measure of the change in the prices of goods and services bought for consumption by the vast majority of households in the UK.
Retirement annuity contract	The forerunner of modern **personal pensions**.
Sandler product	New savings products which are relatively simple and can be sold using a simplified sales process. For more details see HM Treasury's consultation paper *"Consultation on 'stakeholder' saving and investment products regulations"*.
Savings Credit	Part of the **Pension Credit**. It is a means-tested benefit for people aged 65 and over, which is withdrawn at the rate of 40p for each £1 of pre-Pension Credit income above the level of the **Basic State Pension**.
Secondary earnings threshold	See Earnings threshold.
Security	General term for equities, bonds and other investments.
Self-Invested Pension Plan (SIPP)	A **personal pension** where the individual chooses where to invest their funds instead of giving their funds to a financial services company to manage.
Self-administered schemes	An **occupational pension** scheme where the administration is carried out directly on behalf of the trustees and not handed over to an insurance company.
Small and Medium Enterprises (SME)	For statistical purposes, the Department of Trade and Industry usually defines a SME as a firm with 249 or fewer employees.
Small firm	For statistical purposes, the Department of Trade and Industry usually defines a small firm as one with 49 or fewer employees.
Social housing	Social housing is housing of an adequate standard which is provided to rent (or on a shared ownership basis) at below market cost for households in need by Local Authorities or Registered Social Landlords.

Socio-economic class Classification of individuals based on occupation. The Registrar General's Social Class based on Occupation has been used in this Report:

Class	Description	Examples of Occupations
Non-manual		
I	Professional	Doctors, chartered accountants, professionally qualified engineers
II	Managerial & technical/intermediate	Managers, school teachers, journalists
IIINM	Skilled non-manual	Clerks, cashiers, retail staff
Manual		
IIIM	Skilled manual	Supervisor of manual workers, plumbers, electricians, goods vehicle drivers
IV	Partly skilled	Warehousemen, security guards, machine tool operators, care assistants, waiting staff
V	Unskilled	Labourers, cleaners and messengers

Stakeholder pension A **personal pension** product which complies with regulations which limit charges and allow individuals flexibility about contributions.

State Earnings Related Pension Scheme (SERPS) The forerunner of the **State Second Pension**, which provides an earnings-related **National Insurance** pension based on contributions. For more details see Appendix F.

State Pension Age (SPA) The age at which an individual can claim their state pension. It is currently 65 for men and 60 for women. The State Pension Age for women will gradually increase to 65 between 2010 and 2020.

State Second Pension (S2P) The **National Insurance** pension which gives benefits based on an individual's earnings and contributions. For more details see Appendix F.

Term insurance	Life insurance which covers a specific length of time, for example to cover a mortgage.
Third party information	An administrative data source generated from returns to the Inland Revenue by personal pension providers for each individual **personal pension** plan. The data are used for the publication of National Statistics and compliance checking purposes.
Total Fertility Rate (TFR) or Total Period Fertility Rate (TPFR)	The average number of children that a woman would bear if the female population experienced the age-specific fertility rates occurring in a particular year throughout their childbearing lifespan. It provides a measure of fertility that is comparable over time and geography as it controls for the underlying age distribution of the population.
Trading down	Buying a home that is less expensive than one's current home.
Underpin	Another name for the **Lower Earnings Threshold**.
Unemployment	The number of unemployed people in the UK is measured through the Labour Force Survey following the internationally agreed definition recommended by the International Labour Organisation, an agency of the United Nations. Unemployed people are: without a job, want a job, have actively sought work in the last four weeks and are available to start work in the next two weeks, or: out of work, have found a job and are waiting to start it in the next two weeks. For some of the ELSA analysis unemployment is not so strictly defined.
Unfunded	Pension schemes which are not backed by a pension fund. Instead current contributions are used to pay current pensions along with other funds provided by the employer.
Unquoted equity	See private equity.
Upper Earnings Limit (UEL)	The upper limit on earnings for the purposes of calculating entitlement to **S2P**. Also the upper limit for most employee **National Insurance** contributions. In 2004-05 it is £31,720 per year or £610 per week. For more details see Appendix F.

Upper Earnings Threshold (UET)	An intermediate point prior to the **Upper Earnings Limit**, which affects the accrual of **S2P**. For more details see Appendix F.
US treasuries	These are bonds, loans etc issued by the US government. They have very similar characteristics to **gilts**.
Withdrawal rate	The rate at which a **means-tested benefit** is reduced for an additional pound of pre-benefit income. For more details see Appendix F.
Working age population	Generally defined as those aged 16-59 for women and 16-64 for men. However in some of our analysis we have used a starting age of 20.

Glossary

List of abbreviations

Abbreviations	Description
ABI	Association of British Insurers
ACA	Association of Consulting Actuaries
AMC	Annual Management Charge
APP	Approved Personal Pension
AVC	Additional Voluntary Contribution
BHPS	British Household Panel Survey
BSP	Basic State Pension
COB	Conduct of Business
COMP	Contracted Out Money Purchase scheme
COSR	Contracted Out Salary Related scheme
CTB	Council Tax Benefit
DB	Defined Benefit
DC	Defined Contribution
DWP	Department for Work and Pensions
ECHP – UDB	European Community Household Panel Users' Database
ELSA	English Longitudinal Study of Ageing
EPC	Economic Policy Committee
EPP	Employers' Pension Provision survey
ESRC	Economic and Social Research Council
EU	European Union
EU15	European Union 15 Member States
FRS	Family Resources Survey
FSA	Financial Services Authority
FSAVC	Free-Standing Additional Voluntary Contribution
GAD	Government Actuary's Department

GDP	Gross Domestic Product
GNP	Gross National Product
GPP	Group Personal Pension
HB	Housing Benefit
HRP	Home Responsibilities Protection
IFA	Independent Financial Advisers
IFS	Institute for Fiscal Studies
ISA	Individual Savings Account
IPPR	Institute for Public Policy Research
LEL	Lower Earnings Limit
LET	Lower Earnings Threshold
LFS	Labour Force Survey
LLMDB2	Lifetime Labour Market Database
MIG	Minimum Income Guarantee
NAPF	National Association of Pension Funds
NES	New Earnings Survey
NI	National Insurance
NINO	National Insurance Number
NIRS2	National Insurance Recording System
OECD	Organisation for Economic Co-operation and Development
ONS	Office for National Statistics
PAYG	Pay As You Go
PPF	Pension Protection Fund
RIY	Reduction in Yield
RPI	Retail Prices Index
SBS	Small Business Service
S2P	State Second Pension
SERPS	State Earnings Related Pension Scheme
SIPP	Self Invested Pension Plan
SPA	State Pension Age

SPI	Survey of Personal Incomes
TFR	Total Fertility Rate
UEL	Upper Earnings Limit
UET	Upper Earnings Threshold

Abbreviations

Bibliography

ABI, (October 2003), *The State of the Nation's Savings*

ABI, (September 2003), *The Future of the Pension Annuity Market – summary report*

ABI, (2003), *ABI response to HMT consultation on Sandler products*

ACA, (May 2004), *2004 Smaller Firms Pensions Survey: A Divided Nation*

ACA, (March 2003), *Occupational Pensions 2003 Pensions Reform: too little, too late?*

Aegon, (May 2003), *AEGON UK Response to HM Treasury and Department for Work and Pensions Consultation Document: Proposed product specification for Sandler 'stakeholder' products*

Bajekal, M. *Healthy life expectancy by area deprivation: estimates for England, 1994-1999,* National Centre for Social Research, submitted for publication Journal of Epidemiology and Public Health

Balchin, S and Shah, D (May 2004), *The Pensioners' Income Series 2002/3,* DWP

Banks, J., Emmerson, C., Oldfield, Z. (forthcoming), *Prepared for Retirement? The pension arrangements and retirement expectations of older workers in England,* Institute for Fiscal Studies

Barclays Capital, (2004), *Barclays Equity Gilt Study*

Bardasi, E., Jenkins, S. and Rigg, J. (2002), *Retirement and the income of older people: a British perspective,* Ageing and Society Vol. 22, pp131-159

Barker, K. (March 2004), *Review of Housing Supply Delivering Stability: Securing our Future Housing Needs Final Report – Recommendations,* HMSO

Bateman, H., Kingston, G. and Piggott, J. (2001), *Forced Savings Mandating Private Retirement Incomes,* Cambridge University Press

Black, O., Richardson, I. and Herbert, R. (July 2004), *Jobs in the public sector mid-2003,* ONS, Labour Market Trends, Vol. 112, No. 7, pp271-281

Blake, D. and Burrows, W. (October 2001), *Survivor Bonds: Helping to Hedge Mortality Risk,* The Pensions Institute, The Journal of Risk and Insurance, 2001, Vol. 68, No. 2, pp339-348

Blöndal, S., and Scarpetta, S. (February 1999), *The Retirement Decision in OECD Countries,* OECD, Economics Department, Working Papers No. 202

Blundell, R. and Tanner, S. (December 1999) *Labour force participation and retirement in the UK,* IFS

Bobak, M., Kristenson, M., Pikhart, H. and Marmot, M. *A comparison of Russian and Swedish community – based data,* International Centre for Health and Society, University College London, UK and Department of Health and Society, University of Linkoping, Sweden

Breeze, E., Fletcher, A., Leon, D., Marmot, M. and Shipley, M. (2001), *Do Socioeconomic Disadvantages Persist Into Old Age? Self-Reported Morbidity in 29-Year Follow-Up of the Whitehall Study,* American Journal of Public Health, February 2001, Vol. 91, No. 2 pp277-283

Bridgwood, A. (2000), *People Aged 65 and over: Results of an independent study carried out on behalf of the Department of Health as part of the 1998 General Household Survey,* ONS

Brown, J. (1990), *Social Security for Retirement,* Joseph Rowntree Foundation, York

CBI, (June 2004), *Raising the bar. Benchmarking pension provision,* CBI Pension Strategy Group

CBI/Mercer Human Resource Consulting, (2004), *A view from the top: A survey of business leaders' views on UK pension provision*

Cebulla, A. and Reyes De-Bearman, S. (2004), *Employers' Pension Provision Survey 2003,* DWP, Research Report No. 207

Choi, J., Laibson, D., Madrian, B. and Metrick, A. (November 2001), *Defined Contribution Pensions: Plan Rules, Participant Decisions, and the Path of Least Resistance,* NBER Working Paper No. W8655

Connolly, E. and Kohler, M. (March 2004), *The Impact of Superannuation on Household Saving, Reserve Bank of Australia,* Research Discussion Paper 2004-01

Craggs, A. (ed), (June 2004), *Family Spending: A report on the 2002-2003 Expenditure and Food Survey,* ONS

Donkin, A., Goldblatt, P. and Lynch, K. (Autumn 2002), *Inequalities in life expectancy by social class 1972-1999.* Health Statistics Quarterly 15, pp5-15, ONS

DSS, (December 1998), *A new contract for welfare: Partnership in Pensions* Cm 4179, TSO

DWP, (February 2004), *Simplicity, security and choice: Informed choices for working and saving*

DWP, (2004), *Family Resources Survey 2002-03*

Economic Policy Committee, (2001), *Budgetary challenges posed by ageing populations,* ECFIN/655/01-EN final

Edwards, L., Regan, S. and Brooks, R. (2001), *Age old attitudes? Planning for retirement, means-testing, inheritance and informal care,* Institute for Public Policy Research

ESRC, (2004), *Seven Ages of Man and Woman: A look at the Life Britain in the Second Elizabethan era*

Feldstein, M. and Horioka, C. (1980), *Domestic Savings and International Capital Flows,* Economic Journal 90, pp314-329

Fries, J. (December 2002), *Reducing Disability in Older Age,* Journal of the American Medical Association, Vol. 288 No. 24

FSA, (July 2004), *Building Financial Capability in the UK*

FSA, (June 2004), *A basic advice regime for the sale of stakeholder products,* CP04/11

FSA, (December 2002), *Persistency of life and pensions policies Eighth survey*

GAD, (2004), *National Population Projections 2002-based Report giving population projections by age and sex for the United Kingdom, Great Britain and constituent countries,* TSO

GAD, (October 2003), *Government Actuary's Quinquennial Review of the National Insurance Fund as at April 2000*

GAD, (April 2003), *Occupational pensions schemes 2000: Eleventh survey by the Government Actuary* and previous editions

GAD, (1998), *Government Actuary's Department Survey of Expenses of Occupational Pension Schemes*

HM Treasury, (June 2004), *Consultation on 'stakeholder' saving and investment products regulations*

HM Treasury, (December 2003), *Long-term public finance report: fiscal sustainability with an ageing population*

HM Treasury and DWP, (July 2003), *Assessing the likely market impacts of charge caps on retail investment products*

HM Treasury, (July 2002), *Sandler Review: Medium and Long-term Retail Savings in the UK*

IDS, (2004), *Pensions in Practice 2004/05*

Iyengar, S., Jiang, W. and Huberman, G. (2003), *How Much Choice is Too Much?: Contributions to 401(k) Retirement Plans,* Pension Research Council, Working Paper 2003-10

James, K. (February 2000), *The Price of Retail Investing in the UK,* FSA, Occasional Paper Series 6

Joseph Rowntree Foundation, (2004), *Homeowners: Sons and Daughters*

Lunnon, M. (October 1998), *New Earnings Survey data on occupational pension provision,* Labour Market Trends, pp499-505

Madrian, B. and Shea, D. (2001), *The power of suggestion: inertia in 401(k) participation and savings behaviour,* Quarterly Journal of Economics, Vol. CXVI, Issue 4, pp1149-1187

Manton, K.G. and Gu, X. (May 2001), *Changes in the prevalence of chronic disability in the United States black and nonblack population above age 65 from 1982 to 1999,* Centre for Demographic Studies, Duke University, Durham, Proceedings of the National Academy of Sciences of the Unit

Marmot, M., Banks, J., Blundell, R., Lessof, C. and Nazroo, J. (ed), (December 2003), *Health, wealth and lifestyles of the older population in England: The 2002 English Longitudinal Study of Ageing,* UCL, IFS and National Centre for Social Research

Martin, C., Martin, L., and Mabbett, A. (April 2002), *SME Ownership Succession – Business Support and Policy Implications,* Knowledge Management Centre, Business School, University of Central England

Mayhew, V. (2003), *Pensions 2002: Public Attitudes to Pensions and Planning for Retirement,* DWP Research Report No. 193

Mayhew, V. (2001), *Pensions 2000: Public Attitudes to Pensions and Planning for Retirement,* DSS Research Report No.130

Mehra, R. and Prescott, E. (1985), *The Equity Premium: A Puzzle,* Journal of Monetary Economics, March 1985, pp145-161

Miles, D. (1999), *Modelling the impact of demographic change upon the economy,* Economic Journal, Vol. 109, No. 452, pp1-37

Mitchell, O. and Utkus, S. (2003), *Lessons from Behavioural Finance for Retirement Plan design,* Pension Research Council, Working Paper 2003-6

National Association of Pension Funds, (2003), *Twenty-ninth Annual Survey of Occupational Pension Schemes*

OECD, (October 2003), *Monitoring the Future Social Implication of Today's Pension Policies*

OECD, (October 2003), *Monitoring Pension Policies Annex: Country Chapters*

ONS, (October 2003), *New Earnings Survey 2003*

ONS, (2003), *United Kingdom National Accounts The Blue Book 2003,* TSO

Poterba, J. (August 2004), *Population Aging and Financial Markets,* Federal Reserve Bank of Kansas, Jackson Hole Economic Symposium

PPI, (July 2003), *State Pension Models*

Purcell, K. (Summer 2002), *Qualifications and Careers Equal Opportunities and Earnings Among Graduates,* University of the West of England, Equal Opportunities Commission, Working Paper Series No. 1

Rickards, L., Fox, K., Roberts, C., Fletcher, L., and Goddard, E. (2004), *Living in Britain, No 31, Results from the 2002 General Household Survey,* ONS, TSO, London

Samuelson, P. (1958), *An Exact Consumption Loan Model of Interest with or without the Social Contrivance of Money,* Journal of Political Economy 66, pp467-482

Sefton, J. and van de Ven, J. (2004), *Does Means Testing Exacerbate Early Retirement?* National Institute of Economic and Social Research, London, Working Paper 244

Shaw, C. (Spring 1999), *1996-based population projections by legal marital status for England and Wales,* ONS, Population Trends 95, pp23-32

Small Business Service, (August 2004), *Small and Medium-sized Enterprise (SME) Statistics for the UK 2003,* DTI

Smith, J. (Autumn 2004), *Exploring attitudes to housing wealth and retirement,* CML Housing Finance, Autumn 2004, pp22-33

Stark, J. (2002), Annuities – *The Consumer Experience,* ABI

Thaler, R. H. and Benartzi, S. (2004), *Save More Tomorrow: Using Behavioural Economics to Increase Employee Saving,* Journal of Political Economy, Vol. 112, No 1, Pt. 2, pp164-187

Thaler, R. H. and Benartzi, S. (2001), *Naïve Diversification Strategies in Defined Contribution Saving Plans,* The American Economic Review, March 2001, Vol. 91. No. 1, pp79-98

Thomas, M., Walker, A., Wilmot, A. and Bennet, N. (1998), *Living in Britain. Results from the 1996 General Household Survey,* ONS, TSO, London

Tily, G., Penneck, P. and Forest, C. (August 2004), *Private Pensions Estimates and the National Accounts,* Economic Trends No. 609

Towers Perrin, (June 2004), *Survey of Defined Contribution Pension Arrangements*

Tudela, M. and Young, G. (Winter 2003), *The distribution of unsecured debt in the United Kingdom: survey evidence*, Bank of England Quarterly Bulletin, pp417-427

Turner, A. (September 2003), *The Macro-Economics of Pensions,* Lecture to the Actuarial Profession

Watson Wyatt LLP, (January 2003), *Administration Cost Survey 2003*

Whitehouse, E. (June 2000), *Administrative Charges for Funded Pensions: An International Comparison and Assessment,* Pension Reform Primer Series, Social Protection Discussion Paper 0016

Willets, D. (July 2004), *The Pension Crisis: What it Means and What to do About it,* Speech to Politeia

Women and Equality Unit, *Individual incomes of men and women 1996/97 to 2002/03,* DTI

World Economic Forum, (2004), *Living Happily Ever After: The Economic Implications of Ageing Societies*

Yoo, P. (1994), *Age Distributions and Returns to Financial Assets,* Federal Reserve Bank of St. Louis, Working Paper 94-002B

Young, G. (2002), *The implications of an ageing population for the UK economy,* Bank of England Working Paper